PROPHECIES OF

Personal and Small
Group Study Guide

REVELATION
made simple

SETH J. PIERCE

Pacific Press®
Publishing Association

Nampa, Idaho | www.pacificpress.com

Cover design by Gerald Lee Monks
Cover design resources from SermonView.com
Inside illustrations by Marcus Mashburn
Inside design by Kristin Hansen-Mellish

The author assumes full responsibility for the accuracy of all facts and quotations as cited in this book.

You can obtain additional copies of this book by calling toll-free 1-800-765-6955 or by visiting http://www.adventistbookcenter.com.

Library of Congress Cataloging-in-Publication Data:

Pierce, Seth J.
  Prophecies of Revelation made simple : personal and small group study guide / Seth J. Pierce.
     pages cm
  ISBN 978-0-8163-5014-8 (pbk.)
  1. Bible. Revelation—Criticism, interpretation, etc. 2. Prophecies—Biblical teaching.
  3. Seventh-day Adventists—Doctrines. I. Title.
  BS2825.6.P7P544 2014
  228'.06—dc23
                              2014002916

August 2021

Dedication

This book is dedicated to all those who have attended a seminar about, read a book about, or suffered through "beastly" preaching about Revelation and ended up more confused than they were when they began.

Acknowledgments

Thank You to Jesus—First and Last and Everything in between. Your strength and grace during the battles I fought in writing this book will not be forgotten.

Thank you to my loving and patient family. Thank you to my wife for bearing the stress of a husband glued to the computer for weeks and who developed some antisocial disorders due to the stress. I love you. Thank you to my Maddie and Chloe for interrupting my writing with their hugs and love. I can't wait to play for hours and hours and not just a few minutes here and there. I love you too.

To my wonderful church family in Puyallup, Washington, thank you for your prayers and never-ending support during this project. Thank you to Mike for picking up preaching and other duties so I could slay this beast. Know that the whole Demma family is loved and appreciated.

Thank you to Mary Stevens for the care package full of goodies that kept me awake and fed so I could work into the wee hours of the morning. You are a huge blessing.

Much love to the Proctors and the Riters for taking the girls that last Sabbath so I could finish the book.

Thank to Lori Cockerham and Mark Witas for the extended Facebook discussion on wrath that never turned wrathful despite some disagreements. I love you guys and hope you will find my treatment of the subject fair.

Thank You to Jesus—First and Last and Everything in between.

Thank you to Joyce Schilt and to my uncle Ken for giving me books to supplement my studies. They were very helpful, and I have promoted them in the recommended reading section.

To my writers group—now meeting at an even more secret location—thank you for your critiques and encouragement.

To all my seminary professors who let me bask in their wisdom, and to the editor and copy editors who get to clean this mess up, to Tiger Paulsen and his promotional work, and to scholars whose works I read and in which I found ideas—may God continue to bless your work.

Thank you to you, the consumer who has purchased this book. Don't even think about returning it . . . I'll find you.

Of course, thanks to everyone at TDKR, BTAS, and the Avengers Initiative for their help. Cheetos, YouTube, Netflix, chocolate, salsa, Sony PS3, Apple iPad, soap, Snuggie, and Charlie the Unicorn—where would I be without you?

Thank You to Jesus—First and Last and Everything in between.

Also by Seth J. Pierce

Camporee of Doom

The Day the School Blew Up

Prophecies of Daniel Made Simple

What We Believe for Teens

What We Believe: Prophecies of Daniel for Teens

What We Believe: Prophecies of Revelation for Teens

You can also see/hear/read more of Seth's perspective on religion, God, and life in general on his Web site: www.sethjpierce.com.

Contents

Preface

Who Am I?

"I have a confession to make: I'm a Seventh-day Adventist.

"No—scratch that. I'm a Seventh-day Adventist pastor."

These are the words I spoke to a couple hundred people gathered in a gymnasium to hear a seminar on Bible prophecy. They came because we had sent a colorful flyer to about fifty thousand of the people who live near our church. The people had gathered to hear the words of Scripture.

There are a lot of misunderstandings about who Seventh-day Adventists are and what we believe. We are Protestants in the grand tradition of the Reformation and even of the radical reformation. Lutherans, Anabaptists, Mennonites, Presbyterians, Baptists, Methodists, and even Pentecostals are our brothers and sisters. We believe in salvation by grace through faith in Jesus Christ, in believer's baptism by immersion, that the Holy Spirit still empowers believers with special gifts to love and heal a world that suffers from chronic pain.

And we believe that Jesus is coming soon.

We believe that last item because we believe in God's Word above everything else. That Word informs my faith tradition's identity as an end-time movement that seeks to restore truths buried under the man-made traditions and other refuse piled up over the centuries by politically minded members of religious institutions. This means that while we share many things with our Christian brothers and sisters, we do see some things in God's Word that others seem to miss. And it's that Word that I am concerned with.

Revelation is about revealing—not hiding. It *is,* after all, a revelation of Jesus Christ.

Even the scary flyers with beasts tell us something about Jesus—and if Jesus is giving the vision, then who is responsible for those images?

A warning: no book is ever finished—it just runs into deadlines. That means the author is going to miss someone's favorite part. The problem is if we "remembered" everything we read while writing our books, they would never end. Every author has to make choices and consequently runs the risk of missing someone's favorite part.

So, if you need more, go to the recommended reading section—that's what it's there for. Or you can chat with me on my Web site: www.sethjpierce.com. I'd love to hear from you.

Prophecies of Revelation Made Simple is meant to begin dialogue, not to end it. Therefore, the language—not the material—is simple. And I have tried to use humor, something commentaries really struggle with.

Adventists have so much material on prophecy—we've been talking about it so long—that sometimes it's difficult to find a way into the conversation.

This book is an invitation for you to join the conversation.

It's a stepping-stone to deeper study.

A stepping-stone to help you stand on the Cornerstone.

May you see Truth.

May you see Jesus.

Seth J. Pierce

P.S. When you turn the page and start reading chapter 1, you may think you're experiencing a genuine case of *déjà vu*. Or that someone at Pacific Press® made a major mistake. At least you may think that if you've read my book *Prophecies of Daniel Made Simple*. That's because the first four chapters of this book are identical—or nearly identical—to the first four chapters of my book on Daniel.

But you're still sane, and the duplication isn't the fault of Pacific Press®.

I *wanted* the first four chapters of this book to say the same thing as the first four chapters of my book on Daniel. These chapters contain important information about interpreting the kind of prophecy that both Daniel and Revelation contain. People who haven't read my book on Daniel need this information to understand Revelation, so I had to put it in this book too.

In other words, if you've read my book on Daniel, you can skip the first four chapters of this book—that is, if your memory is perfect. If not, you probably should at least skim through chapters 1 through 4 before you go to chapter 5.

Chapter 1
The Interpreter

Going Deeper

Can you think of ways people interpret the Bible without using the Bible?

_____

_____

_____

_____

_____

_____

_____

_____

_____

_____

_____

_____

_____

_____

_____

_____

_____

_____

_____

_____

_____

_____

One of the jobs I worked while attending college was covering the Prescott Hall front reception desk. It was a good job, as I'd usually get four short calls in a four-hour shift, and I could spend the rest of the time doing homework or chatting with friends who stopped by. However, one night I received a call that resulted in a crisis of international proportions. The phone rang, and I answered it: "Prescott Hall—how can I help you?"

A timid voice responded. "Jose?"

"I'm sorry," I said. "I didn't catch his last name. Is he a student here?"

"Jose?" asked the voice again.

OK, she doesn't speak English. That's easily fixed. There were only a few Joses in our dorms, and I knew most of them, so I knew I could find him by the process of elimination. Swiftly I punched the keys on the computer and located the mysterious Hispanic man known only as Jose.

"Here's your transfer, ma'am," I said while she asked again for what I presumed was her son. Then I transferred the call—only to be greeted by a busy signal.

"Uh, I'm sorry," I told the caller, "but his line is busy."

Now the timid voice transformed into something more irate. "JOSE!" the woman cried angrily.

She didn't understand what I was saying. The words I spoke bounced off her ears like bullets off Superman's chest. I had only one option left—I transferred her call to the women's dorm, muttering, "Let's see if they can get anywhere with this situation."

A few moments later, the phone rang again, and I answered dutifully. "Hello, Prescott desk. How may I—"

"JOSE!" the voice shrieked.

I was helpless. This caller wouldn't get off the line. I couldn't make the transfer, and apparently the only word in her vocabulary was "Jose," followed by what sounded like thirty or forty exclamation points. Panic ensued, and all was nearly

Going Deeper

Why have people made so
many different versions of
the Bible?

_____

_____

_____

_____

_____

_____

_____

What are the tools listed
below, and how can they
help you study Scripture?

a.   Concordance

_____

_____

_____

b.   Parallel Bible

_____

_____

_____

c.   Bible dictionary

_____

_____

_____

lost—until my Spanish-speaking Hispanic friend Gil walked into the lobby.

"Gil," I cried, shoving the phone into his hand, "tell this woman what's going on! Her son's line is busy! She is screaming and probably thinks that we've done something to him or are hiding him somewhere, or worse!"

Gil grabbed the phone and in perfect Spanish translated what I had been trying to tell her. The crisis was defused, and eventually the anxious mother was reunited via telephone with Jose—who I hope has acquired call-waiting since then.

Sometimes we need an interpreter to understand the message.

The Bible's interpreter

In the book of Daniel, we see something that seems unlikely—a prophet confused by a message sent from God. The prophet says, "And I, Daniel, was overcome and lay sick for some days; then I rose and went about the king's business; but I was appalled by the vision _and did not understand it_" (Daniel 8:27; emphasis added).

Daniel was even more upset than Jose's mother was because he couldn't understand what God was telling him. It's just as easy for us to become frustrated when trying to understand what God wants to communicate to us today through His Word. Thankfully, there's a way that works.

The great Reformer Martin Luther once said, "Scripture . . . is its own light. It is a grand thing when Scripture interprets itself." This concept has been echoed throughout history by great Christian leaders. As a Seventh-day Adventist, I find this concept supported by a man named William Miller. One of his top three principles for interpreting the Bible states: "Scripture must be its own expositor [explainer], since it is a rule of itself. If I depend on a minister or teacher to explain it to me, and they should guess at its meaning, or desire to have it so on account of their creed, or thought to be wise, . . . then their guessing, desire, creed, or wisdom is my rule and not the Bible!"[1]

In seminary I took an exam in Hebrew and had to dissect each verb to make sure my translation was correct. It would have been easier if I could have used a Hebrew dictionary because it would have helped me with the translation. Using a German dictionary would have done nothing except score me a big fat F—and possibly a psychological evaluation. To understand Hebrew, I needed a Hebrew dictionary. So, if we want to understand Scripture, we need to look at Scripture.

Here's an example. Early on in the book of Revelation, when Jesus is having John write letters to seven churches, the text tells us that Jesus is the One who "walks among the seven golden lampstands" (Revelation 2:1). What does that mean? Does Jesus like lampstands? I don't see why He wouldn't—but there's a little more meaning here.

Golden lampstands were used in the Old Testament sanctuary (see Exodus 25:31). They symbolized light in darkness (the sanctuary had no windows). In describing the effect Jesus has on people, the Gospel of Matthew says, "the people who sat in darkness have seen a great light, and for those dwelling in the region and shadow of death light has dawned" (Matthew 4:16).

Jesus also likens Himself to "light" (John 8:12), and He even tells His followers, "You are the light of the world" (Matthew 5:14). In other words, God and His followers bring light to a dark world. So when we get back to Revelation 2:1, we can see that Jesus is likening His churches to lights in a dark world—meaning we are supposed to be sharing the hope and love we have instead of hiding ourselves away where people can't find us.

By looking at other places in Scripture that have phrases, images, and objects like those in the passage we're studying, we can get a clearer sense of what that passage or that prophecy is saying to us and where things are taking place.

In the case of Daniel, we are greeted with a myriad of time prophecies. Take a look at this important one in Daniel 8:13, 14: "Then I heard a holy one speaking; and another holy one said to the one that spoke, 'For how long is the vision concerning the continual burnt offering, the transgression that makes desolate, and the giving over of the sanctuary and host to be trampled under foot?' And he said to him, 'For two thousand and three hundred evenings and mornings; then the sanctuary shall be restored to its rightful state.' "

You may be tempted to think of these 2,300 days as twenty-four-hour days and come up with the time in this prophecy being somewhere around six years. Problem is, the sanctuary wasn't in its "restored" or its "rightful state," or "cleansed," as some translations have it, six years after this prophecy was given.

So now what?

As we will discuss more in the next chapter, prophecy uses lots of symbols for its descriptions, and symbols aren't to be taken literally. I mean, can you imagine reading Daniel 7:3—which pictures four horrible beasts emerging out of the sea—and thinking Daniel's prophecy means that at some point four monsters will run amok around the planet, ravaging everything in their path?

Maybe you do. But while I agree that it would be incredibly exciting to have a sort of prophetic *Jurassic Park,* I'm going to let you in on something. *Shhh*—hold this book up close to your face, and I'll whisper it to you:

They aren't literal beasts. They represent something else.

OK, back to the timeline in Daniel 8. The point is that the time periods in Daniel's prophecies aren't literal either. We need a different formula so we can understand when the events in these prophecies will occur. When we search Scripture for the answer, we find two texts that help us understand Daniel's time prophecies: "According to the number of the days in which you spied out the land, forty days, *for every day a year,* you shall bear your iniquity, forty years" (Numbers 14:34; emphasis added). And "I assign to you *a number of days, three hundred and ninety, equal to the number of the years* of their punishment" (Ezekiel 4:5; emphasis added).

Going Deeper

What is the "day for a year principle"?

_____

_____

_____

_____

_____

_____

_____

_____

_____

_____

_____

_____

_____

_____

_____

_____

_____

_____

_____

_____

_____

_____

_____

_____

Going Deeper

How do you study the Bible?

_____

_____

_____

_____

_____

How does the way you study it help you to find the meaning of difficult Bible texts?

_____

_____

_____

_____

_____

_____

What could you do to push yourself even deeper into the Bible?

_____

_____

_____

_____

_____

_____

_____

Both these passages come in the context of judgment decrees—as does Daniel 8 and the 2,300 days. These passages indicate that the 2,300 days are actually 2,300 years. When those years start and end is the subject of another chapter. For now, just remember that this way of calculating time is referred to as the "day for a year principle."

Because I am a pastor, I get a lot of weird phone calls, some of them about people's interpretation of the Bible's prophecies. People have called to tell me that the locusts in Revelation 9 are helicopters and that the mark of the beast in Revelation 13 referred to none other than President Franklin Delano Roosevelt—who died sixty years prior to that bizarre call. Other people have suggested the mark of the beast is a computer chip, and that the knowledge that Daniel 12:4 says shall increase refers to the latest gadget at the Apple store. I'm still waiting, though, for a call from a nut who goes to Yellowstone Park, and sees a bear with three ribs from an unfortunate deer in its mouth, and thinks he or she has spotted a prophetic beast wandering around (see Daniel 7:5).

At the time I'm writing this chapter, a popular piece on YouTube features a hippie videoing a double rainbow. While steadying his video camera, he marvels, weeps, and yells about the beautiful sight. After regaining his composure, he asks in hushed tones, "What does it mean?"

Biblically speaking, the rainbow is God's way of reminding us that He won't destroy the world via a flood again. In this guy's case, however, my first thought was, *I'll tell you what it means—it means, "Time to lay off the marijuana, my friend."* People tend to want to look for hidden and obscure meanings in various areas of life. That's true of prophecy too. But when we allow Scripture to interpret itself by giving us the clues we need, we avoid coming up with something crazy and making our faith (and our God) look dumb, unreasonable, and unstable.

CHAPTER 1 IN BRIEF

The study of prophecy is not a quest for some secret, mystical meaning—though this isn't to say that God doesn't know things we don't know or that He has no mystical qualities. Instead, God uses prophecy to reveal things to us. Matter of fact, in the Greek language in which the New Testament was first written, the word translated "Revelation" is *apokalupsis,* which means "disclosure" or "a revealing." In other words, prophecy is about God revealing His message to us in Scripture, not about His hiding it from us.

ENDNOTE

1. William Miller, "Rules of Interpretation," *Midnight Cry,* November 17, 1842.

Chapter 2
Genre

Going Deeper

What does *genre* mean?

_____

_____

_____

_____

_____

_____

_____

_____

_____

_____

_____

_____

_____

_____

_____

_____

_____

_____

_____

_____

_____

_____

_____

_____

_____

What kind of stories do you like to read?

If you're going to sit down and enjoy a book, and you're not reading something just because your job demands it, what do you like?

If you enjoy stories centered on a man and a woman, and they spend the entire story flirting back and forth and misunderstanding each other until finally they kiss and get married at the end (and you don't gag once throughout the entire thing), you enjoy *romances.*

If you enjoy technology, such as spaceships, lasers, light sabers, alien life-forms, and a good measure of explosive action, you probably enjoy *science fiction.*

If you enjoy reading about dead presidents, ancient disputes, old recipes, and how people lived hundreds of years ago, your book of choice is *history.*

If you enjoy feeling tense, angsty, and nervous, and you like having sweat stain the armpits of your shirt, you probably enjoy *thrillers.*

Then again, if you like cowboys, then you enjoy *westerns,* and if you want to find out "whodunit," then you're a reader of *mysteries.*

Whether it's books or movies, these kinds of media are classified in *genres.* A genre is simply a style. Each style has its own rules; each kind of story works in a certain way. Romances usually don't feature zombies; westerns usually don't feature alien spacecraft (and when they do, the result isn't good); histories don't feature fiction; and a mystery means that, well, the story involves some kind of mystery. And too often people think Scripture is a mystery because they don't understand that it contains genres.

Biblical genres

The Bible contains many different kinds of writing, and it has genres all its own. In Psalms, you have poetry and song lyrics that use analogies that aren't to be taken literally. For example, King David, who wrote many of the psalms, says, "I am poured out like water, and all my bones are out of joint; my heart is like wax, it is

Going Deeper

What genres do you see in the Bible?

_____

_____

_____

_____

_____

_____

_____

_____

_____

_____

_____

_____

_____

_____

_____

_____

_____

_____

_____

_____

_____

melted within my breast" (Psalm 22:14).

Obviously, David doesn't mean he has been literally poured out like water, or that every joint is dislocated, or that his heart has melted—otherwise he wouldn't have survived to write Psalm 23. No, David is using descriptive language to communicate how awful he feels.

We use the same kind of figure of speech. When we say that something melted our heart, we mean that we feel warm and soft and fuzzy—not that one of the most important organs in our body has turned into a pile of steaming goo, leaving us for dead.

The same kind of thing happens in Song of Solomon—a book of the Bible in which two lovers are passing love notes back and forth. One of them says, "Your lips distil nectar, my bride; honey and milk are under your tongue" (Song of Solomon 4:11). Now, if taken literally, we could conclude that the woman whom Solomon is describing has a severe drooling problem and doesn't swallow her food. However, since this verse is in the genre of poetry, we can understand this to mean that Solomon thought this woman's lips were sweet for the kissing—which makes a whole lot more sense because pointing out a girl's drooling problem won't get you very far.

The Bible contains other genres too—*narrative,* for instance, which simply means description of historical events. Look at the following from Exodus 4:18–20: "Moses went back to Jethro his father-in-law and said to him, 'Let me go back, I pray, to my kinsmen in Egypt and see whether they are still alive.' And Jethro said to Moses, 'Go in peace.' And the LORD said to Moses in Midian, 'Go back to Egypt; for all the men who were seeking your life are dead.' So Moses took his wife and his sons and set them on an ass, and went back to the land of Egypt; and in his hand Moses took the rod of God."

This passage is simply describing what happened, and it includes some dialogue. Pretty basic and simple, right? There's nothing in the texts surrounding this passage that suggests it is anything other than the recording of a historical event—unless you believe the Bible isn't true.

The New Testament contains a genre that Jesus made popular. Called "parables," these short stories are nonhistorical illustrations told to make a point. One of the best-known parables is the story of the rich man and Lazarus (Luke 16:19–31). It reads as follows:

"There was a rich man, who was clothed in purple and fine linen and who feasted sumptuously every day. And at his gate lay a poor man named Lazarus, full of sores, who desired to be fed with what fell from the rich man's table; moreover the dogs came and licked his sores. The poor man died and was carried by the angels to Abraham's bosom. The rich man also died and was buried; and in Hades, being in torment, he lifted up his eyes, and saw Abraham far off and Lazarus in his bosom. And he called out,

'Father Abraham, have mercy upon me, and send Lazarus to dip the end of his finger in water and cool my tongue; for I am in anguish in this flame.' But Abraham said, 'Son, remember that you in your lifetime received your good things, and Lazarus in like manner evil things; but now he is comforted here, and you are in anguish. And besides all this, between us and you a great chasm has been fixed, in order that those who would pass from here to you may not be able, and none may cross from there to us.' And he said, 'Then I beg you, father, to send him to my father's house, for I have five brothers, so that he may warn them, lest they also come into this place of torment.' But Abraham said, 'They have Moses and the prophets; let them hear them.' And he said, 'No, father Abraham; but if someone goes to them from the dead, they will repent.' He said to him, 'If they do not hear Moses and the prophets, neither will they be convinced if some one should rise from the dead.' "

Whew! I know it was long but it's worth it. Consider the following details, which make it clear that this story isn't historical:

1. Most of Luke 15 consists of parables Jesus told, and Luke 16 begins with another story, this one about a "rich man."
2. If this is literal—meaning if it's about things that actually happened—then people in hell can see people in heaven and vice versa.
3. Even more revealing, if this story is literally true, people in hell can talk to people in heaven. That's awkward.
4. The Bible tells us that God forbids necromancy (communication with the dead; see Leviticus 19:31). So it makes no sense to request that someone be "sent from the dead" to do something good—to warn the rich man's wicked family to change their ways.

The main point Jesus makes in this story is that people with money need to be generous. He also teaches that there are some people who won't give their lives to God no matter who talks to them.

Prophetic genres

By now you should be starting to understand the concept of genre and to realize that since each genre has different characteristics, each must be interpreted differently. The study of how we are to interpret different writings is called *hermeneutics* [*her-men-oo-ticks*]. Now back to the genre of prophecy and the principles we use to understand it.

Prophecy has three major characteristics that I want you to note. The first key to understanding prophecy is described by one of my seminary professors in his book

Going Deeper

Why is it important to understand what genre you are reading?

15

Going Deeper

What are *type* and *anti-type*? (See Genesis 22:8 and John 1:36.)

_____

_____

_____

_____

_____

_____

_____

_____

_____

_____

_____

_____

_____

_____

_____

_____

_____

_____

_____

_____

Revelation of Jesus Christ. He states, "A very distinguishing feature of the book of Revelation is its peculiar and symbolic language. . . . [Revelation] should be approached with a presupposition that the scenes and actions are symbolic or figurative in nature, unless the context clearly indicates that a literal meaning is intended."[1] In other words, when we read prophecy, we come across symbols and strange language that we shouldn't take literally unless the text clearly tells us we should.

In both Daniel and Revelation, there's a fairly easy way to tell when symbols and symbolic language are headed our way. In both books there are cues that tell us when a prophet is entering a "vision" or a "dream," which is our clue that things may be about to get a little strange. Look at the following examples.

"In the third year of the reign of King Belshazzar a vision appeared to me, Daniel, after that which appeared to me at the first. And I saw in the vision; and when I saw, I was in Susa the capital, which is in the province of Elam; and I saw in the vision, and I was at the river Ulai" (Daniel 8:1, 2).

So, here Daniel is giving us the literal time and place where he was when he had a vision.

The very next verse says, "I raised my eyes and saw, and behold, a ram standing on the bank of the river" (verse 3). We have just made the jump to symbols. Daniel shifts from *when* he saw something and *where* he was when he saw it to *what* it was that he saw, and the symbols begin with a ram and go from there to horns, a goat, and the four winds of heaven.

Revelation follows a similar pattern. John says, "I, John, . . . was on the island called Patmos on account of the word of God and the testimony of Jesus. I was in the Spirit on the Lord's day, and I heard behind me a loud voice like a trumpet. . . . Then I turned to see the voice that was speaking to me" (Revelation 1:9, 10, 12). John tells us his literal location: he's on an island named Patmos, and he says he's there because of his telling others about Jesus. The big clue that things are moving toward symbolism comes in his statements that he "was in the Spirit" and that he heard a voice "like a trumpet." That's a form of symbolism called *simile*—when you liken one thing to something else. Next, John turns and "sees" in vision "seven golden lampstands" (verse 12), and then, like Daniel, John is seeing symbols.

So why all the symbols? Why not just speak normally?

Part of the answer may lie in the fact that the prophets were seeing future events and witnessing heavenly scenes that were so wonderful and beyond comprehension that they found them difficult to describe, so they used *metaphor*—which are when one thing is used to represent something else. For instance, if I said, "Susie is a real peach," you would think of something sweet—or maybe even fuzzy. And if I said, "Bob is a dinosaur," you would conclude either that he is old or that he is rather large.

Something else to consider is that within a vision, prophets may be given a glimpse into heaven, where they see supernatural beings. John sees such creatures and says, "And round the throne, on each side of the throne, are four living creatures, full of eyes" (Revelation 4:6). He then uses similes, likening one to a lion, another to an ox, one with the face of a man, and another like a flying eagle. So, are these descriptions literal or symbolic? They may be a mixture of both; we need to be flexible on some points. Perhaps they do actually have wings, but all those eyes are symbolic, representing their never-ceasing gaze.

Another characteristic we need to be aware of is one called "dual fulfillment," which means that a prophecy may have an application at the time of the prophet's vision and another application to the future. This is sometimes called "type and antitype." A *type* is something that foreshadows (points toward) a greater reality, the *antitype.* In Old Testament times, people sacrificed a lamb for their sins; but in the New Testament, Jesus is called the "Lamb of God, who takes away the sin of the world!" (John 1:29), by sacrificing Himself on the cross. The lamb and its sacrifice are types, and Jesus and His sacrifice on Calvary are the antitypes.

The last item to be aware of when studying prophecy has to do with a viewpoint or mind-set called "historical criticism."

Historical criticism

Historical criticism is a method of study that scholars use to figure out the origin of a text—where it came from. While it uses several helpful tools, the perspective of many people who use historical criticism may be flawed. Many historical critics completely deny the existence of God and that miracles can happen. They accept their beliefs *before* they study the text. In other words, before examining what the Bible says, they have already concluded that there is no God and there is nothing supernatural in the world. Consequently, they approach the Bible as if it were nothing more than a book of stories or a history book, and they deny that there can be such a thing as prophecy because that involves the miraculous ability to know the future.

Imagine you are scientist commissioned to study whether or not children like being pushed down the stairs. Yes, I know that's ludicrous but remember that the National Science Foundation spent over half a million dollars to research shrimps running on a treadmill.[2] So, let's not be too quick to judge this important study of pushing children down the stairs.

Now let's say as you begin your study you start, not by interviewing children or doctors, by writing your paper first, making bold claims that kids loving nothing more than to fall down the stairs. You even go so far as to suggest the health benefits of pushing children down as many flights of stairs as you can. You publish your paper and let the public feast their eyes upon your amazing discovery.

Not only do you lose all your credibility but Child Protective Services has their eye on you for the rest of your life.

What ideas do you bring to the Bible before you've seen what it says?

Are there good presuppositions to bring to our reading of the Bible?

What are they?

You completely ignored interviewing kids, examining medical records of people who have tumbled down stairways, getting the testimony of others who have pushed people down the stairs and faced the consequences, and even entertained the possibility that some kids—despite your perspective—may actually *hate* being thrown down the stairs. To have a respectable answer to the assigned question, you would have to include all angles and possibilities in your research of the known facts and testimonies *before* reaching your conclusion.

Now, someone might say the reverse is true for those who believe in God and the miraculous; they come to the Bible automatically believing everything to be true. That would be like someone asking you to write a paper on unicorns and you simply stating that you believe they are real despite the fact that the only place where they're found is in fictional stories. Your case wouldn't be any stronger if you duct-taped a homemade horn on a horse, took a picture of it, and used the picture as evidence. Again, your fail would be epic.

We all have *presuppositions*—things we believe before we've studied about them. We have presuppositions regarding God when we come to the Bible, but we can consciously allow for all possibilities before we examine the evidence instead of automatically discounting one possibility just because it lies outside of our personal experience. Just because you haven't seen or experienced God doesn't mean He isn't there. One evangelist put it this way: "Would you say you know—from experience and study—that you had 50 percent of all the knowledge in the universe? How about 20 percent? Ten percent? Most of us would barely feel comfortable claiming to know 1 or 2 percent of all there is to know. Is it possible, then, that God exists in the other 98 to 99 percent that you don't know and haven't experienced?"

The answer, of course, is Yes.

CHAPTER 2 IN BRIEF

The Bible contains a variety of genres, each of which has its own characteristics. Prophecy is one of these genres, and it has many unique features we need to understand in order to interpret it correctly. These characteristics include clues that tell us when the prophetic message comes in a vision or a dream and the use of symbols and of metaphors and similes in the prophecy.

People vary in the way they approach prophecy. Some discount it before they look at it, and others believe it before they study it. The challenge is to keep an open mind, to let the Bible speak for itself, and to see its words in the light of history.

People who believe that God has inspired the prophecies in the Bible can disagree about how we should interpret those prophecies. In the next chapter, we'll take a look at the various ways people interpret prophecy.

ENDNOTES

1. Ranko Stefanovic, *Revelation of Jesus Christ: Commentary on the Book of Revelation,* 2nd ed. (Berrien Springs, Mich.: Andrews University Press, 2009), 17.

2. Tiffany Gabbay, "Update: NSF Conducts $682,570 Taxpayer Funded 'Shrimp on a Treadmill' Research," *The Blaze,* December 27, 2011, accessed August 14, 2013, http://www.theblaze.com/stories/2011/12/27/update-nsf-conducts-682570-taxpayer-funded-shrimp-on-a-treadmill-research/.

Notes

Chapter 3

Past, Present, Future—and All of the Above

One of the more exasperating educational experiences I had occurred in a kung fu school about a half hour from my house. I had always wanted to try kung fu, and since I had grown up learning from a dad who is an advanced black belt in traditional Japanese karate, I felt that I must already have some skills and understanding that would help me learn the Chinese art. But while it may be true that karate drew on kung fu hundreds of years ago, I would have had an easier time reading ancient Chinese backwards and blindfolded than I did trying to make sense of what the instructors were telling me.

The problem lay in their belief that kung fu was "caught rather than taught." Whenever I felt the urge to ask a question about what we were doing, they would reply, "Talk with the hands." When you're told over and over again to talk with your hands, your hands develop an intense feeling of wanting to communicate upside someone's head!

To make matters even worse, many of the kung fu practitioners—despite the fact that they were living in middle-class houses, shopping at Wal-Mart, and wearing Nikes—acted like they were wandering Tibetan monk philosophers. When they did deign to give a verbal answer to a question I asked, they did it in riddles.

For instance, one time I asked, "Am I punching straight?" The reply I got, in a hushed breathy whisper, was, "Think of your arms as a bow [as in the weapon]. They should be as straight as the drawstring, not curved like the bow."

What on earth was he talking about? A simple Yes or No would have been fine.

I pressed the matter, telling him that his little bow analogy was simply a restating of my question; it wasn't an answer.

"Talk with your hands," he said.

"Don't tempt me," I muttered.

About that time we switched partners, and my former partner practiced with a senior student. In a few moments, I heard the senior student stop the exercise and ask my former partner, "Has anyone ever told you the bow analogy?"

I left the school shortly after that and enrolled in a karate school where the instructors taught in much the same way as my father had when I was growing up. The sensei had a binder that showed what we would be learning, and he answered my questions and helped me with all of my stances, katas, strikes, throws, and warm-ups. The senior students also made themselves available for extra practice sessions, and they were willing to discuss the art openly. Both karate and kung fu are martial arts, both have traditions, and both are taught in classes with one or more instructors, but they view their subjects differently.

Similarly, although you go to only one university, that university will give you many "schools" to choose from. For example, there is the school of psychology (getting inside people's head) and the school of biology (dissecting what's inside people's heads) and the school of education (putting things into people's heads). Each school emphasizes different things, though sometimes they overlap.

This is true even of the Bible's prophecies. There are four major schools of thought about how to interpret them.

Preterism

The term *preterism* has the prefix *pre,* which I guess is also in the word *prefix.* Anyway, *pre* means what comes before—so a pre-game show happens *before* the game, and a pre-made pie is one you bought already made so you didn't have to bother making a far superior, freshly made pie for your company.

Preterism is one of these schools of interpretation of prophecy. Preterists believe that all the prophecies in the Bible happened in the past—*before* the present, in other words. (See Hastily Drawn Figure 3.1.) They consider everything in Daniel and Revelation to be history. Many people are preterists because they believe that the Bible is just a book and that nothing supernatural ever really happens. So they don't believe in prophecy.

While it's true that parts of Daniel and Revelation are about things that happened when Daniel and John were alive, if these books contain no prophecies about later times, how we can apply what they say to the lives we're living now, thousands of years later?

Hastily Drawn Figure 3.1

PRETERISM

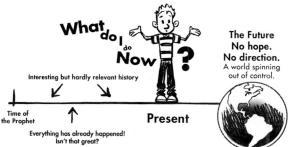

What do I do Now?

Interesting but hardly relevant history

Time of the Prophet

Everything has already happened! Isn't that great?

Present

The Future
No hope.
No direction.
A world spinning out of control.

Futurism

Futurism is the opposite of preterism. Futurists believe that all the prophecies in Daniel and Revelation, and particularly Revelation 8–12, are meant only for the last generation of people on earth before Jesus comes (see Hastily Drawn Figure 3.2). In other words, these prophecies are all about what will happen at the end of time or just before it, and they won't make any sense to you and me until then.

Just like preterism, futurism is partially correct. It's true that Daniel and Revelation have prophecies about events beyond the time we're living in now, but that doesn't mean that none of their prophecies say anything about the past or to our time. And while we don't understand everything these prophecies contain, it doesn't make a whole lot of sense to say that we can't understand God's Word, especially what He's saying in a book titled "Revelation"—which means "to reveal" information.

Hastily Drawn Figure 3.2

FUTURISM
HEADACHE

Time of the Prophet　　Present

Miscellaneous points about the far future that you can't understand, so don't even try or you'll get a headache.

Idealism

Another school of thought about Daniel and Revelation and how they should be interpreted is called *idealism*. Rather than focusing on specific points or actual events, idealists look for and cherish principles, general truths. They believe that the symbols in Daniel and Revelation say nothing about historical happenings. Instead, these books merely paint a very general picture of the ongoing struggle between good and evil (see Hastily Drawn Figure 3.3).

While it's true our application of God's Word and truth to various situations in our lives should be based on principles we find in His Word, this doesn't mean God has never given specific commands or acted in special ways during crucial times—such as when He sent His Son to die for our sins. We need to be aware of God's acting on earth during the past and the present and that He will continue to do things here on earth in the future. And we need to believe that He has given us His Word to guide us at all times.

Hastily Drawn Figure 3.3

IDEALISM

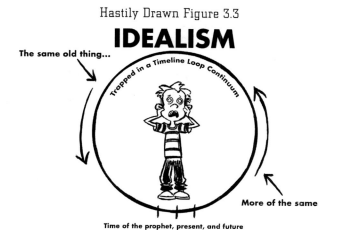

The same old thing...

Trapped in a Timeline Loop Continuum

More of the same

Time of the prophet, present, and future

What are the strengths and weaknesses of each school of thought?

_____

_____

_____

_____

_____

_____

_____

_____

_____

_____

_____

_____

_____

_____

_____

_____

_____

_____

_____

_____

_____

_____

_____

_____

Historicism

Finally, we arrive at the *historicism* school of prophetic interpretation. This is the school most Seventh-day Adventists subscribe to. I believe it is the best because it incorporates, in a balanced way, elements of all the schools above, and it makes the most sense.

In this school, prophecy is viewed as a continuous whole—beginning at the time of the prophet and unrolling like a scroll through history and up to the time of the end (see Hastily Drawn Figure 3.4). This means that we can believe God has been communicating during the long-ago times of the prophets, in recent history, and in the present, and that the prophecies of Daniel and Revelation give us insights regarding actual events that will happen on earth in the future. In the rest of this book, we will be looking at these prophecies from the perspective of the historicist school.

Hastily Drawn Figure 3.4

HISTORICISM

Peace from seeing that God is in control of the past, present, and future

Unrolling Revelation

God Actively Working in History

Prestent

Second Coming

Time of the prophet | 70-week Prophecy Fulfilled A.D. 34 | 2,300-day/year Prophecy Fulfilled A.D. 1844 | Identity/Mark of the Beast | **Time of trouble**

Going Deeper

Many people believe that the schools of preterism and futurism arose during a time when some people were interpreting prophecy in a way that portrayed the pope very negatively, and that to take the heat off him, the church of that time commissioned scholars to develop different ways of interpreting these prophecies. If all prophecy was fulfilled in Bible times, it couldn't refer to the then current pope, and that was also true if all prophecy was to be fulfilled in the future. What can we do to make sure we don't interpret Scripture in such a way as to make it say what we want it to say?

_____

_____

_____

_____

_____

_____

_____

_____

_____

CHAPTER 3 IN BRIEF

There probably are as many ways to approach prophecy as there are people. Individual personalities, preferences, and presuppositions can take readers in a variety of directions. However, in this book we will use the biblical concept that Daniel and Revelation contain prophecies that stretch from the times of Daniel and John and extend through the present and into the future. We can take comfort in knowing that God interacts with humanity throughout the ages and that He is at work in our lives today.

Chapter 4
Eye Exams

Going Deeper

Where do you see people repeating things in life to make a point?

_____

_____

_____

_____

_____

_____

_____

_____

_____

_____

_____

_____

_____

_____

_____

_____

_____

_____

_____

_____

_____

_____

Ever since my eyes failed me in the fourth grade, I have been subjected to the medieval medical practices of eye doctors on an annual basis. Even though my prescription hasn't changed in years, these people won't sell me anything until I pass through their gauntlet of torture.

True, I could bypass their medieval ways and go for refractory eye surgery and be done with it. However, I found out that "refractory eye surgery" is a fancy name for shooting one's eyes with a laser. Other surgeries "reshape the cornea," which is another way of saying they cut your eye with a sharp knife until you see better. I'd have better luck falling down the stairs with a sharp pair of kitchen shears. So I continue to make my sojourn to that person and his or her helpers to pester my pupils for an hour.

The first torture device of the eyeball odyssey is the eye puffer. Supposedly, this machine measures the fluid pressure in your eyes and checks for a disease called glaucoma. Whether or not you have the disease, the experience is a startling exercise in the uncomfortable. You place your head up against the machine, they tell you to look in a particular direction, and then, without warning, they blast your eye with a puff of air. *PFFFT!* The puff blows out all the moisture in your eye—along with your contact lens, if you're wearing one. By the time they puff your other eye, they have just about puffed out your patience as well.

I asked the woman who administered the test how it works, and she said she didn't know—she just pressed the button. I debated walking up to her and blowing in her eye to see how she liked it.

The next phase of this nightmare happens inside the doctor's office. Whatever pleasantries he or she greets you with are simply to set you up for the next round of suffering.

Ever since I was a kid, the people who actually cared about me told me not to look at the sun—it's so bright that looking at it can blind you, which makes sense to me. So why is it the first thing the eye appraisers do when they get you in their

Going Deeper

What things do you view differently now than you did when you were a kid?

_____
_____
_____
_____
_____
_____
_____
_____
_____
_____

What changed your perspective?

_____
_____
_____
_____
_____
_____
_____
_____
_____
_____
_____

office is to take a light with the power of a billion stars, hold it directly in front of your eyeball—so close that your eyelashes give it butterfly kisses—and wave this blazing source of illumination back and forth in front of your eye, sending dazzling effervescent light bouncing around in your brain?

"Yep, looks good," the light-wielding eye looker says. But the only thing I'm seeing is spots. Magical purple spots floating around the room.

Next on the docket: the Metal Facemask Lens Adjuster Machine. Used in conjunction with the MFLAM is the most tedious test ever administered to humankind. There are just two questions, which are repeated incessantly for several minutes. The first half of the question lilts upward in its inflection, and the second half descends in a monotonous—almost discouraging—inflection that makes you wonder whether you really should ever side with it.

The questions go like this: "Number one? Or number two?"

Each number refers to a different setting on the lens of the facemask that you're looking through. The eye investigator rotates through several sets of lenses as you look at a poster full of letters varying in size:

T
HI
SWI
LLHU
RTYOU!

As you move through different lens settings, the poster changes from fuzzy to crystal clear. What a great way to mess with someone!

Well, of course, the letters don't change, but your vision becomes better and you see the letters in their entirety and in sharp focus. This process ends when the eye appraiser finds the lenses that help you see best. Then the prescription is written, you pick out your glasses or contact lenses—and you pay the bill. The final torture.

Prophetic eye exams

As we move through the book of Daniel, you'll notice that the same entities appear several times but are represented by different symbols. Studying Daniel 2's vision of the statue and then Daniel 7's vision of the various animals and finding out they mean the same thing can be confusing. The overlapping applications of prophecy can create overlapping feelings of wanting to poke your eyes out in confusion.

For example, in Daniel 2, "thighs of bronze" represent Greece (verses 32, 39). In Daniel 7, a "leopard, with four wings" represents Greece (verse 6). In Daniel 8, it's a "he-goat" with a "conspicuous horn" that—you guessed it—represents Greece (verse 5).

What gives? Is it just that Scripture is redundant?

It can feel that way—and the writers of Scripture *did* use repetition to emphasize something's importance. But in this case, the repetition is a prophetic lens check. Just as the eye doctor switches back and forth between various lenses to establish clarity, so God used differing pictures and facets of the same entity to make the reader's picture of it as clear as possible.

If I came to your house and asked to see your high school yearbook, you'd be horrified! Looking through your baby book, I'd see pictures of you from infancy to however old you are now. All the candid shots your parents took through those awkward teenage years would be on display for me to laugh at. How embarrassing for you.

I understand.

And hey, I'll do my best to laugh only at the pictures of you in the bathtub wearing bubble beards with your sister and not at anything closer to your present sources of shame.

Time changes the lens

This brings up another important aspect of the Bible that gives us ever clearer lenses to look through as we progress: things change over time.

So, there you are, reading about Babylon the "head of gold" (Daniel 2:36–38), Babylon "the tree" (Daniel 4:20, 21), and Babylon the "lion [with] eagles' wings" (Daniel 7:4, 17), when all of a sudden you notice Babylon isn't in the cast of characters in Daniel 8. As you will see, Babylon is one of the four kingdoms discussed in Daniel 2–7, but then it just drops out of sight.

The fact is, years pass between some of Daniel's visions and between some of the chapters of his book. *Years.* And at a certain point before Daniel finished writing the book, Babylon was defeated and another kingdom took its place. We'll actually see prophetic history unfold within the pages of the book of Daniel.

Remember, the historicist approach to understanding Daniel's prophecies means that we see God working in history from the time of the prophet all the way up to the very end of time. So if something seems missing, just remember that time is moving forward, and, one by one, the prophecies are being fulfilled—from Bible times to our time and into time yet to come.

CHAPTER 4 IN BRIEF

Just as we look through multiple lenses to confirm or change our eyeglass

Going Deeper

What sort of things change your perspective on life now?

_____

_____

_____

_____

_____

_____

_____

_____

_____

_____

_____

_____

Should Christians ever change their views of God?

_____

_____

_____

_____

_____

_____

_____

_____

_____

_____

Going Deeper

How do our views of God change?

_____

_____

_____

_____

_____

_____

_____

What causes them to change?

_____

_____

_____

_____

_____

_____

_____

Is change good or bad?

_____

_____

_____

_____

_____

_____

_____

prescriptions, so we look through multiple "lenses" within the pages of Daniel's prophetic book till we find the clearest picture. The changing imagery in Daniel sharpens the picture of what God is doing in history. And just as people's eyes can require lens changes over time, so, as we move through prophetic history, there will be changes in the symbols and the entities we will be studying.

While truth never changes, our understanding of it does. As we become better acquainted with God, our perception of Him and how He works will become clearer and clearer. If we aren't changing, then we aren't growing. The Christian life is never stale and static; it's constantly moving and growing. Just think how much more you know now than you did last year, and then imagine what you'll learn during the next year. I hope, in fact, that you'll learn more about Him as you read this book. May the Holy Spirit continually give you new lenses through which to see God and His plan in ever-increasing clarity!

Chapter 5
What Do You See?

Going Deeper

Why do you think John used so many images from the Hebrew Scriptures instead of spelling things out?

When we see paintings or hear vivid descriptions, we rely on what we've learned and what we've experienced to help us understand what they mean. When you read the word *campground,* for instance, you might think of the time you were nearly eaten alive by mosquitoes. *Pumpkin* might raise in you thoughts of Thanksgiving and the emotions you feel when your family is together. And pencils might bring back memories of grade school and having to fill out those millions of tiny circles on your exams.

There are images in Revelation that might seem a little, well, crazy. Seeing how they're used in other places in the Bible and what they meant to Christians at the time Revelation was written makes them more—shall we say—sane.

Scroll eater

For example, take Revelation 10:9, 10, in which John writes, "So I went to the angel and told him to give me the little scroll. And he said to me, 'Take and eat it; it will make your stomach bitter, but in your mouth it will be sweet as honey.' And I took the little scroll from the hand of the angel and ate it."

So, here we have a guy who's eating a rolled-up piece of paper. Does this make any kind of sense? What do you see here besides a weird way to increase the fiber in your diet?

Hastily Drawn Figure 5.1

A cosmic ensemble

Then there's the picture described in Revelation 12:1: "A great sign appeared in heaven: a woman clothed with the sun, with the moon under her feet, and on her head a crown of twelve stars." You won't find that outfit at the mall.

Hastily Drawn Figure 5.2*

Now you and I, who are reading this in the twenty-first century, see these images as bizarre and potentially symptoms of insanity—but they would have made sense to John's readers. As I mentioned in chapter 1, John was a Jew who was exiled for his faith in Jesus. His primary audience would have been as familiar with the Hebrew Scriptures (a.k.a. the Old Testament) as we are with lines from popular movies.

What did they see?

Just as the sight of a light saber makes people living today think of *Star Wars,* seeing someone eat a scroll would make a first-century Jew think of the following texts from the Hebrew Scriptures:

- "Your words were found, and I ate them, and your words became to me a joy and the delight of my heart, for I am called by your name, O LORD, God of hosts" (Jeremiah 15:16).
- "He said to me, 'Son of man, eat . . . this scroll, and go, speak to the house of Israel' " (Ezekiel 3:1).

---

* Yes, I know the woman has no arms. Did the text say anything about arms? Did it? Thank you.

John wasn't the only one in the history of God's people to "eat the scroll." As we read these two Old Testament passages in their "context" (meaning we read the verses before and after to get the whole story), the meaning becomes clear. "Eating the scroll" means understanding fully the message God was giving them. In fact, that expression is very similar to one that we use to describe someone who has gotten really caught up in reading. We say that person is "devouring" the book.

As for the cosmic lady of Revelation 12, the Hebrew Scriptures give us the clues we need to unravel the mystery. Throughout the Old Testament, God's people are likened to a woman, a wife (see Isaiah 54:5, 6; Jeremiah 3:20; Ezekiel 16:8–14). Second Corinthians 11:2 and Ephesians 5:25–32 contain the same analogy.

Similarly, the sun, moon, and stars appeared in a dream Joseph had (see Genesis 37). Joseph tells his brothers that he dreamed that "the sun, the moon, and eleven stars were bowing down to me"—which his father recognizes as representing himself and Joseph's mother and brothers (verses 9, 10). The imagery is also found in Song of Solomon 6:10, where Solomon describes his wife as being "as beautiful as the full moon, pure as the sun" (NASB). Given that a woman can refer to a people—specifically God's people, it's a good bet that we are dealing with the church.

So Revelation's images aren't crazy after all. They're full of deep meaning.

SUMMARY AND CONCLUSION

You'll see some weird stuff in Revelation that won't appear to make sense. However, God sometimes doesn't make sense until we pause and reflect on who He is and what He's doing. So Revelation benefits us by making us slow down and digest what God is saying instead of flying through it as if we already know everything it contains—which happens all too often when we study the Bible. Books like Genesis, Esther, and John are naturally easier to read—but I think we miss half of what is in them because we push our way through them so quickly. Many of the people who think the Bible is wacky have never stopped to figure out the deeper meaning of what they're reading.

God uses strange images that are loaded with meaning to make us slow down and realize we don't know everything. So, whether you're reading the verses I've mentioned or some you picked out for yourself, read a little slower and pause every now and then to reread a verse or passage a few times. And ask God to help you understand what you're reading.

Do you ever use symbols or images when you communicate? Why are they more effective than just saying it straight as it is?

Chapter 6
The Significant Seven

Throughout my life I have tended to wander away from the nice ladies who have taken me shopping with them. My mother wanted her trips to the grocery store to be quick ones—only to have her eldest son—me—disappear to the produce section, where I tried to juggle the oranges. While she was picking up those fruits, I would scramble over to the coffee section and pull the lever on the fancy dispenser, releasing the as-yet-unground coffee beans to fall on the floor. By the time my mother had halted the flow of beans, I had made my way to the video game section, where I would drool over the expensive, cellophane-wrapped Nintendo games—which, obviously, my mother didn't buy.

I haven't changed much. From time to time, my wife agrees to take me shopping in public. One of our family's favorite haunts is Pike's Place Market in downtown Seattle. My wife goes for the flowers, the food, and little pretty things she uses to fluff up our house. I, however, have another goal. When I've parked our car, it takes me just ten minutes to locate a special place deep within the bowels of the market.

A collection of exotic nerdery

Golden Age Collectibles (.com!) has one of the greatest collections of exotic nerdery from times past to be found anywhere. Their glorious nonsense ranges from *Star Trek* phasers and Darth Vader's helmet to Spiderman coffee mugs and old toys. Their motto—"Refusing to Grow Up Since 1971"—resonates with me since I've been refusing the same thing since the 1980s, when I received my first pair of Superman pajamas.

The market also has comic books for sale, which is what I was after on my recent escape from my wife's side. Whilst she was looking at lavender soaps and honey-based facial creams, I darted away to my fortress of foolishness.

"Get back here!" she cried. "You'd better not be going where I think you're going!"

But she was too late. I was well on my way to get a very special item. One that I needed. One that had just been released and that won't be released again—perhaps ever again.

Batman.

Issue number 1.

DC Comics decided to re-release all their comics. Since some of the originals were first released as early as the 1930s, first issues are not only rare but also excruciatingly expensive. One expert says that an original of the first Batman comic book is worth $125,000. But the new releases cost only three dollars—exactly the amount that I get for my weekly allowance.

After spending time looking at various comic books, I picked up issue number 1. Now, before I admit to buying it, let me say that many comic books are violent and disturbing, and some of them are beyond vile. I'm not telling you to go out and buy comics. I was mostly on a quest to own a piece of American history—one that now rests in a plastic case high on a shelf where my wife can't reach it.

When it comes to comic books, the most valuable number is one. However, the book of Revelation is different. In this prophetic book, the number that counts is seven.

Book of sevens

Revelation is full of sevens.

- Seven churches—Revelation 1:4
- Seven golden lampstands—Revelation 1:12
- Seven stars—Revelation 1:16
- Seven spirits—Revelation 3:1
- Seven seals (not the animal)—Revelation 5:1
- Seven horns—Revelation 5:6
- Seven eyes—Revelation 5:6
- Seven angels—Revelation 8:2
- Seven trumpets (blown by the seven angels)—Revelation 8:2
- Seven thunders—Revelation 10:4
- Seven thousand people (who are killed)—Revelation 11:13
- Seven heads (on a red dragon that's in a foul mood)—Revelation 12:3
- Seven horns (on a sea monster that's also in a foul mood)—Revelation 13:1
- Seven plagues—Revelation 15:1
- Seven golden bowls (filled with wrath soup)—Revelation 15:7
- Seven mountains—Revelation 17:9
- Seven kings—Revelation 17:10

When people repeat things, whether it be in the warnings broadcast in Scripture or in the shouts of a woman trying to save herself from financial ruin because her

Notes

Search the Bible for places where the number seven is a symbol of perfection (The easy way to do this is to look up the word *seven* in a concordance.)

husband has gotten loose in the comic-book store, you know there's something of importance nearby. John uses the number seven repeatedly because it carries significance, and he uses that to label something as significant.

Why not one?

Or ten?

Or a million billion?

Because in Scripture, seven says perfection.

The significance of seven

Way back when God decided to create the planet we live on, He decided to do it in seven days (see Genesis 1 and 2). In those seven days, everything that makes up our favorite planet came into being: light, air, land, water, flamingos, and so on.* However, only one item on God's divine to-do list received the privilege of being called "holy." "On the seventh day God finished his work that he had done, and he rested on the seventh day from all his work that he had done. So God blessed the seventh day and made it holy, because on it God rested from all his work that he had done in creation" (Genesis 2:2, 3).

The final day of that week, the day known as the Sabbath, is the crown of the world God had just finished making. God didn't even call the first two human beings "holy"† and "blessed" as He did this incredible day. The Sabbath is the cherry on top of God's creative sundae. He considered this sacred moment in time so important that He even made it part of the Ten Commandments:

"Remember the Sabbath day, to keep it holy. Six days you shall labor, and do all your work, but the *seventh day* is a Sabbath to the LORD your God. On it you shall not do any work, you, or your son, or your daughter, your male servant, or your female servant, or your livestock, or the sojourner who is within your gates. For in six days the LORD *made heaven and earth, the sea, and all that is in them,* and rested on the *seventh day.* Therefore the LORD blessed the Sabbath day and made it holy" (Exodus 20:8–11; emphasis added).

The seventh day of our week is a significant reminder of a magnificent Creator. God has given us six days on which we can create all kinds of things. God made the Sabbath to remind us that our creation is not like His. It's a day that reminds us that we are not God.

The wording God used in the fourth commandment appears in Revelation 14:7 too: "Fear God and give him glory, because the hour of his judgment has come, and

---

* OK, so I don't know whether flamingos as we know them existed at the dawn of time. Thanks for pointing that out. Now get a sense of humor, and start reading again.

† *Holy* means "set aside."

worship him who made heaven and earth, the sea and the springs of water" (Revelation 14:7; emphasis added). John says that it's an angel who makes this statement. So it must be an important statement. And the fact that God sends the angel to repeat the words of the fourth commandment tells us that people need to be reminded of the God who made everything, and they need to worship Him—as opposed to worshiping something—or someone—else.

SUMMARY AND CONCLUSION

The number seven points back to Creation, when God completed His construction of planet Earth. Seven signifies completion and perfection.

What then does this tell us about all the symbolic sevens used in Revelation?

Whether it's "seven eyes" that see everything or judgment in the form of "seven bowls of wrath," God doesn't do things halfway. He doesn't turn in half-done homework. He doesn't become bored with humanity or abandon His plans for the future.

As we progress through Revelation, we'll see God's awesome power on display. That should tell us that our Savior is strong enough to carry this world—which includes you and me—to the end of time and beyond.*

---

* Yes, that was a Buzz Lightyear allusion. Thanks for noticing.

Chapter 7

Running the Ball: The Structure of Revelation

Deep in the huddle I made the plan. Since I was both the quarterback and the pastor, my teammates—the young adult leaders—looked to me for the plays we would run against the nefarious teenagers we had challenged in our annual flag football game. We could hear their mockery as we concocted a scheme that would bamboozle them and bring us glory.

The key to a good running play is the element of surprise—and we needed it against this particular group of teens. One of them played on his school's football team. Compared with the rest of us, he was practically a professional. The other teens possessed a genetic anomaly that gave them limitless energy, and, when combined with the Hawaiian punch they brought, created a dynamic admixture that enabled them to reach nearly supersonic speeds.

As for us youth leaders, our well-toned but experienced muscles refused to match the frenetic pace of our sugar-filled challengers. That meant we had to base our plan on something other than physical prowess—we had to base it on cunning. Fortunately, over the years I have created a book of plays that border on the clinically insane, but that work.

One of my plays is what I call the Ring of Fire. The center hikes the ball to the quarterback, who then runs toward the end zone. The rest of the team runs in a tight circle around the quarterback while simultaneously moving down the field. This visually stunning play frustrates the other team because they can't break through the protection to sack the quarterback. The downside of this play is that it doesn't last long because the players become dizzy. However, this play is usually good for a first down.

Next comes the Harvey Knee-Slapper, based on a *Sesame Street* character by the same name. On the children's show, this nutty puppet with googly eyes runs toward other puppets laughing maniacally and slapping letters on them after telling stupid jokes. He's by far my favorite *Sesame Street* character.

Here's how this play works: after the ball is hiked, all but two players on the team begin to laugh and run wildly around, slapping themselves and anyone else within arm's reach while the runningback and a blocker head for the end zone. Unfortunately, I haven't actually tried this play, so I don't know how well it works. I'll allow you the pleasure of trying it the next time you play football. Let me know what happens.

Finally, there's my greatest invention: the First-Down Hail Mary. Most football teams use the Hail Mary when they're at the height of desperation—when the other team has more points and there are only a few seconds left in the game. The play consists of the quarterback making an epically long throw and hoping against hope that someone on his team will catch the ball and score, either tying the game or winning it.

This play is risky and a little stupid—unless you don't have the pressure of the clock winding down. Then it's pure genius. No one expects a Hail Mary on the first play of a down or of a possession—or from a team that is in the lead.

That's why it worked against the youth that day.

Five times.

The sheer audacity of making a play like that goes against every bit of common sense. Frankly, it's appalling—at least it was to the guy who played football in school. It's the sporting equivalent of requesting French fries at an expensive restaurant, burping after eating said French fries, and then dashing out of the dining establishment without paying the check.

Uncouth.

Insulting.

Rude.

And very effective.

We won by thirty or forty points that day—all because we had plans that worked—that moved the ball toward the end zone.

X marks the spot

Football isn't the only activity that works better when there's a plan. Most people who write articles or books make an outline first. The outline is like a map or a blueprint that helps the author move from the beginning to the end in a logical way, getting his or her point across to the reader. The outlines we use generally look something like this:

I. Introduction
    A. My neighbor stares at my house late into the night.
    B. I will prove that my neighbor is a spy.
II. Main Body
    A. My neighbor often stares at my house until midnight.

B. Research on my computer tells me about him.
   1. He is the famous theoretical physicist Stephen Hawking.
   2. He's almost totally dependent on a motorized wheelchair.
   3. His blog says his wheelchair has been malfunctioning.
   4. His "spying" has really been attempts to get help.
III. Summary and Conclusion
   A. My neighbor isn't a spy but someone who needs my help.
   B. I'll call a wheelchair mechanic.

As common as this outline is, though, and despite the fact that many study Bibles and commentaries say John of Patmos used one like it, you won't fully understand what John wrote in Revelation if you look for this kind of outline there. While we tend to organize things chronologically—in order of appearance, 1-2-3, a-b-c, beginning-middle-end—the basic literary structure used by the Jews, including our friend John, is the *chiasm*. A chiasm is a group of parallel ideas and/or words that are arranged in an X shape.

The Greek alphabet has a letter that looks like an X. It isn't an X, though; the letter is a *chi*—which is equivalent to our *c* and *h* put together (as in *chameleon*) and which people generally pronounce as *ky* (as in *sky*).*

The writers of Scripture—of both the Old Testament and the New—often put their main point right in the middle of their outline instead of at the end. They outlined entire books this way—shorter passages, too, and even individual verses. Their outlines, then, resembled a *chi* (X), or half of one, so Bible scholars call this kind of outline a *chiasm*. The point is that when a writer used a chiastic outline, he put his most important point at the middle of his outline. This is one of the primary characteristics of chiastic outlining, of chiastic structure.

The other primary characteristic of chiastic structure has the big, fancy name *parallelism*. When two things are parallel to each other, they're headed in the same direction. In at least that way (and often in other ways too) they resemble each other. For example, parallel lines look like this:

Fascinating, right? Time of your life?

Just hang in there. This will all come together soon.

When writers use parallelism, something that was said or an idea that was set forth at one place in the story reappears in some form or fashion later on in the story. For example, in the Disney movie *The Emperor's New Groove,* the prideful Emperor Kuzco fires his creepy advisor Yzma from her post. When he kicks her out, he tells her, "Just think of it as your being let go, that your life's going in a different direction, that your body's part of a permanent outplacement."

---

* The Greek word *Christ* begins with the letter *chi;* in Greek letters, it looks like this: ΧΡΙΣΤ.

Toward the end of the film, Yzma tries to exact revenge upon Kuzco, and as she does, she says, "Just think of it as your being let go, that your life's going in a different direction, that your body's part of a permanent outplacement."

That is a parallel.

In fact, it's a cruel irony of a parallel, as Yzma points out.

To repeat: a chiasm is a group of parallel ideas and/or words that can be arranged in an X shape. You can see how this works in a small way in verse 12 of Matthew 23: "Whoever exalts himself will be humbled, and whoever humbles himself will be exalted."

Hastily Drawn Diagram 7.1

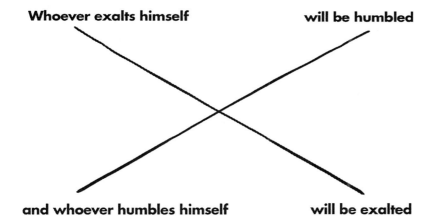

Chiastic Structure of Matthew 23:12

Whoever exalts himself   **will be humbled**

and whoever humbles himself   **will be exalted**

Arranged in sequence, this verse reads:

A. Whoever exalts himself

                      B. Will be humbled,

                      B'. And whoever humbles himself

A'. Will be exalted.

The outline has the form of half of the letter X, so despite the missing half, it's still called a chiasm. Each letter stands for a major point, and A' parallels A, and B' parallels B. A and A' speak of people being exalted, and B and B' speak of being humbled. So we have "exalting" at the beginning and end, and "humble" in the middle—which tells us that the primary idea Jesus meant for us to walk away with is the value of being humble. "Humble" is in the middle. It is central. It's the jelly

Notes

in the middle of the doughnut, if you will.

Mmmm . . . doughnuts.

Revelation's outline

The entire book of Revelation is written as a chiasm, though scholars are still discussing exactly which parts go where, and what's in the center of the chiasm. Here are a couple of my favorite outlines.

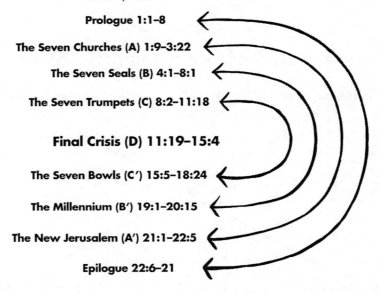

Hastily Drawn Jon Paulien Model[1]

Prologue 1:1–8

The Seven Churches (A) 1:9–3:22

The Seven Seals (B) 4:1–8:1

The Seven Trumpets (C) 8:2–11:18

Final Crisis (D) 11:19–15:4

The Seven Bowls (C′) 15:5–18:24

The Millennium (B′) 19:1–20:15

The New Jerusalem (A′) 21:1–22:5

Epilogue 22:6–21

While it may not be totally apparent, the second half mirrors the first. Obviously, the prologue and the epilogue are related—but what about things like the seven churches and the New Jerusalem? We'll get to these parts of Revelation eventually. For now, just remember that the major point is in the middle, and the first half and the second are reflections of each other.*

Another way to view the chiastic structure is based on the menorah—the seven-branched candlestick or lampstand characteristic of the Jewish faith. Notice that Doukhan and Paulien differ as to what parts of Revelation should make up the various sections.

---

* Such as when you look in a mirror and raise your left hand—but in the mirror image, it's your right hand.

Hastily Drawn Strand/Doukhan Model[2]

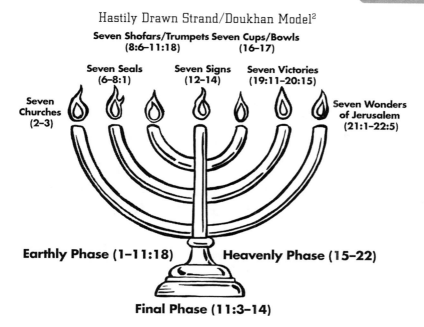

Going Deeper

See if you can pick out any more chiasms in the Gospel of Matthew.

I've built a few models of my own, using Paulien's text references: the Rainbow Model, the Ship Model, the ATARI Pong Model, and the Football Running-Play Model.* We don't have room for all of them, so I'll just throw two in for your consideration.

The Ship Model

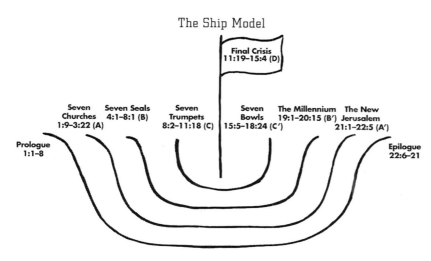

___

* If you don't know what this is, google "ATARI Pong" and witness the greatest video game of all time.

Since we began with football, it's certainly appropriate—in a chapter on chiasms—to end with football.

The Football Running-Play Model

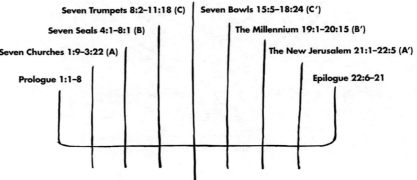

Final Crisis 11:19–15:4 (D)

Seven Trumpets 8:2–11:18 (C) | Seven Bowls 15:5–18:24 (C')

Seven Seals 4:1–8:1 (B) | The Millennium 19:1–20:15 (B')

Seven Churches 1:9–3:22 (A) | The New Jerusalem 21:1–22:5 (A')

Prologue 1:1–8 | Epilogue 22:6–21

SUMMARY AND CONCLUSION

The book of Revelation begins with the story of a man named John who's exiled on the island of Patmos. However, as we move through this book of visions, it will be a challenge to maintain focus because what's in this book doesn't flow like a typical story. Revelation is comprised of a series of visions—all of which are connected. Sometimes these visions take us to future events, but they can also refer back to the past.

The good news is that while the sections of Revelation can seem random and unrelated at first, the book does have a structure and a flow, and those sections become easier to see as we continue to study. God isn't the author of chaos; He has a plan—one that He reveals in Revelation. When our lives seem random or out of control, remembering that God does have a plan does us good.

ENDNOTES

1. Jon Paulien, *Seven Keys: Unlocking the Secrets of Revelation* (Nampa, Idaho: Pacific Press® Publishing Association, 2009), 99.
2. Jacques Doukhan, *Secrets of Revelation* (Hagerstown, Md.: Review and Herald® Publishing Association, 2002), 14.

Chapter 8
Ciphers

The Central Intelligence Agency—better known as the CIA—is a legendary organization that has been training spies to crack codes since 1947. This mysterious organization is characterized by men in dark suits who ride around in big black sedans and exude an air of confidence signaling that they are capable of handling anything—anything, that is, except decoding the sculpture located on the grounds of their headquarters in Langley, Virginia.

You heard me: someone's art project is bamboozling the United States' spy agency right on their own property. And to make matters worse, the CIA commissioned and paid for the sculpture that has them scratching their heads.

Jim Sanborn is the culprit behind the copper statue that plagues the CIA. When the administrators of that agency erected a brand-new building in the late 1980s, they thought it would be great to commission a cool puzzle to commemorate the event. And by cool, I mean really cool—$250,000 cool.

Sanborn is the sculptor who conceived the project and saw it through. His sculpture, named *Kryptos,* consists of four nine-foot-high copper sheets.* Letters that form an encoded text have been punched out of each of these sheets. In the twenty years this sculpture has stood on the CIA's grounds, people, including the employees of the agency itself, have managed to decipher three of the four plates. But section four—known as K4—has remained elusive.

Just in case you feel like cracking the code on K4 in your free time, here it is:

```
NGHIJLMNQUVWXZKRYPTOSABCDEFGHIJL
OHIJLMNQUVWXZKRYPTOSABCDEFGHIJL
PIJLMNQUVWXZKRYPTOSABCDEFGHIJLM
QJLMNQUVWXZKRYPTOSABCDEFGHIJLMN
RLMNQUVWXZKRYPTOSABCDEFGHIJLMNQ
SMNQUVWXZKRYPTOSABCDEFGHIJLMNQU
```

* You can see it at http://en.wikipedia.org/wiki/Kryptos.

Notes

_____

_____

_____

_____

_____

_____

_____

_____

_____

_____

_____

_____

_____

_____

_____

_____

_____

_____

_____

_____

_____

_____

_____

_____

_____

```
TNQUVWXZKRYPTOSABCDEFGHIJLMNQUV
UQUVWXZKRYPTOSABCDEFGHIJLMNQUVW
VUVWXZKRYPTOSABCDEFGHIJLMNQUVWX
WVWXZKRYPTOSABCDEFGHIJLMNQUVWXZ
XWXZKRYPTOSABCDEFGHIJLMNQUVWXZK
YXZKRYPTOSABCDEFGHIJLMNQUVWXZKR
ZZKRYPTOSABCDEFGHIJLMNQUVWXZKRY
ABCDEFGHIJKLMNOPQRSTUVWXYZABCD
```

Have you solved it yet?

Neither has the CIA.

If you do solve it, you could probably get a job in the CIA. Just put that accomplishment on the job application.

Not only is the fourth section still a mystery, but the three sections that have been decoded seem to make very little sense. This may be a hint that there are codes within the codes yet to be deciphered. I mean, take a look at the solution to K1: BETWEEN SUBTLE SHADING AND THE ABSENCE OF LIGHT LIES THE NUANCE OF IQLUSION.

I totally get it—it's crazy talk. Good old-fashioned nonsense, right? Well, the CIA doesn't think so, and it continues to employ its best minds in attempts to somehow break this thing down. In the meantime, the only man who knows the solution isn't revealing it. Sanborn remains silent—and quite delighted—at the difficulty of his puzzle. He has given a few clues and pointed out a few mistakes, but he's not about to give the answer now or even after his death. (He *has* given the answer to someone, though, because in case of his death, he's arranged for that person to tell would-be cryptographers whether their solutions are right or wrong.)

Well played, Mr. Sanborn.

Revelation's cipher texts

Unlike the creator of *Kryptos,* our Creator God has placed clues within the book of Revelation to help us decipher the meaning of seemingly coded passages. We can be thankful that these "cipher verses" make a whole lot more sense than K1 does.

Because of Revelation's unique organization, it can frustrate our attempts to understand what it's saying while it bedazzles our senses.* Fortunately, John has embedded clues—ciphers, if you will—in his prophecy to help us unlock the meaning of the text. He slips the clue to the meaning of a passage in the last part of the preceding passage. And while the message of Revelation may be to some extent hidden by symbols from the Old Testament (to mislead Roman officials who might intercept Rev-

---

* I'm not sure that the word *bedazzle* connotes what I mean, as that word has the aura of little girls putting sparkly things on clothing, furniture, and small animals. My intent was to say that we can easily become confused when we're reading and trying to understand Revelation.

elation and attempt to use it as evidence against the author and the people to whom he sent it), the text isn't double encrypted, and it is understandable.

Let's look at a couple examples. The last verse of chapter 1 states, "As for the mystery of the seven stars that you saw in my right hand, and the seven golden lampstands, the seven stars are the angels of the seven churches, and *the seven lampstands are the seven churches*" (emphasis added). Guess what we see as we move into chapters 2 and 3? That's right—the seven churches. That passage is pretty easy to figure out, but as we move forward, we'll find things that are a little more bedazzling.*

The conclusion of Revelation 3 contains these lines: "The one who conquers, I will grant him to sit with me on my throne, as I also conquered and sat down with my Father on his throne." Notice the four elements here. Taken in chronological order, they are the Father's throne, Jesus joining the Father on His throne, followers of Jesus who conquer, and followers of Jesus joining Him on the throne. *These four lines reveal the subjects of the next four chapters of the book.* Revelation 4 pictures the Father's throne in heaven; chapter 5, Jesus' inauguration as King, following which He sits on the Father's throne; chapter 6, the followers of Jesus who have been faithful unto death in contrast to the fate of those who have turned away from God; and chapter 7, the followers of Jesus surround the throne of God, to which they have been given free access.

What all this means will become clearer. (We'll be spending a chapter on each of these elements.) The point here is that the end of chapter 3 gives us the key that unlocks the next four chapters of the book. We don't have to go to the Internet or to newspapers or learn some weird mathematical formula to unlock the basic meaning of Revelation. Jesus means this book to be understood.

SUMMARY AND CONCLUSION

Revelation can seem like an encrypted puzzle that can be understood only by those who have been given the code. But Jesus, the One who gave the original revelation to John, isn't interested in hiding His messages from you and me. He wants to reveal Himself and His truth to us—to everyone. He has placed the keys to the meaning of this book within its text, and has made them easy to find and to understand.

Significantly, the Greek word translated "revelation" isn't a broad word that means every kind of revealing. This word is quite specific. It means the revealing of something that once was hidden. In other words, Revelation offers us a picture of Jesus that no other book in the Bible contains—one that Jesus doesn't want to be hidden from us. That's an encouraging thought—one that we should remember when we feel that God is hiding from us.

* Again, I'm not thinking of sparkly sequins, but of confusion. Maybe I should stop using that word.

Going Deeper

Why do you think people ignore the biblical ciphers and choose instead to look to newspapers and newscasts to interpret Revelation and last-day events?

Chapter 9

Sync

"Death to the remote." That's what I told my audio-visual team at church when we discovered that I could run my PowerPoint presentations from my iPad. For years I have been plagued by faulty clickers that are too lazy to connect with the computer, preventing me from moving my presentations forward. These little devils pretend they work during the practice run before church starts. Everything appears fine as I press down on the soft little red button that calls for the next slide—wowing the audience with my creative capabilities. However, when the worship service starts and I begin to preach for real, the buttons prove unresponsive.

At first I think, *Hey, no biggie. I must not have pressed the button.* But let me tell you, my friend, that I *did* push the button. I pushed it, all right, but the little black remote in my hand has chosen to disobey my command! That plastic pest has ruined me in front of hundreds of people who are dying from curiosity about what the next slide would have shown them!

I begin tap-tap-tapping furiously on that infernal button—but the screen remains discouragingly dead. Trying to maintain a smile, I nod to my audio-visual team, begging them to do something, but they just shake their heads and throw their hands in the air. They've been bamboozled as well. Nervously, and holding back the rabid-dog-rage swelling in my heart, I try to make light of the situation by pasting a knowing look on my face as I glance at the congregation and say something witty, like, "Technology . . ." while the congregation chuckles nervously. I'm too angry to say anything else.

But those days are over. The diabolical clicker has met its match in the form of a higher technology: Bluetooth. Yes, that glorious thing we call Wi-Fi has come to the rescue. Now, with my iPad, which rests snugly in my iPad pulpit, I can sync with the computer on which the presentation is running. My iPad and the computer have become one. As I touch the screen of my Apple product, it signals the computer effortlessly, and the message flows along without hesitation.

Syncing with Daniel

About six hundred years before John wrote Revelation, the prophetic work named Daniel, after its writer, was written. That book contains prophecies that run from the era of the main human character, Daniel, until the end of time. However, though Daniel wrote these prophecies, many of them were mysteries to him, for he wrote that an angel told him to "shut up the words and seal the book, until the time of the end" (Daniel 12:4). Naturally, this frustrated Daniel.

(You can read all about it in my book *Prophecies of Daniel Made Simple*. There's the shameless book promotion you've been waiting for.)

But what was frustrating for Daniel is exciting for us, because the book of Revelation is synced with Daniel. The second part of Daniel 12:4 hints at this when it says, "Many shall run to and fro, and knowledge shall increase"—implying that as we get closer to the end of time, people would begin to understand Daniel's sealed prophecies.

Enter the book of Revelation.

The first prophecy in Daniel's book gives us an overview of human history and then ends with the words, "a great *God has made known* to the king *what shall be after this*" (Daniel 2:45; emphasis added). The New International Version translates this part of the text in these words: "what will take place in the future." Compare this with the very first verse in Revelation, which says, "The revelation of Jesus Christ, *which God gave* him to show to his servants *the things that must soon take place*" (emphasis added).

While the beginning of Revelation isn't exactly the same as the ending of Daniel, there are enough similarities to link the two books together. Both books indicate that God gave the prophets their content, and they both say that they deal with what "must soon take place." They go hand in hand together.

In Daniel 7:9, we read, "As I looked, *thrones were placed,* and the Ancient of Days took his seat" (emphasis added). So here we have a scene in heaven in which thrones were being set in place. Now look at Revelation 4:2. John is also given a peek into heaven, and he says, "Behold, *a throne stood* in heaven, with one seated on the throne" (Revelation 4:2; emphasis added). So, to recap, Daniel tells us that he saw some royal furniture being set up, and when we reach Revelation, the royal furniture is in place and in use.

In Daniel 7:25, the phrase "time, times and half a time" appears in connection with an evil entity that is attacking God's people. Revelation 12:14 tells us that "the woman was given the two wings of the great eagle so that she might fly from the serpent into the wilderness, to the place where she is to be nourished for *a time, and times, and half a time*" (emphasis added). I'll have more to say about the two times I've noted here. For the time being, just remember that this makes the third sync between the two books that was pointed out in this chapter.

Finally, some scholars believe that the mysterious number 666 mentioned in

Notes

Revelation 13:18 could be referencing the story found in Daniel 3 about the giant gold image that was dedicated to false worship. That pagan image was sixty cubits high, six cubits wide, and (probably) six cubits deep—in other words: 666.[1] That brings the number of syncs in this chapter to four—which I think sufficiently demonstrates how tightly Daniel and Revelation are connected.

SUMMARY AND CONCLUSION

Daniel is intricately linked with Revelation. Not only is Revelation a continuation of Daniel's prophecies, but the wording it uses is familiar because it first appeared in Daniel's book. The book of Daniel, then, is a major key to understanding Revelation.

While Daniel was distraught over the fact that he wouldn't get to see how all the prophecies played out at the end of time, we have the privilege of seeing the fulfillment of the plans God told us about through His prophets. This is a good reminder that even when we can't see how things will work out, the Bible promises that "he [Jesus] who began a good work in you will bring it to completion at the day of Jesus Christ" (Philippians 1:6).

May we, like Daniel, continue to hold on to our faith even when we can't see how things will turn out well.

ENDNOTE

1. See the *Andrews Study Bible* (Berrien Springs, Mich.: Andrews University Press, 2010), 1676.

The Battle Lines Form
Revelation 1–11

Chapter 10
Stranded

Revelation 1

Before our second daughter was born, my wife worked as the principal of a Christian school. Every morning she had to leave the house before I woke up so she could get the classroom ready for the day and prepare to greet the students as they arrived. Several times a year when I woke up and got ready to go to work, I would be sucked into a frantic scramble to find an item critical to my making it to my appointments.

My keys.

Whether it was because of my wife's haste to get to work on time, or because I had carelessly placed the keys near her purse, she would take them to work with her. It's one thing to lose your keys in the house: you still have hopes of finding them and racing off with the possibility of getting to your meetings on time. But it's quite another thing to have the foreboding feeling that your wife has both sets of keys. This feeling is worsened when you ask her about them and she says, "Uh-oh."

Stranded.

Well, I guess I'll be working from the home office today.

The setting

The book of Revelation features a character named John who sees visions and writes them down. While God loves him, and so do the Christians of his day, he finds himself not only exiled, but stranded too. In the first chapter of Revelation, John tells us whom he is writing to and where he is writing from:

> John *to the seven churches that are in Asia:* Grace to you and peace from him who is and who was and who is to come, and from the seven spirits who are before his throne, and from Jesus Christ the faithful witness, the firstborn of the dead, and the ruler of kings on earth. . . . I, John, your brother and partner in the tribulation and the kingdom and the patient endurance that are in Jesus, *was on the island called Patmos on account of the*

Going Deeper

Verse 4 mentions the "seven spirits." Do you have any idea what they are? I'll give you a hint. If the number seven signifies perfection, then "seven spirits" could simply be an allusion to a perfect or complete spirit. Who might that be?

word of God and the testimony of Jesus (Revelation 1:4–9; emphasis added).

In John's introduction to this important book, he says three things—conveniently italicized—that help set the stage for what follows. To be a firefighter or one of those nature photographers who go in cages, underwater, to take pictures of angry sharks is to take on some of today's most dangerous jobs. But back in the first century, being a Christian pastor or leader could get a person killed faster than a raging fire or a hungry shark can.

For example, the Christian church in Ephesus had a leader named Paul.

The government cut off his head.

We'll come back to that in a moment; the point for now is that when Paul lost his head (in A.D. 64) and the church needed a new leader, they settled on John. Like Daniel, John was Jewish. Perhaps significantly, his name means "God is gracious." He led the church in Ephesus for nearly thirty years, and was well known and well liked by its members.

After such an impressive tenure in an influential church, you'd expect the aging preacher to retire and retreat to a tropical island somewhere—one with beautiful beaches, sunny weather, and interesting excursions. Unfortunately for John, he was instead whisked away to Patmos, a rock sticking out of the Aegean Sea.

Several years ago I visited an island prison called Alcatraz located in the San Francisco Bay. As our ferry approached, the ghostly structure emerged from the mist. The fact that it had been closed for decades prior to my visit made it especially eerie. In its thirty-year history, no one managed to escape alive—at least that's what they say. The stone ruins and the dark and gloomy cells still standing—including one called "the hole"—testified to how stranded a prisoner who was being held there would feel.

Patmos was an ancient Alcatraz. It boasted a rugged beach, an active volcano, cave condos dug into the slopes of the volcano, and for exercise, working out in a rock quarry under the scrutinizing glare of soldiers. Patmos' labor camp was its main attraction. Labor camps were kind of like summer camps, except your "vacation" there lasted all year, your cabin was a cave, and the only activity was rock collecting—and if you didn't participate, your counselor, an angry Roman guard, might give you a beating.

Why on earth would the government send an old man to such a place? Let's return to the previous pastor's missing head.

In some ways, early Christians and their churches—including the one in Ephesus—were like the weird kid who gets beaten up in school and can't make friends because he just doesn't fit in. The food sold in the marketplaces and temples of the communities the Christians lived in had been dedicated to false gods before it was put up for sale, the pagan citizens of these communities had disturbing sexual interactions, and because the bread and wine of the Lord's Supper represented the body and blood of Christ (see 1 Corinthians 11), the pagans accused Christians of being cannibals.

In addition, the Roman emperors believed themselves to be gods. So when a group (like the Christians) refused to worship the emperor, they were branded as atheists and persecuted—that's why Paul lost his head.

And finally, there was another religious group—the Jews—who constantly fought with the Romans. They invited the Christians to join in the fracas, but the Christians chose to stay out of it. This didn't endear them to the Jews.

Being Christian at that time was dangerous business. So it's not surprising that as a result of John's uncompromising faith, in A.D. 95 the Roman emperor Domitian sentenced him to two years on Patmos.

Revelation uses the Greek word *thalassa,* which we translate as "sea," twenty-five times. It was the sea that kept John from his loved ones and from his work as pastor at Ephesus. So it's no wonder that when John describes the world as it will be when it's made new after the millennium, he says, "Then I saw a new heaven and a new earth, for the first heaven and the first earth had passed away, *and the sea was no more*" (Revelation 21:1; emphasis added).

The subject introduced

During the time John spent on Patmos, he received seven visions, each of which contains several scenes. So, there are many pieces to this book. Nevertheless, it has a single overarching theme—Jesus Christ, and our worship of Him. Everything in Revelation revolves around this theme. The very first verse in the book describes its contents as "the revelation of Jesus Christ." And as I noted in the previous chapter, the word *revelation* means "to reveal something that was once veiled," or "to reveal that which was hidden." In other words, Revelation shows us a fresh picture of Jesus never before seen—not even in the Gospels. In the book, Jesus describes Himself as "the Alpha and the Omega" (Revelation 1:8). *Alpha* and *omega* are the first and last letters of the Greek alphabet. This phrase, then, means that Jesus is the beginning, the end, and everything in between.

A second major theme that appears throughout the book is expressed succinctly in Revelation 14:7, in which an angel says, "Fear God and give him glory, because the hour of his judgment has come, and *worship him* who made heaven and earth, the sea and the springs of water" (emphasis added). A war permeates this book—a battle over worship. Christians are being persecuted because they refuse to worship false gods, and John is stranded on Patmos because of his worshiping Jesus. Revelation tells us that there is a false system of worship and a true system of worship. Both of them are vying for our allegiance, and the battle between them will get worse before it gets better.

Even the day on which we worship is significant. John tells us the Spirit brought this vision to him "on the Lord's day" (Revelation 1:10). Many people believe that

Going Deeper

Why would Jesus use pagan Greek imagery when He's describing Himself? What lesson does this teach about how to communicate truths about Jesus in our time?

_____

_____

_____

_____

_____

_____

_____

_____

_____

_____

_____

_____

_____

_____

_____

_____

_____

_____

_____

_____

_____

Going Deeper

Revelation 1:7 says "every eye" will see Jesus when He returns. What does this mean for those who believe Jesus will come and secretly rapture people away?

_____

_____

_____

_____

_____

_____

_____

_____

_____

_____

_____

_____

_____

_____

_____

_____

_____

_____

_____

_____

was a Sunday. However, Clement of Alexandria was the first to connect the biblical phrase to Sunday (at least he was the first we know of who put it in writing). But he wrote near the end of the second century—a hundred years after John wrote Revelation.

John, a good Jew, used a myriad of images from the Hebrew Scriptures in Revelation. So, it's likely that he had the seventh-day Sabbath in mind here. And Jesus called Himself the "lord of the Sabbath" (Matthew 12:8). More on the Sabbath later.

The church is in the middle of the worship war. Jesus tells John, "I . . . have sent my angel to testify to you about these things for the churches. I am the root and the descendant of David, the bright morning star" (Revelation 22:16). Through John, Jesus is telling His followers what is happening and what will happen. He is telling them this so they will continue to place their confidence in Him no matter how many beastly things happen on earth.

The worship theme calls those who read this book to direct their worship to God. A related theme tells us where God, the object of our worship, is. He's in the heavenly sanctuary. One study Bible points out that "each sequence of seven (churches, seals, trumpets, etc.) is introduced with a vision set in the heavenly sanctuary."[1] This means that to understand the book of Revelation, we will have to look into imagery connected with the Old Testament sanctuary, which was modeled upon the heavenly sanctuary.

Man of snow and fire

The sound of a trumpet marks the start of John's prophetic experience (Revelation 1:10). When he hears it, he sees "seven golden lampstands, and in the midst of the lampstands one like a son of man, clothed with a long robe and with a golden sash around his chest" (verses 12, 13). Wearing a sash isn't all that unusual, and neither are lampstands—though on Patmos, lampstands might have been out of the ordinary. But John's description of what he saw next indicates that it was something supernatural: "The *hairs of his head were white, like white wool,* like snow. *His eyes were like a flame of fire, his feet were like burnished bronze,* refined in a furnace, and his voice was like the roar of many waters. In his right hand he held seven stars, from his mouth came a sharp two-edged sword, and his face was like the sun shining in full strength" (Revelation 1:14–16; emphasis added).

OK, so either this guy has an amazing body wash/facial scrub, or he is of a wholly different makeup than your average human being. The book of Daniel has an allusion to this same figure: "The Ancient of Days took his seat; his clothing was white as snow, and *the hair of his head like pure wool;* his throne was fiery flames; its wheels burn in fire. *A stream of fire issued and came out from before him;* a thousand thousands served him, and ten thousand times ten thousand stood before him; the court sat in judgment and the books were opened" (Daniel 7:9, 10; emphasis added).

Same hair. Same affinity for fire. We're dealing with the same character.

This allusion would have drawn John's hearers back to Daniel's prophecies—specifically, to prophecies containing a judgment scene. This is a perfect setup, because as we read, we see that the figure John is describing is Jesus—and He is about to lay some judgment on the "seven churches" (verse 11).

You may be tempted to think that this brilliant spectacle is some other creature than a human being. After all, Jesus is generally pictured as a gentle person—the good Shepherd who cares for His sheep and who smiles approvingly when someone does a good deed. But remember, Revelation is showing us a picture of Jesus previously unseen. As we read further, we can see clearly that John is having a vision of his Savior. John says, "When I saw him, I fell at his feet as though dead. But he laid his right hand on me, saying, 'Fear not, *I am the first and the last, and the living one. I died, and behold I am alive forevermore, and I have the keys of Death and Hades*' " (Revelation 1:17, 18; emphasis added). Jesus has already described Himself as being "the Alpha and the Omega" (verse 8), and we know from the Gospels that He died and rose again. So we are justified in saying that this Person in Revelation 1 is Jesus.

The reference to having the keys to Death and Hades is an allusion to the Greek goddess Hekate. In Greek mythology, Hekate was the goddess of revelations and possessed the keys to heaven and hell. Using language that the pagans of John's day would understand, Jesus is declaring Himself to be the *real* God of revelations and of the afterlife.

Cipher alert!

The end of Revelation 1 gives us the key that unlocks chapters 2 and 3. "Write therefore the things that you have seen, those that are and those that are to take place after this. As for the mystery of the seven stars that you saw in my right hand, and *the seven golden lampstands, the seven stars are the angels of the seven churches, and the seven lampstands are the seven churches*" (Revelation 1:19, 20; emphasis added). The Greek word translated "angels" is the plural of *aggelos,** which means "messenger," and Jesus points out that the seven "lampstands" are the "seven churches"—just as we saw in the previous chapter.

So we are about to see the sermon notes that the leaders of those seven church were to share with their congregations. The messages may be short, but they're packed with meaning. People are about to lose their potluck appetite—and it has nothing to do with a greenish mystery loaf that's emitting fumes.†

---

* In Greek, two *g*'s side by side indicate that we're to make an *n* sound before the *g* sound, so the word is actually pronounced *angelos.*

† You know the one. Consider yourself warned—do not eat it.

Going Deeper

Revelation 1:1 says the things this prophecy contains "must soon take place." Which school of prophetic interpretation does this contradict? (See chapter 3.)

_____

_____

_____

_____

_____

_____

_____

_____

_____

_____

_____

_____

_____

_____

_____

_____

_____

_____

_____

_____

SUMMARY AND CONCLUSION
AND WHAT THIS TELLS US ABOUT JESUS

At the very beginning we are told, "Blessed is the one who reads aloud the words of this prophecy, and blessed are those who hear, and who keep what is written in it, for the time is near" (Revelation 1:3). This book is intended to be a blessing to us—not to scare us or confuse us. It's a book written by a man stranded on an island awaiting the day when God will come and restore everything and re-unite him with his loved ones. It is a book that reveals God's plan. It reminds us that when *we* feel stranded and stuck like John was, God will ultimately set us free.

This chapter also reveals that Jesus is supreme and that He cares very much about His servants—those who are working in His church. While no leader is perfect, the fact that Jesus deals with them so carefully should inspire us to be thoughtful and respectful toward our pastors, teachers, and elders.

ENDNOTE

1. *Andrews Study Bible*, 1659.

Chapter 11
What's in a Name?
Revelation 2

Lots of people enjoy collecting weird objects.

Some keep a supply of navel lint, others indulge in hoarding human hair, and still others gather air-sickness bags. Then there are those who collect toilet-seat art. And Arlington, Texas, boasts of a museum dedicated to burnt food.[1]

I collect church names.

You heard me.

Not names like Community Christian Center and First Church of [insert city name here]. I want names that shock, confuse, and inspire. Names like "Beaver Lick Baptist Church."

Facebook it—it's real.

Granted, Beaver Lick is the town name—but how bold is it to include a name like that in your call to worship? The thought of placing your tongue on one of those furry, flat-tailed dam builders is gag-inspiring—and yet here is a church that's proudly willing to put that mental picture in your head as you drive by their sign. Amazing.

The first church name I remember collecting belongs to a congregation in Kansas City, Kansas. When I saw the sign, I did a double take to make sure I'd read it correctly. There, atop the building, were the words "Christ Church of the Jesus Hour."

Naturally, my first question had to do with the identity of the "Jesus Hour." Was it a television or radio program? Why does Jesus get only an hour? Is there one hour during the day that specifically belongs to Him? And aren't Christ and Jesus the same Person? How can Christ own a church with an hour that belongs to Him?

I was confused and delighted at the same time—which inspired me to start the collection. Among the names I've added are these:

- The "Exciting Singing Hills Baptist Church" in Dallas, Texas. (Apparently, as opposed to boring singing hills.)

- The "As You Are Church" in Reseda, California. (Does that mean as I am, or as the church is?)
- The "Guided Missiles Church" in Nigeria. (Church discipline takes on a whole new meaning.)
- The "First Haitian Free Methodist Church" in Stamford, Connecticut. (So I can't bring my Haitian friends?)

All jokes aside, the most important aspect of a good church name is that it says something about the focus and mission of that particular group of believers. Many churches are known for certain characteristics, such as the "Fire Baptized Holiness Church." The name says they are particularly focused on holiness and the Holy Spirit (fire being a metaphor for the Holy Spirit—at least, I hope the fire in their name is metaphorical).

The name of the denomination that I've joined describes our focus and mission perfectly. "Seventh-day" says we worship on the Sabbath God made holy at Creation, and "Adventist" says we look forward to the second coming of Christ, and we do all we can to spread the good news that He's coming soon.

You've got mail

The second and third chapters of Revelation contain letters from Jesus, one for each of the seven key churches in Asia Minor. The letters describe the seven churches and their spiritual problems. These churches were on a circular postal route, meaning that what John was passing along to them would make the rounds. Everybody would be hearing what Jesus has to say to His churches.

Hastily Drawn Map 1
(Please don't use this for your travel over there.)

Asia Minor
First Century A.D.

God particularly wants His light to shine in His churches, but the lamps in some of them had become a little dim. Like a strobe light that causes headaches or a drippy candle that flickers an almost lifeless flame, making the shadows seem even darker, some of these churches were doing more evil than good. They were in danger of losing what little light they had unless they accepted and followed the instructions from Jesus.

Many churches have been able to identify with the struggles of one or another of these churches, some of which receive messages that are full of wonderful encouragements, while others . . .

Well, you'll see.

Ephesus: Church of the first love lost

The name *Ephesus* means "desirable." Ephesus was an important port town. Sailors a great distance from shore could see its lights. No wonder it is the first of the lampstands to be mentioned.

The church in Ephesus was founded by lay people—Aquila and Priscilla (their names rhyme!), who are mentioned in Acts 18. The apostle Paul spent three years there—two of them teaching from 11:00 A.M. to 4:00 P.M. in a rented hall. (And you thought your church service was long!) However, this church had a problem: while its physical light could be seen, the spiritual light it should have had was shrouded in idolatry.

Ephesus thrived on the manufacture of idols. The idol of choice was Artemis—the many-breasted goddess of fertility. (Sorry, no hastily drawn figure.) The temple dedicated to Artemis was considered to be one of the Seven Wonders of the World.

So important to the Ephesians was this trade in idols that the apostle Paul and his buddies caused a riot when they preached against it, so they pulled up stakes and moved on. But the church in Ephesus continued to be influential.

Jesus began His letter to the Ephesian church with affirmations of its commitment: " 'I know your works, your toil and *your patient endurance,* and *how you cannot bear with those who are evil,* but have tested those who call themselves apostles and are not, *and found them to be false.* I know you are *enduring patiently* and bearing up for my name's sake, and *you have not grown weary*' " (Revelation 2:2, 3; emphasis added).

Like a marathon runner enduring aching muscles or a twelve-year-old boy sitting through *The Little Mermaid* (the longest ninety minutes of my life), the followers of Jesus in Ephesus have been beaten on every side by unbelievers and hostile forces—but they have been faithful.

However—there's a problem, and Jesus tells them what it is. " 'I have this against you, that you have abandoned the love you had at first' " (verse 4).

A lot of people think that what the Ephesians had abandoned was their love for Jesus, and to some degree that's true. But the real point here isn't so much that they'd abandoned their love for Jesus Himself. Jesus was telling them that they had lost their love for His people. When we have had to spend a lot of energy defending truth, eventually we're tempted to turn that truth into a weapon and to use it on the people we're trying to lead to truth—the people we're trying to lead to Jesus. Someone has said, "Christians sin the most when they are right." I agree. It's easy for us to consider winning arguments about the "truth" to be more important than winning people to the Lord.

This church loved the truth, but it lost its love for people, and since the character of truth is love, the "truth" they were teaching no longer reflected Jesus accurately. I call this the "Ephesus Effect." Too often there is a false tension between truth and love, as if they were opposed to each other—like peanut butter and pickles. But they always go together. In fact, without God's love, truth becomes a lie.

Jesus doesn't just diagnose the problem. He also tells the believers in Ephesus what to do about it. " '*Remember* therefore from where you have fallen; repent, and do the works you did at first. If not, *I will come to you and remove your lampstand from its place, unless you repent*' " (verse 5; emphasis added).

Yikes.

Jesus says they had better rekindle the light of love, or He will remove their light altogether. Jesus prefers that people have no light than distorted light. The Ephesians need to reclaim the love of Jesus, which enables people to love others even when they have to hold up the truth and disagree with them. Jesus' love enables us to treat people gently and with respect even if they won't let us share our beliefs.

The Ephesians were doing some things right, though. Jesus commended them for this. He said, " 'Yet this you have: you hate the works of the Nicolaitans, which I also hate' " (verse 6).

The Nicolaitans were followers of a guy named Nicolas of Antioch. They were professed followers of Jesus who no longer lived in a way that brought glory to Him. It's tragic when Christian leaders fall—and especially when those who fall take others down with them. Jesus commended the rest of the members of the church in Ephesus because they hated what the Nicolaitans did.

Jesus concluded His message to the Ephesians with the promise of a reward for those who reject the temptations they face: " 'He who has an ear, let him hear what the Spirit says to the churches. *To the one who conquers I will grant to eat of the tree of life, which is in the paradise of God*' " (verse 7; emphasis added).

The promise is an allusion to the Garden of Eden, which humans could no longer enter after Adam and Eve sinned. This promise offers the hope of a return to the perfect world God intended us all to enjoy.

Ephesus, A.D. 31–100. During this period the church was quite pure—its members successfully defended the truth of Christianity. But as a result of doing this while under the constant threat posed by hostile pagan forces and Jews whose religion was in name only, they lost their loving character.

Smyrna: Fellowship of suffering

The name *Smyrna* means "myrrh," which is derived from a root meaning "bitter." Myrrh is a tree resin that was used in the manufacture of perfume, incense, and preservatives used in burials. It has a bitter flavor and can symbolize death.

I don't recommend that you buy any myrrh for your sweetie, as it may not communicate the romantic feelings you intend it to—unless she'd rather be called Bitter than Sweetie and she wants to smell like death. Fittingly, Jesus begins this message by saying that it contains " 'the words of the first and the last, *who died and came to life*' " (verse 8; emphasis added).

Located on an inlet of the Aegean Sea, Smyrna was a commercial rival of Ephesus. (Think Target versus Wal-Mart.) An enormous, three-level market plaza (think ancient outlet mall) also helped Smyrna to swell with financial success.

However, in the midst of all this prosperity, the church was suffering. Jesus knew that. He said, " 'I know your tribulation *and your poverty (but you are rich)* and the slander of those who say that they are Jews and are not, but are a synagogue of Satan' " (verse 9).

While the bank accounts of the Christians in Smyrna were dwindling, their faith accounts were full. Jesus affirmed that they possessed the true wealth. He also extended sympathy and understanding to the suffering church. He knew of the existence of a shady group who professed to be Jews but whose allegiance—in terms of what they did—made them members of Satan's church. He knew this group was oppressing the believers in Smyrna. So Jesus told His church not to " 'fear what you are about to suffer. Behold the devil is about to throw some of you into prison, that you may be tested, and for ten days you will have tribulation' " (verse 10).

While Smyrna was to take a beating, Jesus offered some hope. " 'Do not fear what you are about to suffer,' " He said. " 'Behold, the devil is about to throw some of you into prison, that you may be tested, and for ten days you will have tribulation. Be faithful unto death, and I will give you the crown of life. He who has an ear, let him hear what the Spirit says to the churches. *The one who conquers will not be hurt by the second death*' " (verses 10, 11; emphasis added).

Jesus didn't condemn the Christians in Smyrna—He doesn't kick people when they are down or beat them when they're already suffering. For this church, which was teetering on the brink of death, Jesus promised a crown of life and salvation from the death that's permanent. Since this promise came from One who died and rose again, they could be sure it is as good as it sounds.

Smyrna, A.D. 100–313. During the early part of this period, the Roman emperor Diocletian conducted a severe persecution of Christians. Around this time also, groups such as the Gnostics and the Docetists began to develop. These groups presented distorted pictures of Jesus—the Gnostics saying that Jesus came to reveal "secret knowledge" to His followers, and the Docetists teaching that Jesus didn't really come in flesh and blood.

A man named Polycarp, a student of the apostle John,* led the church in Smyrna for at least forty years. One evening during one of the times of persecution, soldiers came to his home to arrest him. According to the story, Polycarp invited them to eat dinner with him. Then, throughout the two-hour-long meal, he stood to the side and prayed for all the Christians who were suffering.

When the soldiers finished eating, they brought Polycarp to the authorities, who put him on trial and demanded that he renounce his faith in Jesus. His response was epic: "Eighty-six years have I served Him, and never has He done me wrong. How then can I curse my King, who saved me?"

In Polycarp's case, Jesus' prophecy was fulfilled. The ruler of Smyrna ordered that Polycarp be burned to death.

Pergamum: Satan's-seat Christian assembly

Finding the perfect chair can be one of the most rewarding experiences in life. When I attended seminary, I waited six months for a chair I found in the local furniture store to drop in price. Oversized, plush, capable of seating two or three people comfortably, this chair captured and held me in its embrace like a long lost relative. I needed it.

After several months, this heavenly throne was moved to the clearance section and put on sale. Cash in hand, I marched in and made my offer, and the proprietors accepted it. So, as I write this, the chair dwells in my living room, and everyone who sits in it finds themselves trapped by its comfort.

At a recent gathering at my home after church, one of my guests chose to sit upon its cushions. After acquiring his food, he returned to it and spent the better part of three hours in the chair's comforting clutches. It's nearly impossible to escape from a good chair. The church at Pergamum found this to be true, and they were dealing with the seat of Satan himself—and he didn't want to get up.

Located high on a spur of a mountain, the city of Pergamum (the name means "citadel," or "stronghold"†) was a delight to defend when attacked. As in the game King of the Mountain, people who hold a high position are able to knock their opponents down the stairs/sledding hills/Mount Rushmore much more easily than people who are below and are trying to make their way up.‡

But while defending their city from outsiders was relatively easy, fending off the assaults of fellow citizens was another story. Jesus begins His note to the believers who lived in this mountain city with an acknowledgment of this: "And to the angel

---

* According to two early church leaders, Irenaeus and Tertullian.

† "Pergamum" is also a modification of the words *charta pergamena,* which means "parchment." That was fitting because Pergamum had an incredible library that housed some two hundred thousand scrolls.

‡ I'm not promoting this game; it's just an illustration. I hereby abdicate all responsibility for any injuries that may occur on Mount Rushmore.

of the church in Pergamum write: 'The words of him who has the sharp, two-edged sword. I know where you dwell, *where Satan's throne is.* Yet you hold fast my name, *and you did not deny my faith* even in the days of Antipas my faithful witness, who was killed among you, *where Satan dwells*' " (verses 12, 13; emphasis added).

Pergamum was the site of the first temple of the Caesar cult (which has nothing to do with the salad dressing—though that dressing is good and has many fans). The Romans believed their emperors to be gods deserving of worship. Pergamum's temple, dedicated to Caesar Augustus in A.D. 29, had many zealous patrons. A second temple, this one dedicated to Trajan, was built later. A citizen's refusal to take a seat as a good worshiper carried consequences: namely, punishments, such as exile—the reason John was on Patmos recording these visions instead of at home in his own favorite chair.

In addition to worshiping Roman emperors, folks placed their faith in Greek gods, among them Asclepius, whose symbol was a serpent, and Zeus—the god with the lightning bolts. A thronelike altar to Zeus (now in the Berlin Museum) stood on a rocky crag above Pergamum.

A throne-shaped altar dedicated to a pagan god?

Sounds like the kind of "seat" Satan would use to decorate his abode.

Like the Christians in Ephesus, the believers in Pergamum were surrounded by hostile pagan forces trying to cajole them into abandoning their dedication to Jesus. He affirms them for putting up a strong defense against Satan's attacks regardless of the consequences—some, such as Antipas, even losing their lives.

However, all is not well in the mountain city. Jesus says, " 'I have a few things against you: you have some there *who hold the teaching of Balaam,* who taught Balak to put a stumblingblock before the sons of Israel, so that they might *eat food sacrificed to idols and practice sexual immorality.* So also you have some who hold *the teaching of the Nicolaitans*' " (verses 14, 15; emphasis added).

Balak, the king of Moab, approaches Balaam, supposedly a prophet of God, offering to buy his services. Balak wants Balaam to curse Israel, who are on their way from Egypt to the Promised Land (see Numbers 22). Balaam says he'll do it, and he goes to talk it over with God, seeking His support. But God refuses to curse His own people (verses 7–14).

Balak sends a bigger entourage to pull Balaam his way—but again Balaam finds it impossible to curse God's people (see verses 15–21).

Then Balaam heads out with a crew from Moab, but a talking donkey ends the journey, and the results are the same—Balaam has to tell Balak that God won't curse His people (verses 22–41). So Balak tries several changes of scenery, thinking that Balaam may be able to pronounce a curse from a different location (see Numbers 23; 24).

Nothing.

Eventually, however, Israel does falter—because the Israelite men find the pagan

Notes

women from Moab attractive (Numbers 25).

This Old Testament story indicates that members of the church of Pergamum are more than willing to compromise with pagan leaders, and many are falling away from the faith by bringing pagan worship practices into the church—namely, "eating food sacrificed to idols" and "sexual immorality."

Jesus says that if the members of the church in Pergamum don't repent, He will " 'war against them with the sword of [His] mouth' " (Revelation 2:16). Jesus will make an attack of His own in order to preserve the witness of the Pergamum believers.

Amid the threat of war, Jesus makes a promise to the believers in Pergamum: " 'He who has an ear, let him hear what the Spirit says to the churches. To the one who conquers I will give some of the *hidden manna,* and I will give him *a white stone, with a new name written on the stone* that no one knows except the one who receives it' " (verse 17; emphasis added).

Jewish tradition says that a pot of manna (heavenly bread) was placed in the ark of the covenant as a memorial (Exodus 16:32–34) and was later "taken by Jeremiah at the destruction of Solomon's temple and hidden in the cleft in Mt. Sinai; it would stay there until the Messiah comes."[2] The idea is that it will be nourishment in God's new kingdom when the world is made new.

White stones had a variety of uses in the ancient world. One reference could be to a tessera—a token that was the equivalent of a trophy given to the winner of a big game.* Winning athletes had their names inscribed on them, which gave them privileges and prestige.

As for a new name, Scripture contains numerous examples of people having their names changed after they had an experience with God. For instance, Jacob became Israel (see Genesis 32:28), and Simon became Simon Peter (see Mark 3:16).

When I was five years old, I insisted that my parents call me Luke (last name: Skywalker) because after I watched *Star Wars,* I thought I was a Jedi knight. The name *Luke* brought with it a sense of power and purpose that I didn't have as five-year-old Seth Pierce from Minnesota. Fortunately, I dropped that name and found my calling. In the message to the believers in Pergamum, Jesus indicates that names of believers will be changed to reflect their identity in Him.

Pergamum, A.D. 313–538. During this time Christianity became the official religion of the Roman Empire. That brought about some major changes. The terms *Nicolaitans, Balaamites,* and *Jezebel* are symbolic of the idolatry and false religion that began to creep into the church and alter the truths Jesus had taught. (See Revelation 2:14, 15; and *Prophecies of Daniel Made Simple.* Yes, double shameless promotion.)

However, many good things also happened, because this church was faithful to Jesus' name (see verse 13). In 325, during the Council of Nicaea, believers voted to

---

* Related to but not the same as the pieces of stone, ceramic, and glass used in making a mosaic.

affirm that Jesus is God. In 381, at the Council of Constantinople, church leaders concluded that Jesus is both fully divine and fully human. And in 451, at the Council of Chalcedon, they affirmed that Jesus had two distinct natures (human and divine). So, despite the negative things that were happening in the church, important truths about Jesus Christ were being accepted and expressed.

Thyatira: First church of evil-queen tolerance

Some phrases can communicate the content of a message before the entire message is read. While the following phrases appear to be innocent, they let you know that you're in trouble.

"We need to talk."

"Can I ask you something?"

"Would you like a breath mint, please?"

When the church in Thyatira receives their letter from Jesus, they find that it begins with a loaded phrase that lets them know that all is not well. "And to the angel of the church in Thyatira write: 'The words of the Son of God, *who has eyes like a flame of fire, and whose feet are like burnished bronze*' " (verse 18; emphasis added). While these expressions may look innocent, even impressive, the description of Jesus would draw the minds of John's readers back to Daniel 10. There Daniel wrote, "His body was like beryl, his face like the appearance of lightning, *his eyes like flaming torches, his arms and legs like the gleam of burnished bronze,* and the sound of his words like the sound of a multitude" (Daniel 10:6; emphasis added).

These symbols stand for Jesus' ability to see deeply into the human heart and for His unwavering strength and stability. Thyatira is about to come under close examination—and that could mean trouble.

Thyatira was the smallest and least significant of the seven cities. It was known for the production there of a bright-red dye—called "purple," of all things—from madder roots. Many poor laborers lived in Thyatira. One of the problems for Christians working in that industry was the trade guilds. These guilds helped the local business, but they also required members to participate in Thyatira's pagan festivities. Of course, that was a problem, and the businesses of believers suffered.

To make matters worse, the spiritual labors of the members of the church there suffered just as much. Jesus said, " 'I know your works, your love and faith and service and patient endurance, and that your latter works exceed the first. But I have this against you, *that you tolerate that woman Jezebel,* who calls herself a prophetess and is teaching and seducing my servants to practice sexual immorality and to eat food sacrificed to idols. I gave her time to repent, but she refuses to repent of her sexual immorality' " (Revelation 2:19–21; emphasis added).

The church members in Thyatira have made some spiritual progress—their works are better now than they were at the beginning. However, they made one big boo-boo. Her name is Jezebel—and instead of resisting her, they've begun to tolerate her.

Vile Queen Jezebel lived long before the Wicked Queen poisoned Snow White. Jezebel was an idolatrous huntress who killed God's prophets and led Israel into Baal worship. Jezebel married a whiney king named Ahab and instituted worship services that would make you blush—or vomit. You can read about the mess she caused in 1 Kings 16–21. Her persistent wickedness ended in a gruesome death (see 2 Kings 9:30–36).

Clearly, persistent refusal to follow God can have lethal consequences. Jesus warns the church in Thyatira: " 'Behold, I will throw her onto a sickbed, and those who commit adultery with her will I throw into great tribulation, unless they repent of her works, and I will strike her children dead. And all the churches will know that I am he who searches mind and heart, and I will give to each of you according to your works' " (Revelation 2:22, 23).

Fortunately, not everyone in Thyatira tolerates evil: " 'But to the rest of you in Thyatira, *who do not hold this teaching, who have not learned what some call the deep things of Satan,* to you I say, I do not lay on you any other burden. Only hold fast what you have until I come' " (Revelation 2:24, 25; emphasis added).

The "deep things of Satan" is thought to be a reference to the idea that to enjoy forgiveness and grace people must have done some sinning. Paul warned people about this in Romans: "What shall we say then? Are we to continue in sin that grace may abound? By no means! How can we who died to sin still live in it?" (Romans 6:1, 2).

Many in Thyatira were holding on to their faith, believing that they would receive better things in the future. Jesus tells them, " 'Only hold fast what you have until I come. The one who conquers and who keeps my works until the end, to him I will give authority over the nations, and he will rule them with *a rod of iron, as when earthen pots are broken in pieces,* even as I myself have received authority from my Father. And I will give him *the morning star*' " (Revelation 2:25–28; emphasis added).

When I was in high school, I worked for two months (that's right, I quit after two months) at McDonald's. While I worked there, I wanted nothing more than to find something—anything—else to do. Customers treated us like dirt, and when there were no customers, we had to remove the dirt in the place. As a nice break, I was allowed to play with the deep fryer. Burns and greasy hair were my reward—along with minimum-wage pay. I longed for the day when I would have a real career and could order French fries instead of making them.

The poverty-stricken laborers in Thyatira longed for a day when they wouldn't be the bottom rung of the social ladder. Jesus promises that if they will endure, He will give them a place to rule. Interestingly, despite being paid to curse Israel, Balaam spoke a prophecy in their favor. In that prophecy, he spoke of "the morning star" as a "scepter" that will arise out of Israel. That Morning Star is Jesus—and to have Jesus is to have the greatest Gift of all.

Thyatira, A.D. *538–1565.* The Roman Church, or medieval church, had a lot going for it. Jesus said they had "good works" (verse 19), and they did: hospitals, orphanages, schools, and missions. Belief-wise, too, some of them were doing some things right. Jesus mentions believers who "do not hold" to "Jezebel's" teachings and who "have not learned . . . the deep things of Satan" (verse 24)—meaning people who have not indulged in sin. During this period, followers of Jesus such as Jan Milic of Prague, John Wycliffe, John Huss, Peter Waldo, St. Francis of Assisi, the Lollards, Waldensians, and the early Franciscans represented the best of Christianity.

By 1500, though, the medieval Christian church had become like a crumbling house in need of renovations. Monks and priests had such a bad reputation that some people considered being called "monk" or "priest" to be an insult. In His letter to this church, Jesus says He gave people time to repent, but they refused to do it (verse 21).

That refusal resulted in a major break in what had been a monolithic organization. A monk named Martin Luther nailed to the door of a church a document that challenged many of the teachings and practices of the Roman Catholic Church. So, in 1521, the pope kicked Luther out of the church. But, perhaps unexpectedly, many people followed him out of the church.

In response to these "Lutherans," the Catholic Church held the Council of Trent, which affirmed unbiblical doctrines that the church held, such as penance, a continuing human priesthood, justification being available only through the church, and purgatory—most often presented as a hot place between heaven and hell where people suffer until they've reached the level of purification necessary for them to enter heaven.

As for the "great tribulation" that Jesus referred to (verse 22), the Middle Ages were rife with big problems. The Great Famine lasted from 1315–1317, and a few decades later, two-fifths of the population of Europe died from the disease known as bubonic plague or the Black Death. (Thanks, rats.) The Hundred Years' War between England and France continued during the fourteenth and fifteenth centuries, introducing weapons that used gunpowder. Revolts in the country as well as the city by the poor ripped the social fabric, and together with the Thirty Years' War between Catholics and Protestants (1618–1648), resulted in about ten million deaths.

OK, let's take a break. We've been seeing the church spiraling down from where it started. When we return to these lampstands, we'll see movement in the right direction again.

ENDNOTES

1. www.burntfoodmuseum.com.
2. Stefanovic, *Revelation of Jesus Christ,* 123.

Chapter 12

Dolphins, Whac-A-Mole, and Church History

Revelation 3

We're right back into it now, starting with the fifth church of the seven for whom Jesus had messages.

Sardis: The wake-up-or-perish parish

Sleeping in is an underappreciated art form. It takes great skill to ignore the alarm clock, the yells of my wife, and the sun shining directly on my face. The delicate placing of my pillow over my head so I can ignore the day's responsibilities beating down upon me requires unequaled strength. It's not everyone who's willing to sacrifice his productive daytime hours to sleep.

OK, so maybe it isn't an art—but it sure feels good.

Unless, of course, you miss something you really shouldn't have missed: a plane, a test, a job interview that you no longer have. Bye-bye, McDonald's! Cook your own fries!

The church in Sardis is a little sleepy. Like Pergamum, Sardis rested atop nearly perpendicular cliffs that rose a thousand feet above the valley floor. The people who lived inside the city's walls considered their natural defenses to be very valuable. King Croesus of Lydia thought Sardis the perfect place to hide his treasure. It *was* a glorious place at one time. Alas, as is true of every treasure, there are those who try to steal it.

Cyrus the Great made his move in 549 B.C., and Antiochus marched away with the goods in 214 B.C. Both times, soldiers in their armies volunteered to make the thousand-foot climb (without gear from REI) and caught the city sleeping.

Like the literal guardians of the city, the believers there had also been lulled to sleep: "And to the angel of the church in Sardis write: 'The words of him who has the seven spirits of God and the seven stars. I know your works. *You have the repu-*

tation of being alive, but you are dead' " (Revelation 3:1; emphasis added).

The church in Sardis was living in the past. They'd fallen sleep listening to the lullaby of past deeds. Jesus sends them a message that He intends will get them moving again: " '*Wake up, and strengthen what remains and is about to die,* for I have not found your works complete in the sight of my God. Remember, then, what you received and heard. Keep it, and repent. *If you will not wake up, I will come like a thief,* and you will not know at what hour I will come against you' " (verses 2, 3; emphasis added).

Jesus hopes His disciples in Sardis won't die in their sleep. He hasn't rejected them, but they will have to crawl out of the bed they have made and get to work.

" 'Yet,' " Jesus says, " 'you have still a few names in Sardis, people who have not soiled their garments, and they will walk with me in white, for they are worthy' " (verse 4). Here's evidence that they haven't all fallen asleep. Perhaps if the ones who have gone to sleep are willing to listen, the ones who have remained faithful can awaken them by reflecting some "Sonshine" on them.

" 'The one who conquers will be *clothed thus in white garments, and I will never blot his name out of the book of life.* I will confess his name before my Father and before his angels. *He who has an ear, let him hear* what the Spirit says to the churches' " (verses 5, 6; emphasis added).

Cooler than any pair of pajamas, the white robe of righteousness guarantees its wearer to be awake for an eternal reality that is far grander than any dream come true. If the members who live in Sardis can avoid hitting the spiritual snooze button and will instead get up, they can have a future of hope and life.

Sardis, 1565–1740. The fires sparked by the Reformation began to cool—with many Protestants feeling self-satisfied and others embroiling themselves in endless quarrels with fellow Protestants. Melanchthon, a friend of Luther, rejoiced as his death approached because, he said, it would allow him to escape the "rage of the theologians." Nothing worse than a theologian in rage mode.

In 1577, Lutherans formed an agreement among themselves called the Formula of Concord; and by 1580, roughly eight thousand Lutheran pastors and teachers had signed the Book of Concord. Then, instead of carrying on an active search for truth, they proclaimed themselves satisfied with the cold, formal creed. By the 1700s, the movement had become an institution.

Still, Jesus said that a "few names" remained "worthy" (verse 4). Think of believers like George Frederick Handel (composer of *Messiah*), Johann Sebastian Bach (another composer of great church music), George Fox (who founded the Quakers), John Bunyan (the author of *Pilgrim's Progress*), and the Moravians (who helped introduce the gospel to John Wesley, a revivalist and the founder of the Methodist Church). The preaching of Wesley and George Whitefield sparked massive revivals in England and America, which led to the next stage of church history.

Going Deeper

Jesus made promises to the seven churches—one to the first church, two to the second, and so on, up to the sixth church. Find and write down each of these promises.

_____

_____

_____

_____

_____

_____

_____

_____

_____

_____

_____

_____

_____

_____

_____

_____

_____

_____

_____

Philadelphia: The church of the open door

Whenever my mom left our apartment, my brother and I would re-create scenes from the Worldwide Wrestling Federation. We would pull the cushions off the couch to create a soft floor for our takedowns. Then we shed our T-shirts and donned instead plastic grocery bags—which we would then tear off dramatically to demonstrate our physical prowess. And then the beatings would commence.

I, to my shame, wasn't merciful to my brother. Of course, he got his shots in as well. We executed signature moves such as "the people's elbow" by leaping off the arm of the couch and driving our bony appendages into our opponent's back, head, or stomach. Sometimes one of us would enter rage mode and wildly throw a torrent of slaps and punches into the other. This, in turn, would send the other person into rage mode too, and when this happened, one or the other of us usually ended up crying—and that's when Mom would come home.

Occasionally, when my brother and I were at our dad's and stepmother's house, our stepbrother would join in the fracas, which took place on a trampoline. Naturally, our parents forbade this, but when they weren't looking, we would scramble onto the bouncy surface for a three-way beatdown. Fighting on a trampoline offers one great bonus: when you knock your opponent down, he bounces right back so you can hit him again while saying things like, "Oh, so you're back for more, are ya?"

Philadelphia means "brotherly love"—something that was expressed repeatedly in the illicit fighting matches in our homes. However, in the case of Philadelphia—the youngest of the seven cities—love found a healthier expression. Philadelphia was founded by a Pergamenian (a native or resident of Pergamum—not a Pomeranian, which is a small dog). Attalus II, king of Pergamum (159–138 B.C.), loved his brother Eumenes II so much that he was given the nickname Philadelphus—and the city was named after him.

Philadelphia was a gateway or "open door" city located on the imperial post road. It was meant to serve as a kind of "missionary" city, its mission being to spread the Greek language and culture to places like Lydia and Phrygia (great names for twin girls—though I would feel a little sorry for whoever got stuck with the name Phrygia). Philadelphia was a great launching pad for Christian missions to the east.

Jesus' greeting to the Christians who lived in Philadelphia is quite appropriate: "And to the angel of the church in Philadelphia write: 'The words of the holy one, the true one, *who has the key of David, who opens and no one will shut, who shuts and no one opens*' " (verse 7; emphasis added). The key of David secured the king's storehouse. The idea is that Jesus has full authority—full access to the storehouse of heaven. That's reassuring to a church in need.

" 'I know your works,' " Jesus continues. " 'Behold, I have set before you an open door, which no one is able to shut. I know that you have but little power, and yet you have kept my word and have not denied my name' " (verse 8). This church not only has an open door so they can share the message of Jesus with those who need to hear it, but they also have an open door in heaven. Jesus reassures this weakening community that He can supply the spiritual strength they must have to resist the enemy.

Then Jesus makes a promise: " 'Behold, I will make those of the synagogue of Satan who say that they are Jews and are not, but lie—behold, I will make them come and bow down before your feet, and they will learn that I have loved you' " (verse 9).

As in Smyrna, the believers in Philadelphia are being beaten by people who should have been—but aren't—spiritual brothers. They profess to be followers of God, but in their treatment of Christians they reveal that their allegiance is to Satan.

Philadelphia is weak, but Jesus has no rebukes for them as He does for the other six churches. He has only a big promise: " 'Because you have kept my word about patient endurance, *I will keep you from the hour of trial that is coming on the whole world*, to try those who dwell on the earth. I am coming soon. Hold fast what you have, *so that no one may seize your crown*. The one who conquers, *I will make him a pillar in the temple of my God*. Never shall he go out of it, and I will write on him the name of my God, and the name of the city of my God, the new Jerusalem, which comes down from my God out of heaven, and my own new name' " (verses 10–12; emphasis added).

Philadelphia, 1750–1844. John Wesley and George Whitefield, along with other preachers such as Jonathan Edwards and Charles Finney, ushered in the Great Awakening in New England in the 1730s and 1740s and a second Great Awakening in the early 1800s. These resulted in an explosion of conversions in North America and a commitment to missions as the converts took the gospel message to various parts of the world.

Just as Philadelphia was the church of the "open door" (verse 8; referring to its missionary work) in the apostle John's day, so the Philadelphia age of Christianity saw the birth of the Baptist Missionary Society, the London Missionary Society, and the American Board of Commissioners for Foreign Missions (among other missionary societies). In Britain, a man named Robert Raikes launched the Sunday School movement, which benefitted millions of believers. Moreover, people around the world took a renewed interest in the books of Daniel and Revelation. They believed they were living in a time when prophecy was being fulfilled and the world needed to know what the future held!

Laodicea: Spa church

Some of my best thinking happens while I'm taking a nice, hot shower. But for the proper amount of thinking to occur, I need a good hour or three. The hot water heater in my house thinks otherwise because it is selfish and small. So there I am on the verge of breaking through writer's block when the showerhead that has been dispensing a steaming cascade of therapeutic rain shifts to pelting me with icicles. I shriek and nearly fly through the glass shower door. That's neither helpful nor therapeutic.

What I truly want is one of those eight-person Jacuzzis that are on display at the local fair each year—not because I want to share the Jacuzzi with seven other people, but because it would be a source of never-ending warm water for me to soak in. I could think all kinds of great things with the help of the ever-changing LED ambient lighting, the built-in Bose sound system, the pop-up, flat-screen television, and built-in drink holders for something refreshing. And if you buy enough copies of this book to give to relatives, friends, acquaintances, and people on the street as Christmas gifts, I just may be able to afford one—so don't be cheap.

Laodicea, one of the greatest commercial and financial centers of the ancient world, is forty-five miles southeast of Philadelphia. It was founded in 260 B.C. by the Seleucid emperor Antiochus II, who named it after his wife, Laodice. How's that for a gift idea for the next holiday season? I already told you—don't be cheap.

Laodicea rested in the fertile Lycus Valley, at the junction of two major trade routes. This made the city wealthy and proud—so proud that when, in A.D. 60, the city was leveled by an earthquake, they refused the help the emperor offered and rebuilt it themselves. Imagine places like New Orleans after Katrina or Haiti after the earthquakes they suffered refusing help and cutting a check on their own funds to replace what was destroyed.

Serious wealth.

Laodicea's wealth came from a few key products. In the world of fashion and home, it made its mark with a fine, glossy black wool used for carpet and clothes. (Not that people wore carpet. Then again, one can't be too sure that no one did.)

Banking also played a key role in Laodicea's economy, but perhaps what contributed most to the city's wealth and pride was an eye salve called Phrygian powder and medical facilities where people came to have their eyes treated.

However, Laodicea had a problem that was particularly serious for a medical center. Jesus noted it in His message to the Laodiceans, which begins with His sharpest words yet: "And to the angel of the church in Laodicea write: 'The words of the Amen, the faithful and true witness, the beginning of God's creation. I know your works: you are *neither cold nor hot*. Would that you were either cold or hot! So, because you are lukewarm, and neither hot nor cold, *I will spit you out of my mouth*'" (verses 14–16; emphasis added).

Though Laodicea had many advantages, it had one a big problem—there was no local water supply. Springs in Hierapolis supplied the city's water, but the water was full of minerals, and since it started out hot but had to flow through a six-mile-long aqueduct, it was tepid by the time it reached Laodicea—not the ideal for either drinking or bathing. (People with aching muscles will buy lotions and creams named IcyHot, but not Kinda Warm or Slightly Cool.)

Jesus points out that the Laodicean Christians lack all the spiritual counterparts of the city's resources: " 'You say, I am rich, I have prospered, and I need nothing, not realizing that you are wretched, pitiable, poor, blind, and naked. I counsel you to buy from me gold refined by fire, so that you may be rich, and white garments so that you may clothe yourself and the shame of your nakedness may not be seen, and salve to anoint your eyes, so that you may see' " (verses 17, 18).

The Laodiceans think themselves to be models of spiritual health, but Jesus tells them that they are flatlining. He systematically trashes everything they are known for:

- You make eye medicine? You're blind!
- You have nice, glossy black wool? You're naked!
- You have some sweet moolah? You're poor and pitiable!

Their attitude is so distasteful that Jesus says they make Him want to vomit. Ouch. Not the typical picture of our loving Jesus is it? But He explains: " '*Those whom I love, I reprove and discipline, so be zealous and repent.* Behold, I stand at the door and knock. If anyone hears my voice and opens the door, I will come in to him and eat with him, and he with me. The one who conquers, I will grant him to sit with me on my throne, as I also conquered and sat down with my Father on his throne. He who has an ear, let him hear what the Spirit says to the churches' " (verses 19–22; emphasis added).

The busy, indifferent citizens of the Laodicean church need to have their schedules disrupted, so Jesus stands outside, knocking on their doors. He's trying to break into a church community that has shut the door on Him. He wants their friendship and love. To have His, all they have to do is open the door.

While Jesus doesn't find anything in this church to praise, He still promises something to them. He says that if they will repent, they will have a place next to Him on His throne—which, in the ancient world, looked more like a couch than like a high-backed chair meant to hold one person only. Jesus invites even people who are far away from Him to come close and to share in the new world He will create.

Laodicea, 1844 to the present. The problem of the Laodicean church in John's day was a cooling off of people's spiritual experience (verse 15). That was true of the Protestant Reformation too. And in the period represented by this church, the fiery revivals of the Great Awakenings began to chill. Churches forged in the flames of evangelism (for example, the Baptist and Methodist churches) now split over issues such as slavery.

Other events, such as the publication of Darwin's *Origin of Species,* called into question whether God really created the earth and whether the Bible really is true. Advances in medicine and increases in wealth drew people to focus more on what

Going Deeper

In what way does the final promise—the one Jesus made to Laodicea—summarize all the others? What significance do you see in the promises to each church exceeding those made to the previous church?

73

kind of future *they* could create, rather than on the new world Scripture said God would provide for His people. As a result of a better quality of life and impressive advancements in the sciences, humankind has grown self-satisfied. People—even people who consider themselves followers of Christ—are more interested in their comfort than in Christ.

A popular book entitled *unChristian* presents research that indicates modern Christianity is about as hot as a baby's bathwater. The authors state, "Two-third of churchgoers said, 'Rigid rules and strict standards are an important part of the life and teaching of my church.' "[1]

So, it appears that churches still have standards—even sturdy ones—regarding how people live. However, studies continue to paint a less-than-shiny picture:

> In virtually every study we conduct, representing thousands of interviews every year, born-again Christians fail to display much attitudinal or behavioral evidence of transformed lives. . . . When asked to identify their activities over the last thirty days, born-again believers were just as likely to bet or gamble, to visit a pornographic website, to take something that did not belong to them, to consult a medium or psychic, to physically fight or abuse someone, to have consumed enough alcohol to be considered legally drunk, to have used an illegal, non-prescriptive drug, to have said something to someone that was not true, to have gotten back at someone for something he or she did, and to have said mean things behind another person's back. No difference.[2]

In other words, Christians have the talk, but not the walk. Like the Laodiceans of John's day, they have become physically rich; but spiritually, they're poor.

Fortunately, God lets Laodiceans know that they can repent and change. There's still hope.

Seven dolphins

Think of these seven churches as seven dolphins that are swimming together, and one after another break out of the water and soar through the air.[3] All the dolphins are present all the time, but the characteristics of each dolphin show up when that dolphin is airborne and the rest are beneath the surface. Likewise, all the characteristics (idolatry, lack of love, desire for truth, etc.) of all the churches are present throughout history, but in each age, the characteristics of one of the churches predominate.

Hastily Drawn Figure 12.1

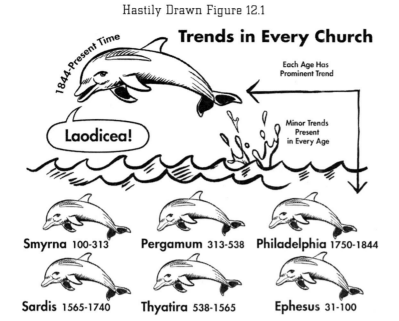

Trends in Every Church

1844-Present Time

Each Age Has Prominent Trend

Laodicea!

Minor Trends Present in Every Age

Smyrna 100-313   Pergamum 313-538   Philadelphia 1750-1844

Sardis 1565-1740   Thyatira 538-1565   Ephesus 31-100

We can also view this in terms of that classic arcade hit Whac-A-Mole, in which several moles "live" under the game board and pop up randomly so we can attempt to whack them. Though there are several moles there, we see only one at a time.

Hastily Drawn Figure 12.2

WHACK-A-CHURCH

Ephesus 31-100
Smyrna 100-313
Pergamum 313-538
Sardis 1565-1740
Thyatira 538-1565
Philadelphia 1750-1844
Laodicea 1844-present

What church fits you personally?

_____

_____

_____

_____

_____

_____

_____

_____

_____

_____

_____

_____

_____

_____

_____

_____

_____

_____

_____

_____

_____

_____

_____

_____

_____

_____

Cipher alert!

" 'Behold, I stand at the door and knock. If anyone hears my voice and opens the door, I will come in to him and eat with him, and he with me. The one who conquers, *I will grant him to sit with me on my throne, as I also conquered and sat down with my Father on his throne*' " (Revelation 3:20, 21; emphasis added). This final and ultimate promise for all of God's people gives us the cypher keys for decoding the next four chapters. Here are those cipher keys and the chapters of Revelation that they unlock:

- Revelation 4: The Father's throne
- Revelation 5: Jesus joins the Father on His throne
- Revelation 6: The saints overcome/conquer
- Revelation 7: The saints join Jesus on the throne

SUMMARY AND CONCLUSION
AND WHAT THIS TELLS US ABOUT JESUS

Jesus tells John to write seven special messages—one for each of the seven key churches in Asia Minor. Each church is unique, with its own culture and victories and shortcomings. Jesus cares about each one, and He meets them where they are, using language and images they understand.

The messages to these seven literal, first-century churches also fit the situation and needs of seven periods of church history and of individual churches all through history, including today. Each letter contains the line: "He who has an ear, let him hear what the Spirit says to the churches." The idea is that members of God's church in every part of the world should learn from these letters. They reflect common temptations and challenges that believers in every place and time must face. Jesus wants to communicate with His followers—even when the message He must deliver is painful.

So, what is your church like? What imagery and wording would Jesus use to reach the church where you choose to worship? Every church has challenges, so don't be discouraged if yours has more than a few. Even if your community of faith is like Laodicea, Jesus wants to be a part of it.

This chapter tells us that Jesus "walks among" the churches no matter how messed up they are. Sometimes it's easy to be critical of the church we attend—and our churches certainly can have real problems—yet Jesus longs to have people work with Him and be happy. How can you walk with Jesus in the church in which He has placed you?

ENDNOTES

1. David Kinnaman and Gabe Lyons, *unChristian* (Grand Rapids, Mich.: Baker Books, 2007), 51.

2. Ibid., 47.

3. I've borrowed this metaphor from C. Mervyn Maxwell, *God Cares* (Nampa, Idaho: Pacific Press®, 1985), 2:94.

Notes

Chapter 13

The Room

Revelation 4

On my Pinterest account (don't judge me), I have a board labeled "Man Cave." The pictures on that board are dedicated to the male equivalent of a Jane Austen parlor. Typically the "cave" is full of masculine comforts, such as the latest electronics, food that is barely approved by the FDA, and comfortable places to sit. After scouring the Internet, I have pictures of rooms with swimming pools, home theater systems, and large showers that simulate rainfall. Sometimes it's the room's location or construction that makes it particularly impressive. Elaborate tree houses, tents linked together to form a mini-city (men never grow out of forts), and bedrooms constructed in a Plexiglas tunnel in the midst of large aquarium. Tragically, I possess no such wonderful room. At the time of writing this chapter, I live with my wife and two girls. Floral patterns, pinks, and Disney Princesses litter my house and I am relegated to what you might call a "man corner."

The man corner consists of a desk with my computer, a couple of shelves featuring adventure films, works of theology and history, and a PlayStation 3. I am frequently interrupted since it is located in my bedroom, and if it weren't for my noise-canceling headphones I may have never finished this book. This is not to say I don't love my beautiful girls—but everyone needs their space and prides themselves on making it their own. To have someone walk into your house, garage, or man corner and comment on its clever construction and contents is a wonderful feeling.

So, how do your special rooms rate? How have you decorated your personal space? Better yet—if you had unlimited resources, how would you design that one special place in your house dedicated to you? Would you put in a waterslide? A lookout tower? A cage full of rhesus monkeys?

John is given an invitation to ascend somewhere, to go through an open door in someone's dwelling to see the events taking place after the ones mentioned in Revelation 2 and 3. He says, "After this I looked, and behold, a door standing open in heaven! And the first voice, which I had heard speaking to me like a trumpet, said,

'Come up here, and *I will show you what must take place after this*' " (Revelation 4:1; emphasis added).

So, where does John get to go? And what does he get to see?

He sees what's in the most awesome room in the universe.

The coolest room in the universe

"At once I was in the Spirit, and behold, *a throne stood in heaven, with one seated on the throne*" (verse 2; emphasis added).

When you see an arcade game in someone's house, it's a safe bet that you're in the game room. Likewise, when you see exercise equipment in a room, don't be surprised when someone tells you that you're in the exercise room. And when someone unlocks a basement door and you see a vast chamber full of chains, ropes, guillotines, thumb screws, red-hot pokers, and a man stretched out on a large wooden wheel and yelling for help, it behooves you to make a break for it, because you've entered a torture chamber.

Seriously, call the police.

So when we see a room containing a throne, either we're with someone who collects ancient antiques that should probably be returned to their country of origin. Or we are in a throne room.

In John's case, it wasn't just any throne room. It was the throne room of the King of the universe—the seat of authority for all reality. And Jesus let John hang out for a moment in His throne room.

Awesome.

Daniel 7:9 makes a subtle reference to this theme when Daniel, in vision, says, "Thrones were placed." Daniel was seeing the beginning of a judgment scene. But by the time John goes into vision, the "throne stood in heaven." So the point at which John's visions begin is later in this earth's history than the starting point of Daniel's vision, though both are about ongoing activities in heaven.

Very few people have witnessed the activities in the throne room. That's because the throne room is closely connected to the heavenly sanctuary. However, Isaiah did experience the incredible holiness of God's throne room (see Isaiah 6). Ezekiel also witnessed a display of fire, explosive torches, and wonderful creatures (see Ezekiel 1). As Stephen was being stoned, the heavens opened so he could see the sanctuary/throne room there—a vision that gave him great peace and comfort. And, of course, John's vision gave him a taste of heaven's worshipful atmosphere, which crackles with supernatural love and power.

Holy décor

John immediately recognized the throne and the One who sits on it, and from there, the ambiance explodes with life and color: "He who sat there had the appearance of jasper and carnelian, and around the throne was a rainbow that had the

Going Deeper

The king of Tyre was adorned with the same precious stones used on the high priest's breastplate and in God's throne room. In Ezekiel 28, the king of Tyre is a metaphor for Satan. What do you think this means?

_____
_____
_____
_____
_____
_____
_____
_____
_____
_____
_____
_____
_____
_____
_____
_____
_____

appearance of an emerald" (Revelation 4:3).

Precious stones have roots in the Hebrew sanctuary system. The breastplate worn by the high priest bore twelve stones inscribed with the names of the twelve tribes of Israel (Exodus 28:17–20). That's fitting, since Jesus is our High Priest (Hebrews 9). The stones are also mentioned as a part of the foundation of the New Jerusalem (Revelation 21:19, 20).

As for the rainbow, well, who doesn't love a good rainbow? The brightly colored bands of light also appear in the Hebrew Scriptures as a symbol of God's mercy. (See Noah's ark; Genesis 6–9).

So, we are dealing with the Royal Priest who rules the universe mercifully. He is the Centerpiece of the new world that will be fully realized when the New Jerusalem descends to the re-created earth. (See Revelation 21; 22.) Any room with God in it would easily win the contest as best room ever—and God's throne room adds to His presence other impressive elements that point to His majesty as well. John writes, "Around the throne were twenty-four thrones, and seated on the thrones were twenty-four elders, clothed in white garments, with golden crowns on their heads" (Revelation 4:4).

Some people believe, based on Revelation 5:8, that these elders are angelic beings who make sure the prayers of God's people get where they should go. In chapter 5, they are portrayed alongside supernatural creatures that hold bowls of incense, which represent the prayers of the saints—certainly a possibility.

(Bowls of incense represent prayers? I wonder what prayers smell like to God? Do some smell better than others? Do some actually stink? Sorry. Random thoughts.)

Others argue very convincingly that these elders represent redeemed humanity. They point out that in Scripture, the term *elder* is never applied to angels. They also note that these elders have *stephanoi* (yay Greek!) on their heads. A *stephanos* was a special crown given to those who won a great battle—here, referring to the victory over sin these elders have won through Jesus.

John also says that these elders are wearing designer white robes that God gives only to His saints (Revelation 3:4, 5, 18). And finally, the number twenty-four reminds us of the twenty-four courses of priests that served in God's temple (see 1 Chronicles 24:4–19), which could be taken as a symbol representing God's church.

But if the elders are human, how did they get into God's throne room in heaven?

When Jesus rose from the dead, other dead people were raised with Him (Matthew 27:52–55). People who read lots of books speculate that they also ascended to heaven with Him. They cite the following text: " 'When he [Jesus] ascended on high *he led a host of captives*' " (Ephesians 4:8; emphasis added). In any case, the twenty-four elders are a great bunch of people who get to hang out in God's throne room—like a sleepover but without the sleep.

Which brings me to the next point: sleep is impossible—and unnecessary—in a place full of such epic glory: "From the throne came flashes of lightning, and rumblings and peals of thunder, and before the throne were burning seven torches of fire, which are the seven spirits of God, and before the throne there was as it were a sea of glass, like crystal" (Revelation 4:5, 6).

While many people have a nightlight in their bedroom, God's throne room gets flashes of lightning and the fire of the seven spirits. Pretty sweet.

Hotels always charge more for a room with a view—especially an ocean view. The rooms that were mine when I was a kid always had a view of the driveway or the parking lot. That kind of view is always free. But John says that God's throne room is right next to a "sea of glass." Living on Patmos, John would have seen beautiful Mediterranean sunsets that illuminated the scene and made it shimmer. He uses the beauty of nature to describe the view from God's throne.

Four mystical creatures lived in God's throne room—creatures cooler than anything that lives in an aquarium (pet fish), a terrarium (pet tarantulas), or even an herbarium (pet herbs). John writes:

> And around the throne, on each side of the throne, are four living creatures, full of eyes in front and behind: the first living creature like a lion, the second living creature like an ox, the third living creature with the face of a man, and the fourth living creature like an eagle in flight. And the four living creatures, each of them with six wings, are full of eyes all around and within, and day and night they never cease to say, "Holy, holy, holy, is the Lord God Almighty, who was and is and is to come!" (verses 6–8).

Obviously these aren't pets—they are far more powerful than any creature people keep in their homes as pets. What exactly are they?

Isaiah 6 and Ezekiel 1 mention heavenly creatures similar to these. Both of these passages picture these creatures as serving God in His sanctuary, and both of the prophets that saw them say that they stood in awe as they watched them serve the Creator.

As impressive as these creatures are, though, there's no denying that they looked weird. When we describe animals or people that we think are cute, we don't say things like "Jenny is so cute—she's full of eyes." If someone caught a bird that had six wings, he'd sell it to a circus sideshow. And four faces on anything is three too many—especially when each comes from a different animal.

So, how do we make sense of these . . . creatures? First, and perhaps most important, it helps to remember that most of the imagery in Revelation is symbolic. Scripture connects "wings" with speed (see Habakkuk 1:8 . . . and my book on Daniel). Being full of eyes can simply mean that nothing escapes the notice of the creature being described; it sees everything that happens, everything that people do. The four faces may represent different characteristics of the angelic forces serving in the throne room—the lion representing strength; the ox, service; the human, intelligence; and the eagle, both speed and perception.

Going Deeper

Read Isaiah 6 and Ezekiel 1. The prophets who wrote these chapters saw God's sanctuary/throne room and the four creatures with the multiple faces. In what ways were their experiences different from John's? In what ways were they similar?

_____

_____

_____

_____

_____

_____

_____

_____

_____

_____

_____

_____

_____

_____

_____

_____

_____

My parents allowed me to have a stereo in my room, but they set maximums on the volume so the rest of my family wouldn't have to listen along with me. However, God's room has no volume control. Everyone present listens to what's happening, and they all participate in worshiping God. The prophet says, "Whenever the living creatures give glory and honor and thanks to him who is seated on the throne, who lives forever and ever, the twenty-four elders fall down before him who is seated on the throne and worship him who lives forever and ever" (verses 9, 10).

In the throne room, worship is a physical experience, not just a mental exercise. Worshiping God impacts every particle of our being—which makes sense since God _made_ every particle of our being.

The lyrics to the worship song in Revelation 4 highlight God as Creator: " 'Worthy are you, our Lord and God, to receive glory and honor and power, for you created all things, and by your will they existed and were created' " (verse 11). This is the best song to get stuck in one's head, because it expresses the truth about life and whom we are called to serve. And when we sing this song, the entire host of heaven joins us—even if nobody around us on earth feels like singing.

SUMMARY AND CONCLUSION
AND WHAT THIS TELLS US ABOUT JESUS

In Revelation 4, John tells us what he saw when he was caught up to heaven and permitted to enter the nerve center of all reality—God's throne room. In this special room, he witnesses the powerful worship that results when God's creatures are in His presence. He also sees amazing creatures unlike any that live on earth today, and he sees beings—either angels or redeemed humans—whose job is to serve God and carry out His will. But the focus of Revelation 4 is on the Father's throne, and in the next chapter we will see Jesus taking His seat on that throne.

The beauty of this passage is that it relates strongly to our prayer life. When John mentions the elders again (Revelation 5:8), he pictures them as holding "golden bowls full of incense, which are the prayers of the saints." This means that our prayers ascend to the most powerful place in the universe, where God hears them and commissions His amazing servants to do what He wants to be done about our prayers.

The writer of Hebrews says, "Let us then with confidence draw near to the throne of grace, that we may receive mercy and find grace to help in time of need" (Hebrews 4:16). God's throne room is much more awesome and holy than we can begin to imagine—but because of what Jesus accomplished on the cross, the door to that room is always open to us, as it was for John. We can rest assured that when we pray, the cosmic forces of heaven will work on our behalf.

Jesus told His disciples—and that includes us—that there are many rooms in His Father's house, and that when He left earth, it would be to prepare a place for us there (John 14:2). Whatever the room that's yours now may look like, the one that Jesus is preparing for you is infinitely more epic. Spend some time there this week worshiping the One who sees and understands.

Going Deeper

Do you find the idea that your prayers ascend to God's sanctuary/throne room intimidating or discouraging? Why? What do you think might change your attitude?

_____

_____

_____

_____

_____

_____

_____

_____

_____

_____

_____

_____

_____

_____

_____

_____

_____

_____

Chapter 14

Can Someone Open This Thing?

Revelation 5

A few days ago my magnificent strength was called upon to handle a potentially dangerous situation: opening a jar. Not a random jar, mind you—this jar contained green olives stuffed with jalapeños and soaking in a spicy liquid. An error in the force of pressure being applied to that infernal lid might result in fiery juice splattering everywhere—including into my eyes. I approached the briny menace carefully and applied pressure while my wife watched in awe.

The seal wouldn't break.

More pressure.

Fortunately, in the case of the jalapeño-stuffed olives, I did possess the might necessary to break the seal. So our guests were able to enjoy their spicy goodness. And I didn't even go blind.

Following the directions of our cipher text (Revelation 3:21), we saw God the Father's throne (Revelation 4), and now it's time for Jesus to take His place on that throne. In the ancient Middle East, thrones were more like couches than chairs, so there was room for more than one person to sit on the throne and rule with authority. According to Revelation 3, Jesus takes His seat after He conquers—that is, after He conquers death and ascends to heaven.

But there's a problem.

A problem that's worse than a stubborn jar of spicy olives.

It's so troubling that it makes John weep—and not because he got something in his eyes. John writes the following:

> Then I saw in the right hand of him who was seated on the throne a scroll written within and on the back, sealed with seven seals. And I saw a mighty angel proclaiming with a loud voice, "Who is worthy to open the

scroll and break its seals?" And no one in heaven or on earth or under the earth was able to open the scroll or to look into it, and I began to weep loudly because no one was found worthy to open the scroll or to look into it (Revelation 5:1–4).

Despite all the power there is in heaven, nobody is found who is able to open it—because power isn't the issue. Only the person to whom the scroll is addressed can open it.

The scroll with seven seals

We all have our favorite books—books that are special to us for one reason or another. I have a first edition of *The Great Controversy*, a book that's very important to our faith tradition. The copy I have belonged to my grandmother.

I also have a first edition of a book written by one of my favorite college professors—with his signature. And standing on my shelf of children's literature is a copy of *The Invention of Hugo Cabret*—now a major motion picture called *Hugo*—that I purchased in Chicago. The author's signature rests on the opening page.

No, you *can't* touch it.

The seven-sealed scroll is extremely special. First, the phrase "in the right hand" is a figure of speech that means "at the right side." This scroll is resting beside the Father on His throne. In ancient Israel, whenever a new king took the throne, he was given the scroll of the covenant. *Covenant* is a word that refers to the agreement God has with His people (see Deuteronomy 17:18–20; 1 Samuel 10:25; and 2 Kings 11:12). The scroll is a symbol of being installed on the throne. The kings of Israel were said to sit at God's "right hand" as co-rulers with Him (see Psalms 80:17; 110:1). The sealed scroll in Revelation 5 appears to be awaiting a kingly figure, some worthy person, before its contents will be revealed.

This scroll has another interesting feature—someone has written on both sides of it. It has words on both the front and the back. This was a practice called *opisthographos* (congratulations for making it through that word), and it can be seen on the two tablets given to Moses—tablets on which God spelled out His expectations for His people (Exodus 32:15). Some people think it may be related to the "little scroll" on which John snacks in Revelation 10.

Seriously, he eats a book. But we'll come back to that later.

The seals that pasted documents closed were made of wax. While the wax was still warm, a signet ring was pressed into it. The wax then bore the impression of the ring, which took the place of a signature. You can still buy these things at craft stores.

When someone wanted to read a scroll that was sealed shut, all of the seals had to be opened—a scroll can't be opened up when even just one seal remains unbroken. As I've mentioned before, the number seven means perfection and completeness.

Going Deeper

How do you find comfort when you feel lonely? Are you surprised that someone who has encountered Jesus so personally—like John—could feel such despair?

_____

_____

_____

_____

_____

_____

_____

_____

_____

_____

_____

_____

_____

_____

_____

_____

_____

_____

_____

_____

_____

_____

Read John 15. What is the Holy Spirit's main assignment?

_____

_____

_____

_____

_____

_____

_____

_____

_____

_____

_____

_____

_____

_____

_____

_____

_____

_____

_____

_____

Sealing a scroll with seven seals indicates that God and His people have reached a special agreement, or perhaps that a special revelation from God that had been tucked away to await the arrival of a special time has now been opened.

What could be so special that it would require so much security?

One scholar points out that Roman law dictated that wills had to be sealed with a minimum of seven seals—which meant seven people had witnessed the sealing—in order to guarantee the will was valid.[1] So we have this legal, royal agreement that has to do with God and His people. Many scholars believe the scroll contained God's will, and others think it's the deed for a property that has been lost and that the owner can reclaim only when the deed has been shown to be valid.

In any case, the next verse reveals who is worthy to carry out the divine will by reclaiming the property.

Lost and found

"And one of the elders said to me, 'Weep no more; behold, *the Lion of the tribe of Judah, the Root of David,* has conquered, so that he can open the scroll and its seven seals.' And between the throne and the four living creatures and among the elders I saw *a Lamb standing, as though it had been slain,* with *seven horns and with seven eyes,* which are the seven spirits of God sent out into all the earth" (Revelation 5:5, 6; emphasis added).

When I entered fifth grade, I was given my very first locker. One day, in the course of dumping all the candy wrappers and homework I hadn't turned in, I found thirty bucks. That's right—thirty big ones. While thirty dollars is a mere trifle for someone as famous and wealthy as I am now (I can make thirty dollars a week, no problem), back then finding that money was the equivalent of finding a unicorn saddled with golden bars jumping over rainbows in my basement. You can imagine my excitement.

However, since I had a moral compass, I turned the money in, thinking it must have been some other kid's lunch money. (A very large kid, because thirty bucks buys a lot of hot lunch.) The school secretary said that if no one claimed the money in the next two weeks, it would be mine. Despite those two weeks being the longest of my life, the day finally arrived when I went to the office to claim the money. I had found it and saved it, you might say, and on that glorious day, the money was returned to me for my purposes—mostly soda, video games, and G.I. Joes.

Property that has been lost can be reclaimed only by the rightful owner. The earth is the choicest piece of property in the universe outside of heaven. God lovingly handcrafted it (Genesis 1; 2) and called it "very good." However, a war that began in heaven carried over to this earth and led to its fall into darkness (Genesis 3), effectively making it a "lost property." The only hope of those who live here is for Jesus to reclaim this world from the cosmic "lost and found" in which it is stuck.

But that would require sacrifice.

All this meant that the scroll wouldn't be opened because no one had the proper credentials. There was no fit person. When John realized this, he wept in despair. But then he was comforted by an angel, who introduced Someone who can fix everything. The term "Lion of Judah" is a term of victory (Genesis 49:8, 9), and the "Root of David" refers to the rising of the ideal King (Isaiah 11:1; 2 Samuel 7:12–16). It's a title of the Messiah (Luke 1:32, 33). The description of Jesus also mentions seven horns (representing perfect strength; Numbers 23:22; Deuteronomy 33:17) and seven eyes (representing perfect perception; Zechariah 4:10).

Then John sees Jesus in a way he has never seen Him before.

The Bible describes Jesus as "the Lamb of God, who takes away the sin of the world" (John 1:29). In Revelation, Jesus is pictured as having obtained the victory over sin through His sacrifice on the cross. He not only won the right to reclaim the earth, but He alone is powerful enough, qualified enough, to break the seals.

Now Jesus takes the scroll representing human history—and the future of human beings—into His hands. "And he went and took the scroll from the right hand of him who was seated on the throne. And when he had taken the scroll, the four living creatures and the twenty-four elders fell down before the Lamb, each holding a harp, and golden bowls full of incense, which are the prayers of the saints" (Revelation 5:7, 8).

Then Jesus takes His seat next to the Father, the Father confers Lordship over the universe to Jesus Christ, and heaven erupts in worship and celebration.

Songs of praise

The first song (verses 9, 10) praises Jesus for His sacrifice. The second song declares Him worthy to receive honor and glory (verses 11, 12). And then the four living creatures and the twenty-four elders exclaim their joy that Jesus is on the throne (verses 13, 14). No one can hold back the tremendous outburst of joy and praise at the inauguration of Jesus. Like a party that wakes up the neighbors, the celebration spills out of heaven and onto earth, waking people spiritually.

John writes, "I saw a Lamb standing, as though it had been slain, with seven horns and with seven eyes, which are the seven spirits of God sent out into all the earth" (Revelation 5:6).

The word *sent* carries the idea of sending out an official representative (see Matthew 11:10; Acts 10:17). Once in a while a salesperson knocks at my door and tries to change my life with a vacuum cleaner, magazine subscriptions, or time-travel machines. Jesus offers something better, something more effective. He sends out His official Representative, and that Representative changes people's lives. In his Gospel, John records Jesus as saying, "Now this he said about the Spirit, whom those who believed in him were to receive, *for as yet the Spirit had not been given, because Jesus was not yet glorified*" (John 7:39; emphasis added). In Revelation 5, Jesus is glorified—look at the lyrics to the songs sung by the four creatures and the twenty-four elders.

Going Deeper

In this chapter, the little scroll has been pictured as a will. A will tells us what the one who wrote it wants us to do with his or her goods. Jesus has the power and authority to carry out the divine will, but in Revelation 5:8, we find that we can participate in Jesus' carrying out of the divine will. What does the incense represent (read the text), and how can you and I help Jesus carry out His will?

_____

_____

_____

_____

_____

_____

_____

_____

_____

_____

_____

_____

_____

_____

_____

Going Deeper

How does Acts 1:14 relate to Revelation 5:8?

_____

_____

_____

_____

_____

_____

_____

_____

_____

_____

_____

_____

_____

_____

_____

_____

_____

_____

_____

_____

_____

_____

_____

_____

The phrase "seven spirits" can be understood to be representing the Holy Spirit, the "perfect Spirit"—seven being the number of perfection. The text says the Spirit was "sent out into all the earth." Peter declares that the Spirit comes in this mighty power as a result of Jesus being "exalted at the right hand of God" (Acts 2:33; see also verses 32–36). Three thousand people came to know Jesus as King of the universe that day, and as the Spirit continues to touch the hearts of people, more and more of them have their lives changed to reflect Jesus.

SUMMARY AND CONCLUSION AND WHAT THIS TELLS US ABOUT JESUS

This chapter pictures Jesus' inauguration as King at the right hand of the Father in heaven. The scroll with seven seals is the deed to a lost property, the earth—a deed that can be opened only by the One who has redeemed the property.

No one in heaven is found worthy or powerful enough to open the seals—until Jesus, the victorious One, appears. His sacrifice on the cross allows Him to take the scroll from the Father. All of heaven rejoices now that a loving Savior is in control of what happens to the earth and its inhabitants. And at the very moment Jesus takes the throne, the Holy Spirit is sent to earth to reveal Jesus in a powerful new way.

While the story told in Acts occurred two thousand years ago, the same Spirit is still active. The Holy Spirit sent to the earth so long ago wants to reveal Jesus in a life-changing way today to you and me. Spend some time asking the Holy Spirit to come into your heart and transform you and fill you with a spirit of worship and joy. After all, Jesus is still sitting on the throne of the universe. He still rules. And He promises us a seat next to Him when He returns.

ENDNOTE

1. Stefanovic, *Revelation of Jesus Christ,* 202.

Chapter 15
History in the Hands of Jesus
Revelation 6; 8:1

From time to time, I have found myself in a café studying or conversing about work only to be interrupted by the music. One time it was Native American chanting followed by Barry White, and then rounded off with Frank Sinatra. Once, while at Starbucks, I noticed the transition from Enya to the Brian Setzer Orchestra, and I inquired of a barista as to what was going on. She shrugged, shook her head, and said, "I have no idea—they just send us CDs to play." They were just as baffled as I was. Each song shifted the mood to the point of it being hard to concentrate. Was the atmosphere supposed to be happy, relaxing, or romantic?

Revelation 5 pictures the inauguration of Jesus as King. It shines with glory, praise, and the outpouring of the Holy Spirit. But then, just as the musical selections incessantly bounced back and forth changing the mood of the café, so the seven seals of Revelation 6 and 8:1 shift the mood immensely. As the seals are broken, the atmosphere becomes intense—and sometimes terrifying. No doubt people's feelings in the café shifted with each genre of music. Some songs irritated patrons while at the same time delighting others. And when the genre flipped again, those who were happy with the previous selection were now disappointed with the music blaring over the sound system. The feelings about the seven seals vary too. What is terrifying from one perspective is beautiful from another.

Revelation 6 contains one of those "eye exams" we discussed earlier. The seals go through much of the same Christian history as the seven churches do. The difference is that previously we saw things from the perspective of Jesus. Now we see them from the vantage point of God's people—what they will do, what they will endure.[1]

The good news is that no matter what happens, history is in Jesus' hands. It has a point and a destination. As the seals break, John sees the world move toward a glorious climax, and hope flares to life even though some of the images that stand between us and that climax are intimidating and even terrifying.

We begin with horses.

The four horsemen

Many people associate horses with birthday gifts for girls who are turning sixteen. From their earliest years, people give young females toys like My Little Pony and books like *Black Beauty*. Girls are groomed for that glorious day when they have the chance to saddle a real steed and trot elegantly around the countryside.

But there are other kinds of riders. The first American work of fiction, published by Washington Irving in 1820, features a Hessian soldier who has lost his head due to an unfortunate encounter with a cannon ball. Irving pictures this decapitated soldier, known as the headless horseman, as wielding a blade and sometimes a fiery jack-o-lantern and riding around on a jet-black horse that breathes flames. The effect is anything but sparkly.

In another famous work of fiction, author J. R. R. Tolkien uses a group known as "the Nazgûl," "the Nine," and "Ringwraiths" to add tension to his story. These mythical creatures thunder through the realm trying to hunt down the hero. These shrieking and hissing beings are devoid of anything cute or fluffy. They won't be stuffed-animal gifts at anyone's birthday party.

But the wraiths don't win the prize for petrifying the most people either. The horsemen who have inspired the most fear throughout human history appear with the breaking of the first four seals of Revelation 6. Books, music, film, and art have all depicted these mysterious riders as supernatural signs of the end. Their identity is the subject of endless speculation. Fortunately, the Bible provides us the key that unlocks who they are.

The book of Zechariah uses the imagery of horsemen. In the first chapter of his book, Zechariah says he saw in vision red, sorrel (brown), and white horses that have patrolled the earth. In chapter 6, the horses bring vengeance.

In Revelation 6, these harbingers of the future are portrayed as breaking forth in the colors white, red, black . . . and dead.

Seal one: Rider on a white horse

John begins Revelation 6 writing about a white horse: "Now I watched when the Lamb opened one of the seven seals, and I heard one of the four living creatures say with a voice like thunder, 'Come!' And I looked, and behold, *a white horse*! And *its rider had a bow*, and *a crown was given to him*, and *he came out conquering, and to conquer*" (Revelation 6:1, 2).

In the book of Revelation, the color white is always used in relation to Christ and His people. Jesus has snow-white hair (Revelation 1:14). God's conquering people are given white stones (Revelation 2:17). The twenty-four elders sitting on thrones are clothed in white (Revelation 4:4). God's people are given white robes (Revelation 6:11; 7:9, 14; 19:14). And Jesus rides not only on a white cloud (Revelation 14:14), but also on a white horse (Revelation 19:11, 14).

In ancient times, Roman generals used to ride a white horse through town to celebrate their victories. The crown worn by the rider in Revelation is called a *stephanos*. This kind of crown didn't identify its wearer as being a member of the royal family. Instead, it indicated that the one who wore it had won a victory. The white horse and its rider represent victory. Bible scholars say it represents the early church's victories as it spread the gospel.

When we think of a bow, we think of Robin Hood. But in the Old Testament, the bow is often connected with God (Psalm 45:3–5; Habakkuk 3:8, 9). Armed with the fiery arrows of the gospel, He rides a horse as He carries out His mission of thwarting the powers of darkness.

Bible scholars consider this first horse and rider to represent the Christian church when it was first founded. This symbol covers the same period represented by Ephesus, the first church of the seven. It would be great if this were the only horse, and it galloped through every phase of history. But unfortunately, some people rejected the loving message of Jesus, and the results have been messy.

Seal two: Rider on a red horse

John continues: "When he opened the second seal, I heard the second living creature say, 'Come!' And out came another horse, bright red. Its rider was permitted to take peace from the earth, so that people should slay one another, and he was given a great sword" (Revelation 6:3, 4).

The word translated "slay" here is the Greek word *sphazō,* which isn't the word used most often to indicate death in battle. Throughout Revelation, *sphazō* is used to refer to the deaths of Jesus and the saints (Revelation 5:6, 9; 6:9; 13:8; 18:24). Some commentators speculate that this horseman and the "living creature" that has the face of an ox (Revelation 4:7) are the same. Note that the ox is a symbol of sacrifice.

The Bible says that those who reject God's goodness have no peace (Isaiah 57). And Jesus warned that the gospel would bring division (Matthew 10:34; Luke 12:51–53). Even as early as the Exodus, God's people experienced bloody divisions between those who were faithful and those who weren't (Exodus 32:27–29). The passage indicates that while the early church experienced success (Acts 4:32–35; 5:12, 13), it also provoked the ire of those who felt threatened by its message.

In the early centuries of the Christian faith, Rome didn't see life the same way the followers of Jesus did. And when Rome had a problem, it had a whimsical way of dealing with it: shoot first and ask questions later. Christianity was a threat to emperor worship, so the Roman authorities tried to stamp it out—sometimes with the aid of hostile Jews. Apparently, all of Jesus' disciples other than John died violent deaths.

Going Deeper

A scholar named Uriah Smith believed that the events described in the seals should be taken literally. That is, that in Revelation, John was writing about real earthquakes, actual darkness, and so forth. He argued that the language in this prophecy changes because Daniel 12:4 describes an increase in prophetic knowledge. Do you think this makes sense? Why or why not?

However, every effort the Romans made to stamp out the church only made it stronger. A leader of the early church named Tertullian wrote, "The blood of the martyrs is the seed of the church!" Generally, people won't sacrifice their lives to preserve a lie, so one of the strongest arguments for the truth of Christianity is the willingness of the early Christians to die rather than give up their faith.

The red horse represents the persecutions of Christians in the second and third centuries—the same period represented by the church at Smyrna. Unfortunately, as we continue, the light that was a brilliant white at first then turned red as the sunset now fades to black.

Seal three: Rider on a black horse

John writes: "When he opened the third seal, I heard the third living creature say, 'Come!' And I looked, and behold, a black horse! And its rider had *a pair of scales* in his hand. And I heard what seemed to be a voice in the midst of the four living creatures, saying, *'A quart of wheat for a denarius, and three quarts of barley for a denarius, and do not harm the oil and wine!'*" (Revelation 6:5, 6; emphasis added).

The description of the black horse and its rider contains the language of famine. A denarius was considered a day's wages, and a quart of wheat was a daily ration of food for one person. Currency is being equated with food, which says that all the buffets around town have closed. People are starving, and since they can't eat coins (well, I guess they could; but coins are low in nutritional value), food becomes more valuable. In times of plenty, a denarius would buy twelve or fifteen times what these verses picture as being offered.

The Old Testament contains several references to famines like this one in Revelation (see, for example, Leviticus 26:26; Ezekiel 4:16). The prophet Amos pictures God as angrily correcting His people for their lack of genuine love for Him and for each other. But there's more than just food at stake here: " 'The days are coming,' declares the Sovereign Lord, 'when I will send a famine through the land—not a famine of food or a thirst for water, but a famine of hearing the words of the Lord' " (Amos 8:11, NIV).

Food is often used as a metaphor for God's Word. (For example, see Matthew 4:4.) As we transition from a time of persecution for God's people, we enter a period of spiritual famine—namely, the exclusion of God's Word from people's spiritual diet.

One example of people being denied access to God's Word is recorded in canons 6 and 14 of the Council of Toulouse, which convened in the year 1229. It says, "We prohibit also that the laity should be permitted to have the books of the Old or New Testament; unless anyone from motive of devotion should wish to have the Psalter or the Breviary for divine offices or the hours of the blessed Virgin; but we most strictly forbid their having any translation of these books."[2]

The penalty for disobeying this prohibition of the church was large: "the house in which any heretic shall be found shall be destroyed."[3]

These kinds of sentiments are strewn about all through the Middle Ages and right down to the 1800s. Great efforts were made to keep Scripture cloaked in the language that only the clergy could understand (go, Latin!), instead of giving it to people in the language they spoke.

The Middle Ages are often also called the "Dark Ages"—and with good reason. The medieval Christian church had been transformed into a political entity hungry for power and control, and spiritual darkness swept over the landscape of faith. Scholars suggest that the dark horse of Revelation 6 represents this period, when the church attained religio-political power but did so to the spiritual detriment of the people who lived at that time. Seventh-day Adventists generally believe this period to have reached from the year 538 to 1798. Some scholars believe that the seal bearing the black horse and its rider corresponds with Pergamum, the third church of the seven—the church known for spiritual compromise that resulted in a scarcity of truth and an obscuring of the teachings of Jesus. In any case, it portrays a time in which the light of the gospel was darkened.

Now death comes riding.

Seal four: Rider on a dead horse

"When he opened the fourth seal, I heard the voice of the fourth living creature say, 'Come!' And I looked, and behold, *a pale horse!* And *its rider's name was Death, and Hades followed him.* And they were given *authority over a fourth of the earth, to kill with sword and with famine and with pestilence and by wild beasts of the earth*" (Revelation 6:7, 8; emphasis added).

Revelation's fourth horse makes people's skin crawl. While most English translations render the word *chloros* as "pale," the word means something else. *Chloros* is the word from which we get the English word "chlorine"—the stuff people put in their swimming pools to kill bacteria and algae. Too much chlorine, and they close the pool down—leaving you standing there in your swimsuit with nothing to do, because if you jumped in, you'd burn your skin. *Chloros* is lethal. It's the color of death—a sickly green.

No wonder Death and Hades (the Greek term for the grave) enjoy riding on this beast.

As famine leads to death, so spiritual famine leads to spiritual death. But as awful as Death and Hades are, they don't inflict their power on their own. Jesus controls them (Revelation 1:18).

In Old Testament times, God warned that He would bring four disastrous instruments of judgment—"sword, famine, wild beasts, and pestilence"—upon the people who claimed to be His but didn't give their full allegiance to Him. He said this would cut "man and beast" from the land He had given them (Ezekiel 14:21).

Going Deeper

Read Matthew 24 and see if you find any similarities in what Jesus describes there and what the seven seals reveal.

Whenever God allows such calamities, He does it to wake His people from their spiritual slumber, their spiritual death, so they'll look to Him for life and help.

Today, especially in Europe, Christianity has faded from the culture. Cathedrals once full of worshipers now stand empty. And attendance at Protestant churches has also dwindled. People claim the name of Christ, but their lifestyles reveal they are more concerned about pleasing themselves than about honoring God.

This seal portrays a church that has died spiritually. The few remaining true followers of Jesus have been abused and feel abandoned—which cues the fifth frightening image: the altar of souls.

Seal five: The altar of souls

"When he opened the fifth seal, I saw under the altar the souls of those who had been slain for the word of God and for the witness they had borne. They cried out with a loud voice, 'O Sovereign Lord, holy and true, how long before you will judge and avenge our blood on those who dwell on the earth?' " (Revelation 6:9, 10).

Sometimes it seems as though time is dragging along like a two-legged cat.

Sorry, that was morbid.

But seriously, we can find ourselves in situations that slow time to a painful crawl. When we're hungry and waiting for Thanksgiving dinner, when we're thirsty and can't find a drinking fountain, or when we're standing in line at Disney World for the Space Mountain ride (actually, that is a long wait), time feels like it has just stopped moving.

The cry of those mysterious souls under the altar points us back to the time when a "holy one" in heaven asks, " '*For how long* is the vision concerning the regular burnt offering, the transgression that makes desolate, and the giving over of the sanctuary and host to be trampled underfoot?' " (Daniel 8:13; emphasis added). The question comes because of extreme grief and suffering. People are crying for God to intervene, to bring holy justice into human experience.

The altar was essential to the Old Testament sanctuary services. Actually, there were two altars in the ancient sanctuary. The first one, located *outside* the temple, was used for burnt animal sacrifices. The second one, located *inside* the temple, was used for burning incense. (You can read about them in Leviticus 4.) The image in Revelation 6 of God's people under the altar says these people have been sacrificed for their faithfulness (their "witness," ESV; their "testimony," NIV, NASB). Since the altar for sacrifices stood outside of the sanctuary, the imagery in John's vision refers to the believers on earth.

The Bible frequently uses personification in its descriptions. Personification is a literary device in which an author writes as though nonhuman creatures or things have human traits. We use it today too. When a man says his car "choked" or a woman says her phone "died," they're applying to nonliving things terms that really are true only of living creatures.

When, in Genesis 4:10, God says the blood of Abel was "crying" to Him from the ground, He doesn't mean that a puddle of red liquid was actually screaming. The idea is that the blood is clear evidence that Cain has hurt Abel, and when God sees that blood, it moves Him to act.

While suffering makes time move along in what seems to be an unbearably slow way, God isn't absent or hard of hearing. Revelation continues by saying, "Then they were each given a white robe and told to rest a little longer, until the number of their fellow servants and their brothers should be complete, who were to be killed as they themselves had been" (Revelation 6:11). The salvation of those who have perished for Jesus is secure.

This fifth seal parallels the church at Sardis. The members of that church held on despite being beaten down with persecution.

At that point, the future looks dark. People cry out for God to act. And then the sixth seal is broken.

Seal six: Bad weather

"When he opened the sixth seal, I looked, and behold, there was *a great earthquake,* and *the sun became black as sackcloth,* the full *moon became like blood,* and *the stars of the sky fell* to the earth as the fig tree sheds its winter fruit when shaken by a gale. The sky vanished like a scroll that is being rolled up, and *every mountain and island was removed from its place*" (Revelation 6:12–14; emphasis added).

During my junior year of college, I was the vice president of the student organization that was responsible for arranging various activities that would enrich the students' experience with Jesus. Without fail, it rained during every event I planned. Rain actually forced me to move one annual event to the middle of January.

Do you hear me? To J-A-N-U-A-R-Y, when the days are cold, crisp, and perhaps fluffy with snow.

It rained that day too.

People were good sports about it, but I longed to inflict bodily harm on the falling liquid that continually sabotaged my plans. However, weather refuses to be controlled. All we can do is predict what will happen when, and even then, we're more likely to find gold nuggets in our underwear drawer than to understand the rhythms of weather.

As the news too often reports, other happenings in the natural world can be more than irritating. They can be devastating. Tsunamis, earthquakes, fires, and tornadoes can rip people apart—sometimes hundreds of thousands of people in mere moments.

The sixth seal reveals some unique changes of the natural world that humans will have to live with in the future. However, as strange and devastating as these disasters are, they point toward a hope rooted in Jesus. And every single one is rooted in imagery from the Hebrew Scriptures. What's more, many students of prophecy

Going Deeper

What relationship do modern disasters have to those that Bible prophecy talks about? What do they reveal about our time?

considered natural disasters to be preludes to the coming of the Lord.

Bible prophecy became a favorite topic in the eighteenth and nineteenth centuries as massive revivals known as the Great Awakenings drew people into a personal relationship with Jesus and created hope and expectancy for His return. A massive earthquake occurred in Portugal in 1755. The ground-shaking event was felt throughout four million square miles in Europe, Africa, and America, and ninety thousand people perished in this natural disaster. Many people saw the event as a confirmation of Revelation, and that motivated them to search Scripture more deeply than they had in the past.

Revelation 6 also speaks of the sun becoming dark and the moon turning red like blood (see verse 12; and see also Isaiah 13:10; 50:3; Joel 2:31; Matthew 24:29–31). In May 1780, an event known in history as the "Dark Day" occurred in New York and southern New England. Thought to have been caused by massive brush fires rampant in northeast North America, sunlight disappeared from 10:00 A.M. through the rest of that day. It became so dark that in the middle of the afternoon, people couldn't read without the aid of candles or other man-made sources of light. The fires also affected the light of the moon, turning the moon a tawny dark color—like the blood moon described in Revelation.

An extraordinary "falling" of the stars is another event that was to occur with the breaking of the sixth seal. (See also Isaiah 34:4; and Matthew 24:29.) On the night of November 13, 1833, sky watchers witnessed a spectacular meteor shower that some described as "raining fire." (Not to be confused with the singer Adele's setting "fire to the rain" in one of her songs.) The star cascade ran from nine to midnight.

Those who were alive during these spectacular events believed themselves to have witnessed the specific, historical fulfillment of prophecy. Others see these events as the kind that recurs naturally, but they say that their increasing intensity reminds us that Jesus is coming soon.

When these events happen, they're like alarm clocks ringing on Monday morning, letting you know that you need to get out of the night's warm, sleepy stupor—the one that has made your pillow wet with drool—and get ready for school. It's time to wake up.

The rest of the imagery, such as the rolling up of the sky (see Isaiah 34:4), all revolves around the second coming of Jesus. This is the perfect response to those who are suffering persecution and even death for their faith. Jesus is coming—soon.

The wicked try to hide (Revelation 6:15, 16).

The righteous rejoice.

The end is coming.

The sixth seal ends with a question (taken from Malachi 3:2): Who is able to stand? That question introduces the subject of Revelation 7—which is an interlude between the sixth and seventh seals. We'll look at that interlude in chapter 16. But first, we'll skip to the final seal, which is found in Revelation 8:1.

Seal seven: The silence

"When the Lamb opened the seventh seal, there was silence in heaven for about half an hour" (Revelation 8:1).

In most human gatherings, a phenomenon known as the "seven-minute lull" crops up. The theory says that after about seven minutes of chit-chat, an awkward silence slips in, and people, suddenly having nothing to say, just stare at each other or at their drinks or their smart phones, or maybe even excuse themselves and join another group of people. Eventually, the conversation in the first group picks up again, but seven minutes later, it will dwindle into another awful silence.

The opening of the final seal brings about a thirty-minute silence within the boundaries of heaven. Most scholars believe that "half hour" simply means a short period of time and don't assign anything specific to it. They say the main idea is the period of silence.

The Old Testament mentions several silences that can help us out. It speaks of a silence at the beginning of creation (Genesis 1:2), and when God's judgment comes into sight (Habakkuk 2:20; Zephaniah 1:7; Zechariah 2:13). The silence of the seventh seal could be a dramatic pause before God executes judgment. The calm before the storm.

In light of the chronology of the seven seals, the seventh seal could also refer to the time when Jesus leaves heaven with all His angels to return to the earth. The silence occurs in heaven because, well, no one is there. The final seal, then, is the great moment when Jesus makes the journey to redeem the faithful from their formidable struggle with sin.

SUMMARY AND CONCLUSION
AND WHAT THIS TELLS US ABOUT JESUS

One Bible scholar describes the seven seals as "life between the cross and Second Coming."[4] As the seals break open, we see parallels between the time periods they represent and the experiences of the seven churches. The history revealed within the scrolls is presented from the perspective of those who follow Jesus. While there are experiences that test human beings—even to death—Jesus is still in control. In the end, Jesus leaves heaven to save those who have placed their faith in Him, and He takes with Him all those who dwell in that supernatural realm.

The book of Revelation lets us know that we will have difficult experiences in this life. The Bible nowhere suggests we can expect a problem-free existence. Jesus doesn't hide the reality of human history and of the future from us. But He does promise us that pain will eventually end. The fact that He presents this theme multiple times within the pages of prophecy highlights just how important it is that we realize this. Our lives are filled with so many

Notes

distractions and discouragements that it is easy to forget the hope we have. Spend time in the books of prophecy whenever you feel that God has forgotten humanity or that He has forgotten you. These books will sharpen your perspective and refresh your faith.

ENDNOTES

1. Roy Naden, *The Lamb Among the Beasts* (Hagerstown, Md.: Review and Herald®, 1996), 106.
2. The Bible Prohibited to the Laity, http://www.justforcatholics.org/a198.htm (accessed April 15, 2013).
3. Ibid.
4. Stefanovic, *Revelation of Jesus Christ,* 255.

Chapter 16
Warriors
Revelation 7

Every year I, along with many other people who feel brave, embark on a quest known as the Warrior Dash. More than just a race, the Warrior Dash is more than three miles of obstacles that test one's physical and mental limits. It also tests how grossed out a person is by mud. Serious mud. Deep, black, wet earth. The kind of filth that sucks the shoes right off your feet.

To get through Barricade Breakdown, contestants must leap over a four-foot-high wall, roll under barbed wire, and then leap over another four-foot-high wall. Road Rage requires runners to clamber over a series of junkyard cars while being blasted with icy water. Cargo Climb involves scaling a twenty-foot-high wall of nets. And to get across Warrior Roast without burning their legs, they must jump over three-foot-high flames.

To reach the finish line, the contestants must swim through a pit that looks like it's been filled with chocolate milkshakes. But the filling is mud. And just above this mud are rows of barbed wire, with sharp metal points that greet the runners' skulls should they bob their heads too high. The Warrior Dash isn't the hardest race on the planet, but only those who are physically fit and have a lot of determination can finish it.

The obstacles described above are the reason potential contestants have to be at least fourteen years old—and they have to sign a waiver saying that if they die, the friendly people who designed and built the Warrior Dash cannot be held responsible. I read and signed the waiver anyway.

Revelation 6 indicates that those who live during earth's last days will face a kind of test of their endurance or perseverance too. It concludes with the question, "Who can stand?" (verse 17). Revelation 7 reveals who will be able to and why they are able to. Before we get into that, though, let's look at the place of chapter 7 in the book of Revelation.

The form of punctuation called the *parenthesis* looks like this: ( ). Well, not really, because when we use them, we place words in between them (like this).

Going Deeper

Taking the 144,000 of Revelation 7 as the actual, literal number of believers alive on earth at Jesus' return requires also that all of them be Jewish. Read James 1:1 and ask yourself who James is expecting to read his letter. Was he addressing only Jewish people—Jews that had become followers of Jesus?

_____

_____

_____

_____

_____

_____

_____

_____

_____

_____

_____

_____

_____

_____

Sometimes when we're writing, we come up with ideas or comments that are good but that might confuse the reader if kept in the sentence we're writing. By putting those ideas or comments in a parenthesis, we can be sure we won't lose them but keep them from confusing the reader too. Here's an example of a parenthesis: My current car (which I wish someone would steal) has engine trouble.

Pretty easy, right?

Another example (and this is the last one) would be to insert a parentheses in the sentence you are reading now. So if I were to outline the seven seals within a sentence (using parentheses)* it might look like this: Seal six asks who is able to stand during the final judgment (chapter 7 says, "The 144,000"), and the seventh seal reveals silence in heaven.

Revelation 7 is a parenthesis between seal six (Revelation 6:12–17) and seal seven (Revelation 8:1). The chapter is broken up into two parts, the first featuring a special group on earth and the second, a group in heaven. But before the Lord's end-time "warriors" are revealed, we are given a glimpse into some angelic preparations being made before Christ's return.

Angelic actions

"After this I saw four angels standing at _the four corners of the earth, holding back the four winds of the earth,_ that no wind might blow on earth or sea or against any tree" (Revelation 7:1; emphasis added).

The four corners indicate that this is an event of worldwide importance, and the four winds represent God's destructive powers, which are reserved for the day of judgment. The angels are holding them back because something special is supposed to happen before the winds are allowed to do their work.

Another angel—not one of those restraining the winds—pops up (verse 2). This angel comes from the direction of the rising sun (which, if you paid attention in science class, you know is the east). This heavenly messenger is carrying "the seal of the living God," and he calls out "with a loud voice to the four angels who had been given power to harm earth and sea, saying, 'Do not harm the earth or the sea or the trees, until we have sealed the servants of our God on their foreheads' " (verses 2, 3).

Now, I'm all for taking care of the environment—people waste resources all the time. However, the angel in this passage isn't speaking of nature conservation. In the first place, when John wrote about the "rising sun," he wasn't referring to Japan (you get that joke if you know your geography), but rather to the direction east. Eden was in the east (see Genesis 2:8), and the glory of God comes from the east (Ezekiel 43:2).

The words _sea_ and _earth_ serve as indications of the relative density of the population of an area—the sea being heavily populated, and bare earth representing desert land that supports only a relatively few people (see Daniel 7:2, 17; Revelation

---

* OK, so _this_ is the last one—as far as examples go, anyway. You can thank me for helping you write better.

17:15). (The writers of Scripture also used the word *trees* to designate people; see, for example, Psalm 1:3; Isaiah 7:2; 10:19.)

I've heard of people covering their plants when they know a cold wind is coming. They cover their plants to keep them from freezing. They cover them so there'll be a harvest. This is a great idea if you love to garden.

Like those tender plants, God's people have to be "covered" before the winds are let loose so they'll be protected. The seal has to do with ownership—like writing your name on a plastic cup at a party so no one will drink—or backwash—your soda. Your name is your seal of ownership. In Scripture, God uses the seal to designate those who serve Him (Ezekiel 9:1–11).

Some people believe there will be a special sealing of the generation of Christians who are alive on earth when Jesus comes. Others believe the seal is the Holy Spirit, whom people receive in a special way when they give their hearts to Jesus (Ephesians 4:30). Having a seal on your forehead doesn't mean that you have an awesome barcode there that the cashier at your favorite store scans. The seal simply refers to an indication of who owns your mind, your life.

We'll discuss this more when we consider the mark of the beast. For now, just remember that the Holy Spirit does something significant in the people of God in the last days—something that protects them. In Revelation 7, the focus is on the end-time function of the Spirit. This chapter tells us the number of those who have this special seal.

The 144,000

"And *I heard* the number of the sealed, 144,000, sealed from every tribe of the sons of Israel" (verse 4; emphasis added).

This passage has sparked a great deal of stress in Bible students. They wonder whether it specifies the actual number of Christians who will be alive and faithful when Jesus comes or whether it's symbolic. I've witnessed some passionate arguments about this, so I realize some readers may strongly disagree with what I'm about to write.

Well, here we go.

Notice that John "hears" the number 144,000. I've already pointed out that what John hears often differs from what he sees. Early in Revelation, John heard a trumpet but saw a person (Revelation 1:10–13), and later, he hears talk about a lion, but he sees a lamb (Revelation 5:5, 6). In chapter 7, after John hears the description of the 144,000, he turns and sees a "multitude that no one could number" (Revelation 7:9). So right away we have a hint that the number 144,000 may not be literal.

Ancient Israel organized into military units by family name (Numbers 1:1–20). There is evidence that the military units were made up of one thousand warriors (Exodus 18:21; Numbers 31:4–6; 1 Samuel 22:7). How does this one thousand

Going Deeper

How can washing clothing in blood turn that clothing white (as in Revelation 7:14)?

_____

_____

_____

_____

_____

_____

_____

_____

_____

_____

_____

_____

_____

_____

_____

_____

_____

_____

_____

_____

_____

_____

_____

_____

Going Deeper

Careful students will no-
tice that two Israelite
tribes (Dan and Ephraim)
are missing from John's
list. Read the following
texts and see if you can
discover why—Genesis
49:17; Judges 18:27-31; 2
Chronicles 30:1, 10; Hosea
4:17.

_____

_____

_____

_____

_____

_____

_____

_____

_____

_____

_____

_____

_____

_____

_____

relate to 144,000? Hold on, and I'll explain.

The Bible says that the New Jerusalem—the city of God that will be flawless, beautiful, and free from litter, crime, homelessness, and rush hour—will be built on the foundation of the twelve apostles (Ephesians 2:20). John also writes that the 144,000 come from the twelve tribes of Israel (Revelation 7:4).

Now for some math.

What sum do you arrive at when you multiply twelve times twelve?

One hundred forty-four.

So, multiplying the Old Testament allusion to military units (1,000) by the number of Israelite tribes (12) and the number of apostles (12), we arrive at 144,000. The idea is that this number represents all of those who make it through the time of trouble. They are Christ's perfect fighting force—His warriors who have pushed through to the finish line, having overcome obstacles far worse than muddy shoes.

Some suggest the initial verses describing this group (verses 4–8) picture them while they are on earth and that when we move to the conclusion of the chapter, we see them victorious in heaven. John writes, "After this _I looked, and behold, a great multitude that no one could number, from every nation, from all tribes and peoples and languages,_ standing before the throne and before the Lamb, clothed in white robes, with palm branches in their hands, and crying out with a loud voice, 'Salvation belongs to our God who sits on the throne, and to the Lamb!' " (verses 9, 10; emphasis added).

This verse expands the idea from Israel's tribes to people from every nation under heaven. They have been given white robes as a reward and now bask in the light of God's glory and grace.

When one of the elders asks John if he can identify the great multitude of verse 9, John asks him for the answer, and the elder says, "These are the ones coming out of the great tribulation. They have washed their robes and made them white in the blood of the Lamb" (verse 14). This is a reference to Daniel 12:1, which warns about a "time of distress" (NIV; NASB), the likes of which have never before been seen. Those who are still standing when it's over—those who have remained faithful regardless of the obstacles placed in their path—are warriors for Jesus.

Revelation 7 ends with a description of the new life with God that the saved enjoy. Having crossed the finish line of history, they enjoy the prize: life with God (verse 15)—a life in which they have everything they need (verse 16), a life in which they never again are hurt (verse 17). God's warriors will never fight again. Instead, they'll have a peaceful eternity full of love and joy.

SUMMARY AND CONCLUSION AND WHAT THIS TELLS US ABOUT JESUS

Revelation 7 functions as a parenthesis between the sixth and seventh seals. It answers the question asked in the last part of chapter 6: Who can stand the temptations and troubles earth's people face? The answer chapter 7 gives to that question is that those who are able to stand in the final days of human history are those who continue to hold on to Jesus no matter how difficult that becomes. The angels at Jesus' command hold back the four winds of destruction so God's people can be sealed with the Holy Spirit.

The number of God's people, 144,000, symbolically represents the church as military units—not because God's people are violent, but because they've made a life-or-death commitment to Jesus and have been fortified by the Spirit of God. As a reward for their choices, they are given white robes and an eternal home with God, where they'll never experience pain again.

Many people have worried about who will be alive when Jesus comes and whether they have to do something special to be among them. They look at their problems and panic, because they know they can barely make it through a day of school or work—much less the "end times." They become afraid of the Second Coming.

Amid all their speculation, they've lost sight of one little detail. Verse 14 states that those who are in heaven aren't there because they are especially strong or possess superpowers, but because "they have washed their robes and made them white in the blood of the Lamb." This means they have given their hearts to Jesus and trust in His goodness and protection. *Jesus* is the One who makes us warriors and gives us the strength we need. *Jesus* is our hope and our victory.

May we give our hearts and minds to Jesus, so we will be sealed by the Spirit and rest upon the power He gives so we can be victorious warriors for Him.

Going Deeper

Read Exodus 12. How could this narrative have influenced John's portrayal of blood as a way to make someone clean? How does it relate to the concept of a seal?

Chapter 17

Nature Goes Nuts

Revelation 8:1–8

We don't respect or appreciate cymbals nearly enough. Mastering them may require relatively little time or effort compared to other instruments, but they have the power to change the mood of a performance completely though struck just once.

I had come home during the holiday break, and one of my childhood friends and I were sitting in the balcony of the church we had both attended while growing up. The worship service was to feature the band from the church's elementary school—of which both of us were alumni—and our expectations were rather low.

As the musicians tentatively worked their way through "Away in a Manger," the percussionist became nervous. Perhaps he lost his place in the piece, or he thought the 250 people in the church were staring at him. Whatever the case, he panicked, and the Christmas carol usually intended to be a soft, reflective piece was awakened to new life when the cymbals sounded.

The student recovered quickly and immediately silenced them, but, unfortunately, his mistake opened the way for the rest of the band to add their own miscounts, missed cues, and miss-timed toots. Through the rest of the service, my friend and I and much of the rest of the audience winced at notes that soared past their intended resting places and at others that died trying to reach them.

Surprisingly, the misplayed notes and mishandled timing that wreaked havoc with my senses didn't bother the moms, dads, and grandparents in the audience. Apparently, people's relationship to the musicians determines their response to the performance.

The next vision given to John involved trumpets. Shiny, brassy, and loud, these instruments are played by angels who have far more skill than those middle-schoolers did. But their sounding produces widely differing responses—even proving to be lethal to many who hear them. The adverse effect doesn't indicate insufficient practice. It's the musicians' relationship to the Composer/Conductor that most affects their response to the performance.

Background

"Then I saw *the seven angels who stand before God,* and *seven trumpets* were given to them. And *another angel* came and stood at the altar with *a golden censer, and he was given much incense to offer with the prayers of all the saints on the golden altar before the throne,* and the smoke of the incense, with the prayers of the saints, rose before God from the hand of the angel. Then the angel took the censer and filled it with fire from the altar and threw it on the earth, and there were peals of thunder, rumblings, flashes of lightning, and an earthquake" (Revelation 8:2–5; emphasis added).

These angels are part of an elite group that serves in God's presence and helps execute the sentences that follow judicial findings (like "Guilty!"). The group may include such luminaries as Gabriel (see Luke 1:19). As to their instrument of choice, one might ask: Why trumpets? Why not guitars, or drums, or even an epically long xylophone? Xylophones are way scarier-looking than trumpets. But trumpets are louder, and they have a rich history within the pages of Scripture.

One of the festivals in ancient Israel was the Feast of Trumpets, which was held ten days before the great Day of Atonement (Leviticus 16; 23:27). The Day of Atonement was an annual day of judgment, and the Feast of Trumpets reminded Israel that it was coming. The trumpets, known as *shofars,* blared aloud for ten days to call Israel to worship and spiritual preparation.

Trumpets also played a role in Israel's military life. They helped rock the walls of Jericho (Joshua 6:4–21) and played a role in Gideon's victory over the Midianites (Judges 7:15–23). At the close of earth's history, you'll hear the sound of trumpets regardless of which station you've set your Pandora to play (Joel 2:1, 2).

(For those who happen to be technologically illiterate, Pandora is a customizable Internet radio station. It isn't to be confused with Pandora's Box, which contains unpredictable, diabolical substances. However, sometimes the Internet Pandora *does* play weird music regardless of what station you set it to. I myself have been burned many times while listening to my favorite music, only to have Céline Dion start her "controlled screaming," as my father-in-law would say.)

Sometimes, the trumpets even sound to call unbelieving nations to punish those who had been God's people but who have abandoned their faith despite God's pleading with them as a desperate parent pleads with a disobedient child (Jeremiah 4:5, 19, 21; 6:1, 17). Finally, and most important for our purposes in this chapter, trumpets announce the final punishment of those who have rejected God and persecuted His people (Isaiah 18:3–7; 27:12, 13; Zephaniah 1:14–18).

No cosmic concert would be complete without a few pyrotechnics, which is a fancy word for controlled explosions. (Yes, you can go to school to learn how to make them, and yes, you're welcome.) Another angel appears with a pile of smoking incense to mingle with the prayers of the saints. When that's done, the angel fills the incense holder with coals from the altar and chucks them at the earth, causing booms, bangs, and blasts unlike anything you can buy at a fireworks stand. Only heaven has that kind of firepower, and it's not for sale. (Don't try to make this stuff at home.)

Let's deal with the furniture first.

The altar of incense

While some of us may have incense burners at home, my guess is that the home versions aren't as big or as fiery as an altar. Certainly, an altar of incense would be an interesting conversation piece to be able to display to guests as you led them on a tour of your house: "This is our living room; over there is the dining room; and right in the middle of the backyard, next to the barbecue, is our altar of incense."

That would be nice, but unfortunately, only one altar of incense still exists, and it's in heaven.

In the Jerusalem temple, the altar of incense stood in front of the veil that separated the Holy Place from the Most Holy Place (Exodus 40:26). The smoke that arose from the burning incense symbolized the prayers of God's people ascending to heaven (Psalm 141:2; Luke 1:8–20). On the Day of Atonement, the high priest would carry a censer full of coals of incense into the Most Holy Place, and the puffs of sweet-scented smoke would cover something called "the mercy seat" (see Leviticus 16:11–13).

The mercy seat was the lid of the ark of the covenant—a special golden box that housed the Ten Commandments (Exodus 20; 25). Those commandments represented God's perfect will—something we humans repeatedly fail to fulfill. The clouds of incense brought by the high priest covered the stone tablets inscribed with God's law—representing God's forgiving grace, which covers the sins we confess.

Many people believe the "altar angel" to be Jesus Christ. In the Hebrew Scriptures, God is often pictured as an angel (Genesis 48:15, 16; Exodus 3:2; 14:19; 23:20–24). So, Jesus could be called an angel here—not as a reference to His nature (He is divine and not a created being), but simply as a title. The altar angel's work of mixing incense with the prayers of the saints points to Jesus' ministry in heaven (Hebrews 9:11, 12). The scary moment depicted in this passage occurs when Jesus wraps up His work as our High Priest and starts to implement the verdicts of the judgment.

Running out of time

Buzzers, alarm clocks, and whistles all produce annoying sounds meant to awaken people to the realization that time has run out. Throughout history, God has used prophecy to wake people up to the fact that, unless changes are made, things will take a turn for the worse. Unfortunately, people have always treated prophets as if they wore snooze buttons. Prophets were told to run away (Amos 7:12), were thrown in big pots (Jeremiah 38:6), were locked in lions' dens (Daniel 6:16), and even were crucified (Mark 15:24). But though people may silence a prophet, they eventually have to deal with the consequences of their sin. God's people have felt the effects of His judgment repeatedly throughout their history—whenever they've abandoned His truth.

From the perspective of the wicked, trumpets provide a countdown to the end of time. Revelation 6:10 refers to the wicked who persecute the saints as "those who dwell on the earth." That verse pictures God's people as praying for justice. As the trumpets begin to blow in chapter 8, and horrifying events take place on earth, the final verse lets us know that these disasters fall on "those who dwell on the earth" (verse 13). The beginning of chapter 8 has Jesus responding to the prayers of His loved ones. The events connected with the blowing of the trumpets are a response to the people of God who are crying out for God to bring to justice those who have persecuted them.

By now you should be seeing a cyclical pattern to the visions. At the beginning of this book we talked about prophetic "eye exams" in which the biblical author repeatedly shows us the same events through different lenses. The seven churches reveal history from the perspective of Jesus, and the seals reveal history from the perspective of Jesus' people; and now we will view history from a much darker perspective—the viewpoint of those who have rejected Jesus.

Hastily Drawn Figure 17.1

History From the Perspective of...

The seven trumpets function as a kind of countdown from the Cross to the Second Coming. Each blast shatters the peace of the wicked. And as in the case of the seals, so in the trumpets there's a parenthesis between the sixth and the seventh items in the series. Note also that both the seals and the trumpets are "arranged in groups of four and three."[1] We'll look at all the trumpets first and then deal with Revelation 10, the parenthesis.

One of the most confusing aspects of Revelation is its disjointed chronology—meaning that things can overlap and make it hard to locate what part of history is being spoken about. The trumpets span salvation history, and they continually refer to "thirds"—not wholes or completes. The trumpets do *not* picture final judgments—they picture *partial* judgments that are meant to get people's attention so they will repent. Later, the plagues, which do their thing at about the same time as the seventh trumpet, will bring the final judgments upon evil.

OK now, let's begin what I call The Concert of Consequences.

The first trumpet: The fall of Jerusalem in A.D. 70.

"The first angel blew his trumpet, and there followed hail and fire, mixed with blood, and these were thrown upon the earth. And a third of the earth was burned up, and a third of the trees were burned up, and all green grass was burned up" (Revelation 8: 7).

Hail *and* fire?

How weird and horrifying.

The first mention of this combination of elements is in the story of a stubborn pharaoh who refused to let God's people go (Exodus 9:23–25). Another allusion to this kind of epic burning comes in Deuteronomy 29, in which God tells His people that if they don't listen, the "whole land burned out . . . where no plant can sprout" (verse 23).

John the Baptist used this imagery in which trees and grass represent people. He warned that "every tree . . . that does not bear good fruit is cut down and thrown into the fire" (Matthew 3:10). The "trees" were the religious people whose actions reveal they have very little of God's love in their hearts.

Jesus called Himself a "green tree" (KJV), and said that, in contrast, the Jewish leaders were "dry" trees (Luke 23:31). The first trumpet seems to target people who claim to be children of God but have actually rejected Him.

Most scholars see this trumpet as referring to the fall of Jerusalem at the hands of the Romans in A.D. 70. As a nation, the people who for centuries had belonged to God rejected His Son, and consequently, God withdrew His protection. The text says a third were destroyed—symbolically meaning that the destruction would be only partial rather than complete. Of course, it's better to experience a portion of God's wrath than all of it. But it's much better not to experience any of it at all.

The Bible says, "For it is time for judgment to begin at the household of God; and if it begins with us, what will be the outcome for those who do not obey the gospel of God?" (1 Peter 4:17). Few things are as irritating as parents who can't see how monstrous their kid is. While everyone else in creation experiences their offspring as a diabolical plague, those blind people see only a sweet little angel who might be a bit mischievous at times. Their delusion makes them frustrating to work with—one has to summon a vast amount of patience and strength to suppress the natural slap reflex that being around them arouses. Yet often these same parents are quick to point out the faults of other children.

God isn't that kind of parent. He sees His kids clearly—and He doesn't hesitate to discipline them. The first trumpet is judgment against God's unfaithful people, who, as a nation, rejected Jesus, and consequently, in A.D. 70, fell to a mighty army of the Roman Empire.

The second trumpet: The fall of the Roman Empire

"The second angel blew his trumpet, and something like a great mountain, burning with fire, was thrown into the sea, and a third of the sea became blood. A third of the living creatures in the sea died, and a third of the ships were destroyed" (Revelation 8:8, 9).

Ever tasted water from a drinking fountain that made you wonder if the fountain was hooked up to the same water source as the toilets? They sometimes look as dirty and stained as the toilets. And the H_2O that spews forth when you turn the handle produces an explosion of rancid flavor on your tongue that stays with you for hours.

The second trumpet pictures a massive mineral—a flaming mountain—being tossed into the earth's water supply, killing a third of the creatures in the sea (again, not total destruction), and destroying a third of the ships.

Mountains represent nations that are the object of God's wrath (Isaiah 41:15; 42:15; Zechariah 4:7). In the Bible, ancient Babylon is pictured as being destroyed by the sea. Babylon is the religious-political power that captured God's people in the time of Daniel and tried to force the Hebrews to worship false gods. (You guessed it—see *Prophecies of Daniel Made Simple*.) The Bible tells us that the sea will wash over Babylon (Jeremiah 51:42). John uses Jeremiah's imagery to describe the fall of spiritual Babylon (false religion; see Revelation 18:21). As for the ships, they symbolize a nation's wealth and power (Isaiah 43:14). The text lets us know that when you play Battleship with Jesus, your boats will always be sunk.

So, what is this mountain that is thrown into the sea, and whose ships are destroyed?

The followers of Jesus called the Roman Empire *Babylon*. The Romans persecuted the early Christians severely and also played a role in crucifying Jesus. The first trumpet shows that God's judgment begins at home, with the people who claim to be His. But it moves on, to others who also have rejected the message of God's love.

History tells us that what was once the powerful Roman Empire broke up as barbarian tribes ran wild over it with clubs, swords, axes, and fire. Some scholars believe the first trumpet extends to the fall of the Roman Empire, while others consider the second trumpet as covering the second and third centuries.

OK, let's take a break. The trumpets are long, and we can listen to only so much of their music at a given time. When you're ready to continue the concert, you may move forward.

ENDNOTE

1. Stefanovic, 287.

Notes

Chapter 18
Rise of the Locorpions
Revelation 8:9–9:12

This chapter picks up where the previous one ended in our study of Revelation's trumpets. Its subject is what those who have rejected Jesus are doing and experiencing during the time between John's vision and the Second Coming.

The third trumpet: The fall of the church

"The third angel blew his trumpet, and a great star fell from heaven, blazing like a torch, and it fell on a third of the rivers and on the springs of water. The name of the star is Wormwood. A third of the waters became wormwood, and many people died from the water, because it had been made bitter" (Revelation 8:10, 11).

Like the previous trumpet, this one brings us a water problem—this one caused by a different mineral contaminant and affecting a different source of the H_2O. Most of us enjoy stars and associate them with lyrical masterpieces that lull us to sleep (such as "Twinkle, Twinkle . . .") or with romantic evenings with our sweeties (unless your parents have forbidden you to date, in which case refer to "Twinkle, Twinkle . . ." again). However, this singular star kills people—which always destroys the mood. And it bears the cute little name *Wormwood,* so you probably aren't going to write any lullabies or love songs about it.

The name comes from a plant used in the ancient world to prevent pregnancy. This bitter biological blight is often associated with death. Here in Revelation, it kills people by poisoning the rivers and springs from which they get their water. The flaming mountain of the second trumpet corrupted the sea. The third trumpet pictures a fallen star that corrupts the very sources of water and of life.

Isaiah tells us another name of the fallen star that poisoned the world: *Lucifer* (Isaiah 14:12). The imagery of making water bitter would have been familiar to John's readers; they would have remembered the story from the Exodus, during which God's people were wandering the wilderness and feeling a little thirsty. Well, OK, they were dying of thirst. Eventually, they find water, but it's so bitter that they can't—or don't want to—drink it (Exodus 15:22–27). The wilderness is deadly to those who have no water.

Scholars, following the line of history, say this trumpet warning of contaminated water points to the time when the Christian church was corrupted. The streams of truth that flowed from the source of life—Jesus—dried up as the medieval Christian church began to embrace teachings that are contrary to God's Word. This period is thought to cover either the fourth and fifth centuries, or, combined with the fourth trumpet, the sixth through the tenth centuries.

The fourth trumpet: The fall of truth

"The fourth angel blew his trumpet, and a third of the sun was struck, and a third of the moon, and a third of the stars, so that a third of their light might be darkened, and a third of the day might be kept from shining, and likewise a third of the night" (Revelation 8:12).

Darkness can be deadly.

Especially when I'm walking down the stairs in my house, headed for a midnight snack.

In addition to an assortment of dolls, tea cups with corresponding saucers, and the occasional box that camps out at the foot of the stairs, I have to contend with a treacherous black cat named Shinobi that runs between my feet and trips me. After thudding down the stairs—utilizing all my highly developed reflexes and strength to stay upright—I arrive in the kitchen.

Naturally, my stairway escapade has awakened my wife, who rudely asks if I'm OK.

"Of course I'm OK," I snap, irritated. "Why shouldn't I be? I just skipped a few stairs because I'm really hungry."

When lights dim, the potential for random cat encounters—and falls, and crashes, and injuries—escalates exponentially. The sounding of the fourth trumpet causes a cosmic drop in power that darkens the sun, moon, and stars—all the bodies that light the world.

In Scripture, the sun represents God (Psalm 84:11, 12), spiritual leaders (Genesis 37:9; Psalm 72:5; Micah 3:5, 6), God's faithful people (Judges 5:31), and Christ (Matthew 17:2). Looking at Jesus is like looking at the sun (Revelation 1:16). So, when this trumpet pictures the light as being dimmed, it's pointing to a time when the light of God would be eclipsed.

During the Middle Ages (538 and on), the Christian church eclipsed Christ by making the pope, the human priesthood, and man-made tradition the focus of religion. The Protestant Reformation restored the focus to faith in Jesus, but scholars of religion fought among themselves, damaging people's faith. And the rise of the Enlightenment increased people's trust in human reasoning and downplayed faith in anything else (cf. Micah 3:6). The result was a loss of spiritual truth.

Scholars see trumpet number four as reflecting the same period as the church of Thyatira.

Notes

Woe!

"Then I looked, and I heard an eagle crying with a loud voice as it flew directly overhead, 'Woe, woe, woe to those who dwell on the earth, at the blasts of the other trumpets that the three angels are about to blow!' " (Revelation 8:13).

English 101: *Woe* isn't the word you use to tell a horse to stop. And it isn't the word you use to get your idiot friend to stop telling another lame joke—as in "Whoa, man, you've said enough stupid for one evening." *Woe* is the feeling of great grief or misery, or the thing that causes great grief or misery. The eagle that cries "Woe! Woe! Woe!" isn't telling "those who dwell on the earth" (a reference to the wicked) to cease and desist doing evil. It's declaring that the payback the wicked are experiencing is about to get a shot of Red Bull—or Red Vulture, if you will.

In Scripture, vultures herald disaster and death that come as a result of judgment (Deuteronomy 28:49; Ezekiel 32:4; Hosea 8:1). Jesus includes them in the bleak word picture He paints of the wicked slain by the Second Coming (Matthew 24:28; Luke 17:37). And in Revelation 19, John speaks of birds dining on the bodies of the dead.

To summarize: the first two trumpets dealt with God's judgment on those who crucified Jesus. The third and fourth trumpets pointed out the darkness that fell upon the medieval church. The fifth, sixth, and seventh trumpets (which we'll go into next) describe the final, desperate flailings of evil.

If the score is tied when time runs out in a hockey game, the game goes into what is called "sudden death." That means that the first team to score a goal wins the game. At that point the game is over. Finished.

As time runs out for humanity and the final trumpets sound, the world enters into "sudden death" between Team God and Team Evil.

Game on.

The fifth trumpet: Rise of the locorpions

"And the fifth angel blew his trumpet, and I saw a star fallen from heaven to earth, and he was given the key to the shaft of the bottomless pit. He opened the shaft of the bottomless pit" (Revelation 9:1, 2).

"Close the door!" my frantic parents yelled as I stood in the doorway contemplating whether to take my shoes off outside the house or to leave them on as I wandered into the kitchen for a soda. My contemplations lasted only a moment— but the damage had been done. Not only did precious cool air escape into the muggy Minnesota atmosphere ("We're not paying to cool off the entire neighborhood!"), but a sinister presence slipped inside to torment those who dwelt within the house.

Mosquitos.

It has been said that the mosquito is the Minnesota state bird. Naturally, this is hyperbole—intentional exaggeration, as the state bird is the loon. However, weighing in at sixty-five pounds or so, the Minnesota mosquito is a formidable foe as it gulps human blood much the same way I gulp soda after playing in the hot sun. Flyswatters are useless. They have to be exchanged for slingshots, throwing stars, and baseball bats—preferably aluminum. Similarly, the blowing of the fifth trumpet is connected with the opening of something that results in a major insect problem.

The text begins with a fallen star—not the kind you catch and put in your pocket so you can make a wish on it someday. This fallen star represents Satan (Isaiah 14:12; Revelation 8:10).

The Greek verb translated "fallen" is in a tense called the "perfect." This cool grammatical form means much more than do the mere past, present, and future tenses. It means something that was completed in the past but is so powerful that its effects are felt into the future. John wasn't writing about a literal meteorite crashing into the earth and leaving a crater that no one cares about today. He was talking about a powerful being that crashed here and has been hurting human prospects ever since.

And this being is given permission to open something that my parents—and most human beings in their right minds—want to stay closed.

The bottomless pit.

The fifth trumpet is extremely detailed, and there are a number of ways to interpret what happens next, so I'll give you a quick version of what is generally agreed upon and then a few different ways people choose to make sense of the images.

When the pit is opened, smoke explodes from it (Revelation 9:2)—as it does from pizza rolls that have been put in the oven and forgotten there because you're playing games (which has *never* happened to me). In Scripture, smoke is associated with attacks from God's enemies (Isaiah 14:31). The smoke from the pit is so thick that it crowds out the fresh air and hides just about everything else. The point is that whatever comes out of the pit functions as a weapon to deceive.

Cue the bugs.

A torrent of locusts swarms out of the smoke (Revelation 9:3). These charming creatures call to mind the eighth plague on Egypt (Exodus 10:4, 12–14) as well as warnings about what will happen to God's people if they refuse to turn away from evil (Deuteronomy 28:38). Scripture also calls the hostile nations that God uses as instruments of judgment "locusts" (Judges 6:5, 6; 7:12).

Scientists perform all kinds of miracles these days, such as genetically enhancing watermelons so they don't have seeds in them. Similarly, these locusts have received an upgrade—they have "power like the power of scorpions" (Revelation 9:3). Scorpions are known for the stingers that top their long, curved tails. They like to hide in sleeping bags, pillowcases, and shoes and wait for people to offend them so they have an excuse to make their life miserable.

Fortunately, God says He won't allow these flying plagues to harm His people, who are likened to green grass and trees, and who are identified as having the seal of the Holy Spirit (verse 4). However, those who have rejected God and His Spirit will have an eschatological (last days) escapade with an entomological (bugs) enemy.

Revelation says the "locorpions" (I made up that word. Awesome, right?) will be allowed to torture the wicked for five months but not to kill them. It also indicates that the stings, while not lethal, will be so painful that people will long for death (verses 5, 6).

The text says this period of torture will last "five months," which, if a month has thirty days (and the months in prophecies did), works out to 150 days—or 150 literal years when we apply the day/year principle. We'll come back to this in a moment, but before we do, let's take a look at the more detailed account of the locorpions Scripture gives us here. The locorpions

- Looked like war horses that had human faces and wore golden crowns (verse 7).
- Had hair like a woman and teeth like a lion (verse 8).
- Wore iron breastplates and had wings that when beating sounded like chariots rolling into battle (verse 9).
- Had tails with stingers like those of scorpions (verse 10).
- Had as their king the angel who had the key to the smoky pit, whose Hebrew name is *Abbadon* ("destroyed") and whose Greek name is *Apollyon* ("destroyer"; see verse 11).

Hastily Drawn Figure 18.1

Beware the Locorpions
Revelation 9:7–11

People mostly agree that the locorpion king is Satan, because he is called a destroyer in John's Gospel (John 10:10) and because all throughout Scripture, destruction is portrayed as Satan's favorite activity.

Near the beginning of the Middle Ages, one of the Roman emperors moved the capital of the empire from Rome to Constantinople (named after Emperor Constantine). There, Eastern Christians were under constant attack by Turkish Muslims. The warriors of the Ottoman Empire (founded by a guy named Othman) fought their first major battle at Bapheum on July 27, 1299. The Islamic warriors were known as exceptional horsemen; they had long hair (like a woman—though I wouldn't say that to their faces), curved scimitars (like a scorpion's tail), iron armor (breastplates), and turbans (like golden crowns). The five-month/150-year period takes us to July 27, 1449, when the new Byzantine emperor (who was to rule from the eastern part of the Roman Empire) had to ask Turkish permission before he took the throne.

When you have to ask permission to sit on a throne, someone else is doing the ruling. You just get to sit in a fancy chair.

It should also be noted that many people who accept this interpretation see the prophet Muhammad (Islam's founder) as the "fallen star" of verse 1.

Hastily Drawn Figure 18.2

Persecution of Ottoman Turks Timeline

150 years (Rev. 9:15)

Attack of the Locorpions

| Battle of Bapheum
A.D. July 27, 1299 | Eastern Christian Emperor
Needs Permission to Rule
A.D. July 27, 1449 |

The fifth trumpet involves judgment on those who profess to follow God but deny Him in their heart and in their actions. Some say this trumpet pictures judgment falling on the eastern Christian church of the Middle Ages. Others say that it's corrupt Christianity in general. The main point is God's protection of His children. If we give ourselves entirely to Jesus, we have nothing to fear. In the ears of God's family, the trumpets play a symphony of justice; while to those who have rejected His love, they sound out the dirge of destruction.

As for the sixth trumpet, it continues to sound the notes played by the fifth trumpet—only with more intensity. We'll see that in the next chapter.

Chapter 19
The Return of the King
Revelation 9:13-15; 11:15-19

Now, on to the last two trumpets.

The sixth trumpet: The locorpions close in for the kill

"Then the sixth angel blew his trumpet, and I heard a voice from the four horns of the golden altar before God, saying to the sixth angel who had the trumpet, 'Release the four angels who are bound at the great river Euphrates.' So the four angels, who had been prepared for the hour, the day, the month, and the year, were released to kill a third of mankind" (Revelation 9:13–15).

In the movie *The Avengers,* Dr. Bruce Banner is brought onboard to fight alongside heroes such as Iron Man and Thor in the hopes of stopping an alien invasion of our planet. At first he is a mild-mannered scientist who's using his intellect in the battle. However, as the heroes face what has become overwhelming odds, Dr. Banner is called upon to release his . . . uh . . . full potential.

You see, Bruce has an anger problem. Due to an unfortunate incident with radioactivity, when something sets Bruce off, he morphs into a massively muscular green being known as the Hulk, and then he smashes things. All kinds of things. Even very big things.

What ensues when Bruce enters his rage mode is quite unfortunate for the aliens. The Hulk crashes, smashes, and bashes everything in sight. The alien leader has portrayed himself as a god, but when he's right in the middle of touting his diabolical evil and his invincible superiority, the Hulk picks him up like a rag doll and slams him into a concrete wall over and over again. When he's finished with him, he snorts, "Puny god," and walks away.

The sixth trumpet ushers in the wrath of God against evil. God has been angry ever since the first deception plunged humanity into darkness. Not an out-of-context, arbitrary kind of anger—like when someone says you've spent enough time destroying your brain on the Xbox—but a broken-hearted, righteous anger that comes from watching sin destroy everything you've created. Up to this point, though,

He has released only a portion of His wrath. But Revelation 6:10 tells us that the voices of those slain for the sake of the gospel ignite the fullness of God's holy wrath, and He begins to act. And in Revelation 9:13, we hear a voice from the altar where Jesus hears the prayers and cries of the saints. The voice from the altar is telling the four angels—the same angels who in chapter 7 hold back the four winds—to release the full onslaught of judgment.

God is in righteous-rage mode.

Everything is intensified—on both sides of the battlefront.

The horses that before had lions' teeth now have lions' heads. The iron breastplates now glow molten red. The stinging tails are now lethal. And now fire and sulfur accompany the smoke (Revelation 9:17–19).

God's foes number two hundred million. (See verses 15, 16. However, the number isn't literal; it represents an uncountable multitude; see Psalm 68:17.) In any case, their army is every bit as intimidating as the army of the alien invaders in *Avengers.* Now, the one who has set himself up as god of this world is about to meet the real Power behind creation. The fire and sulfur remind us of the judgment poured out on Sodom and Gomorrah (Genesis 19:24, 28; Luke 17:29) and the final destruction of the devil (Revelation 14:10, 11).

At this point we encounter several symbols:

- The timeframe of the "hour, the day, the month, and the year" (Revelation 9:15)
- The three plagues of fire, smoke, and sulfur coming out of the horses' mouths (verse 17) and the "power" in their "tails" (verse 19)
- The rest of the people, who worship "demons, and the idols of gold and of silver and of brass" (verses 20, NASB)

The fifth trumpet pictured the horsemen of the Turks wreaking havoc upon Eastern Christianity. In the message proclaimed by this trumpet, number six, God continues to use these forces to inflict judgment on those who have turned away from Him and on their enemies. The four angels stand for the four chief sultans of the Ottoman Empire. Their armies grew until they were countless (the symbolic "two hundred million"). The fire and sulfur have a literal fulfillment in the gunpowder (you know, the stinky stuff that makes fireworks explode) that the Ottomans introduced into warfare and with which they killed thousands.

As for the prophetic time period of an hour, a day, a month, and a year (Revelation 9:15), those who interpret the prophecy quite literally say the time involved amounts to 391 years and 15 days.

I know, I know—you're wondering how they got that number. Let's do some prophetic arithmetic:

Going Deeper

What big ideas regarding prayer can we learn from the trumpets? (Hint: they don't start blowing until God's people cry out for justice.)

Going Deeper

Do you think God is violent? One issue people wrestle with in Revelation is the concept of God's wrath. Perhaps one way to think about it is that God's wrath is a righteous, controlled response to evil. And while the idea that God becomes angry might be uncomfortable, what would you think of a God who didn't ever become angry—not even when people hurt each other?

_____

_____

_____

_____

_____

_____

_____

_____

_____

_____

_____

_____

_____

_____

- One prophetic day equals one literal year
- One prophetic month (thirty prophetic days) equals thirty literal years
- One prophetic year (360 prophetic days) equals 360 literal years
- $1 + 30 + 360 = 391$

Easy, right? But the fifteen days is a little more complicated.

- An hour is 1/24th of a day.
- Since a prophetic day equals one literal year of 360 literal days, then 1/24th of 360 literal days equals 15 literal days.
- So the period in this prophecy amounts to 391 years and 15 days.

I hate division, but there you have it.

When we add the 391 years and 15 days to July 27, 1449, we arrive at August 11, 1840.

What's the significance of this time period?

The first date is the end of the 150 years spoken of in the fifth trumpet—the day when it became obvious that the Byzantine emperor (the ruler of the last bit of the Roman Empire) was subservient to the Ottoman Turks. And the second date is the day on which it became obvious that the Ottoman Empire had lost its power. The Ottoman Turks had been involved in a long fight with Egypt, and on April 11, 1840, they threw themselves on the mercy of Europe to save them. In response, the European nations produced an ultimatum (Make peace or else . . .) and sent it to Alexandria via ship for the military leader of Egypt to read. On August 11, 1840, a fog that had kept ships away lifted enough for them to enter the harbor, among them, the ship with the ultimatum, which eventually made Egypt back off.

When you're in a fight and you have to yell for help, you're admitting that you are weak. After the Ottoman ruler asked Europe for help, his "empire" went into decline, and the surrounding bully nations nicknamed what was left of it "The Sick Man of the East."

The sixth trumpet, then, covers major events from the fifteenth century to the mid-nineteenth century—and the next spiritually significant event is Jesus' return to this earth.

So, like the sixth seal, the sixth trumpet pictures an intensification of God's judgment. The sixth church, Philadelphia, was a missionary church. From the perspective of the wicked, deception flourishes as the zeal of the missionaries increases.

The seventh trumpet: The note of triumph and the song of the saints

"Then the seventh angel blew his trumpet, and there were loud voices in heaven, saying, 'The kingdom of the world has become the kingdom of our Lord and of his

Christ, and he shall reign forever and ever' " (Revelation 11:15).

A parenthesis separates the sixth and the seventh seals, and similarly, a two-chapter parenthesis stands between the sixth and seventh trumpets. We will explore this parenthesis in the next two chapters of this book. At this point we can take comfort in the heavenly music that rings out with the final trumpet. Jesus has come, and the world is free from pain. The song that resounds when the trumpet plays its victorious note is sung by the human beings whom God has saved. In this song they thank God for His protection and power. The evil nations were enraged, but their wrath couldn't match or overpower God's wrath (verse 18). The kingdom of this world is now the kingdom of Jesus (verse 15).

Whew.

Finally!

If the seventh trumpet mirrors the seventh seal, which is silence in heaven, then perhaps the seventh trumpet has to do with the silencing of conflict and persecution. The world is at peace.

If the seventh trumpet mirrors the seventh church (Laodicea), perhaps it has to do with Jesus being so close (as when He stood at the door and knocked; Revelation 3:20). From the perspective of the wicked, this trumpet means that God has finally spewed those who are lukewarm out of His mouth.

The seventh trumpet concludes the song with an important statement: "Then God's temple in heaven was opened, and the ark of his covenant was seen within his temple. There were flashes of lightning, rumblings, peals of thunder, an earthquake, and heavy hail" (Revelation 11:19). This is God opening up the inner parts of His dwelling to reveal His eternal law—the Ten Commandments, which was kept in the ark of the covenant. We'll return to this verse during our exploration of the parenthesis. For now, think of it as stating that God's rule is eternal.

Amen.

SUMMARY AND CONCLUSION AND WHAT THIS TELLS US ABOUT JESUS

In this chapter and the two that preceded it, we've seen that the time of the seven trumpets mirrors the historical periods covered by the seven churches and the seven seals. The trumpets contribute to our understanding of salvation history by covering that period from the perspective of God's fallen people and their enemies. The calamities we read about in this portion of Scripture occur because God has allowed them to happen to those who forsake Him and persecute His people.

Fortunately, Jesus has always been in control of events on this earth—and He will continue to be in control all the way to the end. Despite the persecutions and trials that the evil powers bring on the righteous, Jesus emerged

Uriah Smith, who was one of the premier nineteenth-century Adventist commentators on biblical prophecy, suggests that Muhammad, the prophet of Islam, is the star portrayed in the fifth trumpet as falling from heaven. What are the implications of this interpretation as opposed to the usual interpretation that the star represents Satan?

Going Deeper

The high priest was to enter the Most Holy Place, where the ark of the covenant was kept, on only one day of the year. Read Leviticus 16 and find there what day that was.

_____

_____

_____

_____

_____

_____

_____

_____

_____

_____

_____

_____

_____

_____

_____

_____

_____

victorious, and so will His people. Many people are terrified of the trumpets and of the plagues described in Revelation 16. They dwell on the judgments the wicked will suffer and lose sight of the hope that Jesus intends those who love Him to have.

If you want to strengthen your faith and hope, try this: Get a highlighter in a color that you haven't used in your Bible (green, for instance, since God likens His people to green grass and trees) and highlight verses that speak of God's protection (such as Revelation 9:4). Each time you read Revelation and see the green highlights, they will remind you not to lose hope, but to instead take comfort in Jesus' love and protection. While the music of the trumpets is horrifying to those outside of God's family, it brings visions of heaven to those within because they know Jesus is coming soon.

Revelation reveals the mercy of Jesus. Mercy doesn't mean giving someone what they deserve. If that were mercy, Jesus would long ago have annihilated humanity. Instead, mercy is love shown toward the undeserving. Because Jesus is merciful, He works through circumstances to wake people up so they can be ready for His return. Revelation shows Him repeatedly trying to break through to even the most stubborn people—because He loves them.

Two parentheses (found in Revelation 10 and 11) separate the seventh trumpet from the preceding six. They elaborate on what is happening at the end of history as the final trumpets sound. We'll look at these parentheses next.

Chapter 20
Prophetic Food Poisoning
Revelation 10

Going Deeper

What sweet experiences have you had as you've shared Jesus with others? What bitter experiences have you had while talking about Him?

Revelation 10 is the first of two parentheses inserted between the sixth and seventh trumpets. As we've seen, there's a parenthesis between the sixth and seventh seals too. That one, found in Revelation 7, answers the question "Who can stand?" (Revelation 6:17). The parentheses of Revelation 10 and 11 answer a question about what God's people are supposed to be doing when judgment is crashing down around them and they're about to be sealed and Jesus is about to come.

The answer is: They're supposed to be preaching the gospel.

A strong angel with a little scroll

"Then I saw another mighty angel coming down from heaven, wrapped in a cloud, with a rainbow over his head, and his face was like the sun, and his legs like pillars of fire. He had a little scroll open in his hand" (Revelation 10:1, 2).

Some clothes let people know what you are all about. For example, cowboy hats tell folks you are into country music and the culture of the Southwest.

The description of the "strong" angel in Revelation 10 immediately identifies Him as Christ. The rainbow is a symbol of God's agreement—His covenant—with His people (see Genesis 9:12, 13), and the sunshine face, fiery feet, and thunderous voice all mirror the description of Jesus in the first chapter of Revelation (see Revelation 1:7, 15, 16). And just as Revelation 5 pictures Jesus being given the seven-sealed scroll, so the supernatural being pictured here also holds a small scroll.

Daniel 12 tells of a book that the prophet is to keep closed until "the time of the end" (Daniel 12:4, 9). The difference between the time of the end and the end of time is best illustrated with turkeys in the month of November—when Americans celebrate Thanksgiving. For most Americans, turkey is the main dish of the celebratory dinner. That means November 1 marks the "time of the end" for turkeys, and the day before Thanksgiving is the "end of time" for those that aren't already in your local grocery store.

Many people believe that the little scroll mentioned in Revelation 10 is the little

Notes

scroll that long before, Daniel was told to seal. In fact, speaking of its contents, the angel even says there will be "no more delay" (verse 6). Finally, the time has arrived when the visions given long ago will be understood.

So, when exactly did the "time of the end" begin?

The time of the end

You can find the answers by shelling out some of your hard-earned money for a shiny new copy of *Prophecies of Daniel Made Simple*. In that book I explain in detail the prophetic timelines revealed in Daniel 8 and 9. Among them are the seventy weeks (490 years), the forty-two months (1,260 years) and the twenty-three hundred days (2,300 years). Since I've explained these timelines in detail in that book, I'll give you just a quick explanation here.

A study of the prophecies found in Daniel 8 and 9 reveals that the biblical "time of the end" begins with the endpoint of the 1,260-day/year prophecy. The first event spoken of in 1,260 day/year prophecy took place in A.D. 538. From that date, the prophecy stretches more than a millennium toward our time, ending in 1798. That time period covers the rise of the medieval Christian church and its metamorphosis into a power that tries to usurp Christ's ministry in heaven.

As for the 2,300 day/year prophecy, it began in 457 B.C. and ended in 1844. This period starts with the seventy-week prophecy of Daniel, which includes the first coming of Jesus—specifically, the beginning of His public ministry in A.D. 27 and then His death and resurrection in A.D. 31. (The seventy-week prophecy covers the first 490 years of the 2,300 day/year prophecy.) The deceptions carried out by the medieval Christian church take place during the last third or so of the 2,300 days/years. This prophesied period ends in 1844 with the beginning of the "time of the end." So, what the Millerites thought was the Great Disappointment was actually the beginning of Jesus' final ministry in the heavenly sanctuary, which involves a work of judgment in heaven that parallels the Day of Atonement in Leviticus 16.

Got it?

No? Then reread the paragraph.

Still don't get it? Then it's time to get *Prophecies of Daniel Made Simple*. (Wow! How many advertisements can I fit into one book?)

In this time between the last two trumpets, as God's people are being sealed just before Jesus comes, they are to receive a special message. The fact that the heavenly being holding the scroll stands on earth and sea (Revelation 10:2, 3) indicates that this message will go to all the world before Jesus returns.

In short, Scripture indicated that people would begin to understand the prophecies of Daniel and Revelation in the years leading up to 1844. Interestingly, that year was preceded by two huge spiritual revivals—the Great Awakening, and the Second Great Awakening. These revivals drew people—eventually including William Miller and many others like him—to study Daniel and Revelation. Their study convinced them that Jesus was coming in their day. They told this good news to everyone they could. Estimates are that in the United States alone, as many as one million people began to look for His return around that time.

But the time of the end is not the end of time.

We'll come back to Will Miller in a little bit. First, the angel begins to speak to John again.

Sealing the seven thunders

And he "called out with a loud voice, like a lion roaring. When he called out, the seven thunders sounded. And when the seven thunders had sounded, I was about to write, but I heard a voice from heaven saying, 'Seal up what the seven thunders have said, and do not write it down' " (Revelation 10:3, 4).

Like clothing, our voices tell a lot about us. When your significant other calls you on the phone and whispers, "Hello," you instantly recognize that laryngitis has struck again. Likewise, as a child, when my mother used to call out my full name at the top of her lungs, I could be sure that whatever she planned on doing to me wasn't going to be pleasant.

The voice of the angel is likened to a lion's roar and to seven thunders. The lion is a common metaphor for Jesus, and both Psalm 29 and John 12:28, 29 liken God's voice to thunder. Jewish tradition says that when God spoke from Mount Sinai, His voice "was heard as seven thunders." Since the number seven means perfection and/or completion, it is easy to deduce that God is the One who's talking.

As for the content, it appears to be restricted or sealed, just as Daniel's book was to be sealed (Daniel 12:4). The next parts of Revelation, though, are meant for everyone.

John wrote, "And the angel whom I saw standing on the sea and on the land raised his right hand to heaven and swore by him who lives forever and ever, who created heaven and what is in it, the earth and what is in it, and the sea and what is in it, *that there would be no more delay, but that in the days of the trumpet call to be sounded by the seventh angel, the mystery of God would be fulfilled,* just as he announced to his servants the prophets" (Revelation 10:5–7).

The picture of an angel raising his hand and letting John know that "there would be no more delay" before the mystery is revealed is not only a welcome relief to the prophet, but it is also the answer to a question asked a long time ago in the middle of the story of the great conflict between good and evil. At that time Daniel had asked how what he's seen will end, and he's told, in effect, to forget about it. He's to seal up the book until "the time of the end" (Daniel 12:8, 9).

Many believe the sealed book is the book of Daniel. The angel tells Daniel to "seal the book" for now, but in the same verse he assures him that "knowledge shall increase" in the last days. In other words, the prophecies of Daniel would be understood then—in the last days.

Going Deeper

Why do you think God waited until the mid-1700s before He allowed people to understand the content of the book of Daniel?

Correspondingly, Revelation 12 announces that the mysteries of the gospel that have been sealed so long are about to be understood. When the judgment and the Second Coming are about to take place, God will give His people a full disclosure, a full understanding, of the message of Jesus.

Surprisingly, the grand revealing of the final act in the great conflict between good and evil begins with a snack.

Prophetic food poisoning

"So I went to the angel and told him to give me the little scroll. And he said to me, 'Take and eat it; it will make your stomach bitter, but in your mouth it will be sweet as honey' " (Revelation 10:9).

I've eaten paper before.

Don't laugh—you probably did too when you started getting hunger pains during math class.

While I can't recommend paper for its flavor (it doesn't have any), I can say that it never caused me any problems. However, the angel said that the little book that we understand to be the prophecies of Daniel would start out great ("be as sweet as honey"), but have an adverse effect ("make your stomach bitter").

It's like eating pizza at midnight. The pizza tastes good when you're eating it, but a few hours later . . . Well, I'll spare you the smelly details.

This strange scene is not the first time Scripture pictures scroll sampling. The prophet Ezekiel was told to "feed your belly with this scroll that I give you and fill your stomach with it" (Ezekiel 3:3). He said, "Then I ate it, and it was in my mouth as sweet as honey" (verse 4). But just as John got a case of paper indigestion after he ate the scroll, so shortly after Ezekiel ate the scroll he was given, he said he went to do what the Lord asked him to do "in bitterness in the heat of my spirit" (verse 14).

So, is Heaven passing around some bad paper here?

In both cases, the scroll represents a message from God. The message is about restoration, but also about judgment. So, it's full of joy and hope, but also of bad things for those who won't accept it. In fact, they may become hostile to the message— and fire a few messages of their own toward the messenger. That can be bitter for the messenger—and so can seeing people reject God and choose self-destruction.

Nevertheless, John was told, " 'You must again prophesy about many peoples and nations and languages and kings' " (Revelation 10:11). Just as we have to continue eating even when we've had a bad culinary experience, so prophets—and all the other followers of Jesus—can't let bad experiences prevent them from speaking the words of life. So, Revelation 10 ends with the point that John has still more to share.

Historically, Adventist Christians have found tremendous meaning in this passage. When, based on Bible prophecy, William Miller preached that Jesus would return in 1844, many people believed. And their expectation of His coming and their preparation to meet Him were sweet.

However, as you may have noticed, we aren't in heaven. Jesus didn't come in 1844. That was the Millerites' Great Disappointment. They were dazed by shock and drained by bouts of weeping—and all the while newspapers and mean people mocked them. The bitterness was nearly unbearable.

However, hope dawned in the wake of disappointment. Some of those who still believed God had been leading in their expectation of Jesus' coming turned again to Scripture to see what had gone wrong. They discovered there a powerful message from God. So, despite their bitter experience, they felt compelled to prophesy again.

The next chapter marks the midpoint of Revelation. It expands on the mention in chapter 10 of the preaching of the gospel, informing the believers who were so bitterly disappointed of what must still be told to the world before Jesus returns and reminding them of the power of God's Word. Chapter 11 also contains the cipher for chapters 12 through 22.

SUMMARY AND CONCLUSION
AND WHAT THIS TELLS US ABOUT JESUS

Chapter 10 is a parenthesis between the sixth and seventh trumpets. It occurs at the same time as does the silent period between the sixth and seventh seals. As God's people are being—or are about to be—sealed, they are given a powerful message to share with the world. The little scroll presented to John is believed to represent the unparalleled understanding of prophecy—particularly of the prophecies in the latter half of the book of Daniel—in the "time of the end" spoken of in Daniel 12.

The imagery of a scroll tasting sweet but then turning bitter reflects the experience of believers—particularly, of those believers who preached that Jesus was coming in 1844 to a sometimes receptive but mostly hostile world. Speaking the truth brings joy when people receive it and pain when people reject it. It's a bittersweet experience. However painful it may be, though, we cannot let the bitter moments give us "faith poisoning" or "prophecy poisoning" and cause us to abandon our calling. Now, more than ever before, the world needs to hear about Jesus and His return to earth.

Chapter 10 tells us that while Jesus loves us, He doesn't always give us jobs that are easy to do. In fact, He often places us in difficult—even bitter—places so we have to learn to depend on Him. In return, Jesus promises us that we will see Him work in powerful ways.

You and I are called to speak of Jesus' return no matter how bitter our experiences may be. Like Noah, we are to speak the truth as long as we can—not in a confrontational way or because preaching makes us feel morally superior, but out of a genuine love for those around us.

Going Deeper

In what way or ways is the gospel a mystery?

_____

_____

_____

_____

_____

_____

_____

_____

_____

_____

_____

_____

_____

_____

_____

_____

_____

_____

_____

_____

_____

_____

_____

Notes

Carrying God's message to the world is hard work.

It's God's work, and it's our work too.

May He give us His love and power as we present His truths to the world.

Chapter 21
Strong Words
Revelation 11

Going Deeper

The Bible uses the word *temple* to refer to the sacred building in Jerusalem, but it also calls our bodies *temples* (1 Corinthians 6:19). If Jesus is the standard by which we are to be measured, what does that say about how we should live? What hope does Jesus offer those who don't measure up?

_____

No kids like being sent to their rooms.

Least of all me when I was eight years old.

I don't remember what I'd done on the day when I was sentenced to imprisonment in my room, but I do remember sitting there stewing while my parents chatted with our company. Filled with wrath, I scrawled out the strongest message I could think of to express my displeasure: "I Hate You."

I folded the paper carefully into a neat square, and venturing out to the kitchen table, where the adults sat merrily enjoying one another's company, I handed my note to my dad. He unfolded it, read the message with a raised eyebrow, and then looked at me—and I met his gaze smugly. Then he whispered, "Maybe I should share what you wrote with our friends."

Oops.

I hadn't thought about how my words would affect other people, and suddenly I heard how strong and horrible those words were. I shook my head, took my note back, and returned to my room.

Well played, Dad.

Words are powerful. They can move people to action, inspire a range of emotions, and unlock mysteries.

Revelation 11 gives us a glimpse of how powerful God's Word has been throughout history, and it also gives us a preview of the strong words God's people will preach in the end times.

"Then I was given a measuring rod like a staff, and I was told, 'Rise and measure the temple of God and the altar and those who worship there, but do not measure the court outside the temple; leave that out, for it is given over to the nations, and they will trample the holy city for forty-two months' " (Revelation 11:1, 2).

Chapter 10 indicated the time when the prophecies would be unlocked so that God's people could understand them. Those whose faith survived the bitter experience they had because of Miller's misunderstanding of the prophecy returned to their study of the sanctuary. They were told to "measure"—in other words, to study— the sanctuary. They concluded that the 2,300 day/year prophecy laid out in Daniel 8 (by now, you know where to go for more information on that!) indicated that rather than returning to earth in 1844, Christ entered the Most Holy Place of the heavenly sanctuary to begin the ministry He was to perform there—cleansing His people from sin. In doing so, He ushered in the "time of the end" (Daniel 12:4).

As those early Adventists pushed their way deep into Scripture, truths from God's sanctuary began linking the prophetic pieces together, and they formed a theological construct that has been preached all over the world, resulting in a movement that now has more than fifteen million members. The rest of the book of Revelation contains the final message that these followers of Jesus are to preach.

Two witnesses

"And I will grant authority to my two witnesses, and they will prophesy for 1,260 days, clothed in sackcloth. These are the two olive trees and the two lampstands that stand before the Lord of the earth" (Revelation 11:3, 4).

My favorite holiday movie of all time is *Miracle on 34th Street*. It's about a crazy old man who gets in trouble because he thinks he's Santa Claus. In the course of the film, he's put on trial because of his claims, and his lawyer friend—who may be even crazier than he is—supports his claims.

Toward the end of the trial, the judge demands authoritative proof that the defendant is Santa Claus. This impossible demand is met when the U.S. Postal Service delivers thousands of letters addressed to Santa Claus to the courtroom where the trial is being held, burying the judge. When the judge has dug himself out, he reaches for his gavel, bangs it on the only part of his desk that's visible, and declares the old man to be Santa Claus. Joy and warm feelings ensue, and now you can ruin the end of the movie for your friends like I've ruined it for you.

For our purposes, though, the point of the story is the value of having an authoritative witness on your side. When the respected U. S. Postal Service recognized the defendant as being Santa Claus, the judge ruled in his favor.

The Bible says everything should be established by two to three witnesses (Deuteronomy 17:6; Matthew 18:16; 2 Corinthians 13:1). The two witnesses in Revelation 11 confirm the message they bear to be authoritative.

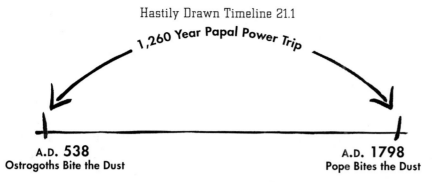

Hastily Drawn Timeline 21.1

1,260 Year Papal Power Trip

A.D. **538**
Ostrogoths Bite the Dust

A.D. **1798**
Pope Bites the Dust

Adventists learned the basic points of God's prophetic messages in the nineteenth century. Do you think they—we—are the only ones God wants to use in the end times? How can Adventists share the work with other Christians?

———————————

———————————

———————————

———————————

———————————

———————————

———————————

———————————

———————————

———————————

———————————

———————————

———————————

———————————

———————————

———————————

———————————

———————————

———————————

———————————

———————————

———————————

———————————

In Scripture, the wearing of sackcloth—the material of mourning—says that something deeply loved and valued has been lost (Genesis 37:34; Jeremiah 4:8; Daniel 9:3). The two witnesses of Revelation 11 are communicating in a time of loss—specifically, in the time of the loss of God's Word, which oppressive forces such as the medieval Christian church, and later, the leaders of the French Revolution, tried to suppress and control during the 1,260 years prophesied.

Now don't get confused, but Revelation 11 contains a prophetic time period within a larger prophetic time period—both of which are based on the number three and a half. By now, you're well acquainted with the three-and-a-half prophetic years/1,260 literal years. Within this time period, there's another one of three-and-a-half prophetic *days*/three-and-a-half literal *years*. We see in the longer time period God's Word bearing witness in the face of strong opposition. In the shorter one, we see the death and then the resurrection of God's two witnesses (Revelation 11:7–12).

The Bible says that during those three-and-a-half literal years, people would celebrate the death of the two witnesses. This actually occurred during the French Revolution, which occupied the decade that began in 1789. In 1793, the French legislature banned the Bible, and on November 11 of that year, a festival "in honor of Reason and Truth" and meant to elevate human beings above God was held in a large church. The celebrations were made up of offensive ceremonies and militant atheism—for instance, people chanted, "Crush the wretch," meaning Christ. Pretty awful, isn't it? Truly, God's Word "lay dead in the streets."[1]

However, the Bible continues: "But after the three and a half days a breath of life from God entered them, and they stood up on their feet, and great fear fell on those who saw them" (verse 11). Three-and-a-half years after the legislature suppressed Scripture, a decree passed by the same assembly reinstated it. And in 1798, at the end of the 1,260 day/year period, God's Word flourished again—especially as seen in the Second Great Awakening (see chapter 12 of this book). John writes, "Then they heard a loud voice from heaven saying to them, 'Come up here!' And they went up to heaven in a cloud, and their enemies watched them" (verse 12). Scripture was revived and made more prominent than it had ever been before. Since those days, it has been translated into nearly three thousand languages, and millions of copies have been distributed worldwide.

Finally, Scripture says, "And at that hour there was a great earthquake, and a tenth of the city fell. Seven thousand people were killed in the earthquake, and the rest were terrified and gave glory to the God of heaven" (verse 13).

Commentators differ regarding what this refers to. Some contend that it recalls 1 Kings 19:18, which says that despite the apostasy of most of Israel, seven thousand refused to bow to false gods. They say this number is symbolic of all the people who, during the French Revolution, chose to die rather than give up their faith. Others think this earthquake should be linked to the Great Lisbon Earthquake of 1755. And still others say it represents those who are still unrepentant as the time of the end approaches—the number seven referring to the completeness of human history as when the seventh trumpet is blown.[2]

The seventh trumpet

As we have seen, this trumpet triumphantly announces the end of human history—or at least, the end of the current segment of human history, with all its bloodshed and pain and death and sorrow. Jesus is victorious, and those who have lived and died for the gospel are vindicated. This trumpet shows the climactic end, filled with hope, to those who are about to make the final call to repentance before Jesus returns. The chapter we have just been through has given us a glimpse of the unstoppable power of the Word in order to inspire us to communicate the truth regardless of the persecution doing so may bring (Revelation 11:15–18).

"Then God's temple in heaven was opened, and the ark of his covenant was seen within his temple. There were flashes of lightning, rumblings, peals of thunder, an earthquake, and heavy hail" (verse 19).

Seventh-day Adventists find this final verse significant. It parallels the first verse of the chapter and confirms the validity of the sanctuary as a subject of study for God's people. This verse tells us that at that time, the Most Holy Place will be opened. We know this because that is where the "ark of God's covenant" stood. God directed His people to see if any truth lost during the 1,260 years of religious persecution had not been recovered yet. They concluded that the fourth commandment—the one that calls God's people to observe the seventh-day Sabbath—had been swallowed up by the keeping of Sunday, the first day of the week. The call to observe *all* the commandments of God without compromising the gospel became extremely important as Jesus began His final work in the heavenly sanctuary in 1844. As we move into the second half of Revelation, we will see every aspect of Jesus' message.

Cipher alert!

"The nations raged, but your wrath came, and the time for the dead to be judged,

Going Deeper

and for rewarding your servants, the prophets and saints, and those who fear your name, both small and great, and for destroying the destroyers of the earth" (verse 18).

Couldn't God convince everyone that His way is right? What reason do you think He has for allowing His people to be persecuted?

The second half of Revelation can be even more confusing than the first. Fortunately, John has embedded a cipher to help us see how his visions are organized. The final verses of the seventh trumpet contain four elements, each of which is the subject of several of the forthcoming chapters. Here's what the cipher says about how Revelation 12–20 is arranged.

- The nations rage (Revelation 12–14): The Dragon's War
- God's wrath comes (Revelation 15–18): The Wrath of God
- The dead are judged (Revelation 19; 20): The Final Exit of Evil
- The righteous are rewarded (Revelation 21; 22): The Reward of the Righteous

SUMMARY AND CONCLUSION AND WHAT THIS TELLS US ABOUT JESUS

As God's people recover from the Great Disappointment that they suffered when Jesus didn't return in 1844 as they had expected, they are told to explore the sanctuary. When they reexamine prophecy, particularly Daniel 8, they realize that Jesus began the final phase of His heavenly ministry in 1844. That's when the "time of the end" began.

Before John's vision moves on to the events of the last days, he receives a glimpse of the painful yet ultimately victorious preaching of the gospel that God's people would do during times of persecution. The fact that God's Word has triumphed in the past lets us know that no matter what resistance we face in the future, the truth will win.

After this encouraging view of the successful preaching of God's Word, the seventh trumpet sounds and current history is wrapped up at Jesus' return. At the very end, the innermost part of God's heavenly sanctuary opens and reveals that God's law, so long trampled upon, holds the place of highest honor in heaven.

After the disappointment caused by Miller's misunderstanding, the people who continued to study Scripture saw that the seventh-day Sabbath and all that comes with it must be preached in the last days. So, the Sabbath became part of the message this remnant of the Millerites were commissioned to bear to the world. The final verse of the song of the seventh trumpet gives us the cipher that unlocks the rest of Revelation and helps us understand what God's people are to preach as part of the prophetic gospel.

As we look around the world we live in today, we can see that God's Word still faces opposition. Many of us have friends and family who don't exactly appreciate our faith—much less our talking to them about it. When we hear that the church we attend is presenting meetings on Bible prophecy or handing out literature about Jesus, we find it easy to slump down in our pew and avoid making eye contact with those who could use our support. However, we are told that the gospel will prevail despite the persecution it raises. The next time you have an opportunity to talk about your relationship with Jesus or to help with a prophecy seminar, say Yes. There's no better way to experience the power of God's Word.

Revelation 11 shows that Jesus reveals Himself progressively to His people. While truth never changes, our understanding of it does. So as we follow Jesus, our understanding of biblical truths will both broaden and deepen. Jesus never leaves His people stale and crusty—He wants to give us increasingly clearer pictures of Himself and how He works.

ENDNOTES

1. Roy Allan Anderson, *Unfolding the Revelation* (Mountain View, Calif.: Pacific Press®, 1974), 109, 110.

2. For more amazing information on Revelation 11 and the French Revolution, see the sections on Revelation 11 in Mervyn Maxwell's *The Message of Revelation,* God Cares, vol. 2.

The Dragon's War
Revelation 12–14

Chapter 22
Cosmic Christmas Card
Revelation 12

Luke 2:15–20 pictures the Christmas-pageant players: Mary, Joseph, angels, shepherds, and Baby Jesus. Bright stars and singing contribute to the multisensory experience that glows brighter than any holiday light display. But this event that we commemorate by dressing kids up in bathrobes and towels and then forcing them to sing to us has far more significance than what is visible in our typical Christmas pageants. While the whole passage is full of descriptions that dazzle the senses—lying just below the surface is a prophetic undercurrent. The birth of Christ is saturated in prophecy.

Both Isaiah and Daniel pointed forward to the birth of a Messiah. The angel of the Lord prophesies to Mary that she will have a Baby who will "save his people from their sins" (Matthew 1:21–23, pointing to the fulfillment of Isaiah 7:14). And Luke's account reminds us of prophecy in Daniel 2 when it says that Jesus' kingdom will have no end (Luke 1:33). So when Scripture says that the "time came" for Mary to give birth, it is not only describing the end of the nine months of pregnancy but also the long-awaited fulfillment of the prophecies of Jesus' arrival as Messiah.

It is this reality that inspired me to design a Christmas card of my own.

Cosmic Christmas

My card idea would never make it to Hallmark's production line because it would offend just about everyone who saw it. The cover of the card would picture a woman in stirrups on a delivery-room table, ready to give birth. (The background reveals that this is happening in outer space.)

I've watched a birth, so I know that the sounds produced during the process communicate well how painful it is—so I'd make this an audio card. When you opened it, you'd hear screams as the woman begins to give birth.

But the best part of the card is the picture inside. It portrays a giant red dragon that's waiting right in front of the woman, mouth open, ready to devour the baby as soon as it's born.

What do you think?

Disturbing?

Gross?

Try biblical.

What I've just described is Christmas from heaven's point of view. The Bible says:

> And a great sign appeared in heaven: a woman clothed with the sun, with the moon under her feet, and on her head a crown of twelve stars. She was pregnant and was crying out in birth pains and the agony of giving birth. And another sign appeared in heaven: behold, a great red dragon, with seven heads and ten horns, and on his heads seven diadems. His tail swept down a third of the stars of heaven and cast them to the earth. And the dragon stood before the woman who was about to give birth, so that when she bore her child he might devour it (Revelation 12:1–4).

For us, Christmas is a time of warm fuzzies and stockings overflowing with worthless junk we'll forget about the next day when we've broken and/or eaten it. For heaven, Christmas was nothing less than the day on which the devil and his kingdom of darkness tried to assault the Baby Messiah. This is the theme of the Cosmic Christmas card. Philip Yancey says, "In heaven the Great Invasion had begun, a daring raid by the ruler of the forces of good into the universe's seat of evil."[1]

Christmas is a celebration of an invasion.

God often uses a pure woman to represent His people (Isaiah 54:5, 6; Hosea 2:19, 20; John 3:29). Conversely, when His people abandon Him, He likens them to an unfaithful wife (Ezekiel 16). The twelve stars in the woman's crown represent the twelve tribes of Israel, the people who hoped for the coming of the Messiah—and from whom the Messiah would come. As for the celestial symbols, the moon has no light of its own. Instead, the moon reflects the light of the sun. As followers of Jesus, we have no light ourselves; we reflect the light Jesus has given us.

The flaming red beast hardly needs interpreting. Who would be likened to a flying serpent bent on the destruction of human hope? It was, of course, the devil who was at work through the pagan powers to bring about the destruction of the Messiah. Ezekiel 29:2–4 likens Egypt to a dragon—the same power that tried to slaughter all the baby boys born to the Israelites when Moses was born. At the time of Jesus' birth, a narcissistic ruler named Herod executed the very strategy the pharaoh had tried so long before (Matthew 2:13). There is a dual application here as well. In this passage we see not only the birth of Christ, but also the birth of His church—and the devil's attempts to eliminate both.

Scholars say the seven heads likely refer to the great monarchies that down through history have persecuted God's people,* or the "seven" may be a symbol

---

* Egypt, Assyria, Babylon, Persia, Greece, pagan Rome, and papal Rome.

indicating fullness or completeness—that *all* God's people will be persecuted through *all* the time this world exists, right up until Jesus comes again. The crowns the dragon wears represent kingly authority and the devil's constant attempts to usurp God's throne. And the horns allude to Daniel 7 and the beast that had ten horns, which there symbolized the ten barbarian tribes that broke up the Roman Empire.

Fortunately, the Baby was born, and He survived the devil's attempt on His life.

The great controversy and the remnant

"She gave birth to a male child, one who is to rule all the nations with a rod of iron, but her child was caught up to God and to his throne, and the woman fled into the wilderness, where she has a place prepared by God, in which she is to be nourished for 1,260 days" (Revelation 12:5, 6).

This passage pictures Jesus' ascension and the persecution of God's people for 1,260 years. Much of what follows is a review of what we call the "great controversy"*—the battle between God and Satan. You can read more about it in my book *What We Believe for Teens*. I'll give the quick version here.

War breaks out in heaven, and eventually the devil is booted out of heaven to earth—along with his evil hench-angels (Revelation 12:7–9). The next verses declare that Jesus is the winner thanks to the plan of salvation—even though the devil pesters God's people "day and night." God's people overcome the demonic harassment through Jesus' sacrifice and their willingness to share the good news (verses 10, 11). The devil's time is short, so we have reason to rejoice—but also reason for concern, because he knows his time is short and so he is in rage mode and messing up everything he can (verse 12). The devil pursues God's people, and they are delivered into the "wilderness" for "a time, and times, and half a time"—those 1,260 days of oppression from 538–1798 again (verses 13, 14).

Next, the dragon vomits water.

Look, I'm well aware that dragons aren't supposed to vomit water; they're supposed to breathe fire—especially red dragons like Smaug.† But the Bible says, "The serpent poured water like a river out of his mouth after the woman, to sweep her away with a flood. But the earth came to the help of the woman, and the earth opened its mouth and swallowed the river that the dragon had poured from his mouth" (verses 15, 16). In Scripture, water can represent destructive forces moving against God's people (Psalm 69:14, 15; Isaiah 43:2). The idea is that the devil will sweep away God's people with a flood of deception. Fortunately, we've seen that God's Word always prevails.

---

* Ellen White wrote a book by that name. The five books in her Conflict of the Ages series trace that great controversy from its beginning even before the creation of this world to the end of evil and the restoration of the perfect world, the perfect universe that God originally made.

† Fire-drake, from the famous book *The Hobbit,* who torches the dwarves' mountain kingdom and steals all their treasure.

Going Deeper

In what ways have you experienced persecution? How can what you have read in Revelation 12 give you hope?

The last verse of this passage is important because it gives us a glimpse of God's people during the end times. They are a people who fluster the flying red reptile. Scripture refers to them as "the rest of her [the woman's] offspring" (Revelation 12:7), a.k.a. known as the "remnant" (Isaiah 28:5; Jeremiah 50:20). They are the faithful people—those who have not fallen to the deceptions of the devil, but instead have firmly held on to "the commandments of God . . . and the testimony of Jesus" (Revelation 12:17).

Some people seem to believe that God's remnant—His end-time people, His end-time church—must isolate themselves from other Christians. They believe themselves to be the only source of truth, and the pride they feel because they belong to the remnant* makes them arrogant, exclusive, intolerant, and no fun to hang out with. Their view looks like this:

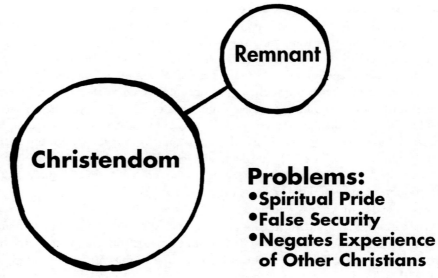

Remnant

Christendom

Problems:
- **Spiritual Pride**
- **False Security**
- **Negates Experience of Other Christians**

People who follow this model can become self-satisfied and believe they are saved by their church affiliation instead of by having a relationship with Jesus.

However, we know that all truth is God's truth. In fact, Jesus Himself is Truth, and He doesn't speak to only one special group of people. For crying out loud—He gave prophetic dreams to Babylon's heathen king! (See Daniel 2 and 4.) Here's a better way to view the remnant concept:

---

* Or because they think they belong to it.

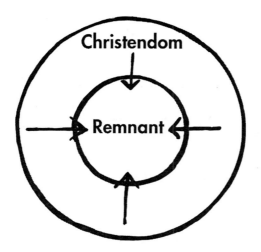

What are some of the deceptions that flood the lives of Christians today?

_____

_____

_____

_____

_____

_____

_____

_____

_____

_____

_____

_____

_____

_____

_____

_____

_____

_____

_____

_____

_____

_____

_____

_____

This model demonstrates that everyone everywhere is called to embrace the truths in God's Word. In my experience, however, only the Seventh-day Adventist Church is willing to step up and share Christ's message in these last days. (I should also note that this model does change in chapter 18. For now, just be aware that the eternal gospel is going everywhere, and that God is calling everyone to be a part of the remnant.)

As we've already noted, Revelation 12:17 says God's remnant people "keep the commandments of God and hold to the testimony of Jesus." In the end times, the commandments of God will be under attack. The early Adventists discovered this when they realized that the fourth commandment—the one about the seventh-day Sabbath—had been buried under human tradition that had accumulated for years, centuries, millennia. Forces allied against God and Christian believers will pressure people to abandon the Decalogue (a fancy term for the Ten Commandments) before Jesus comes.

Revelation 19:10 tells us that "the testimony of Jesus is the spirit of prophecy." (It is the Holy Spirit who gives prophetic insights to God's servants; 1 Corinthians 12:10.) This indicates that in the end time, the gift of prophecy will be a distinguishing feature of God's people. Certainly, the Adventist tradition was born amid intense interest in and study of prophecy. The gift manifested itself particularly in the life of a woman named Ellen White.

I've addressed this in more depth in *What We Believe for Teens* (yes, another commercial), so I'll be brief. Shortly after the Great Disappointment, a young woman with only a third-grade education experienced visions that encouraged God's people in their study of the Bible. Some people abuse her writings, but she *never* claimed to be perfect or that her writings were equivalent to Scripture. Her role, in her own words, was to serve as "a lesser light to lead men and women to the greater light."[2] She didn't supersede the Bible; she directs our attention back to it.

Going Deeper

Sometimes people speak of God's "remnant church" in a way that makes it an exclusive institution from which its members look down on other Christians. How can we encourage people to be faithful to God's commandments and to respect the gift of prophecy without feeling or acting condescending toward other Christians who don't accept what we say about these things?

_____

_____

_____

_____

_____

_____

_____

_____

_____

_____

_____

_____

_____

_____

Her ministry was instrumental in developing the largest Protestant educational system in the world, and it laid the foundation for groundbreaking medical ministries such as Loma Linda University in California and Celebration Hospital in Florida (which works in conjunction with the Disney company). Her writings—she wrote more than 100,000 pages on a variety of subjects—have inspired millions of people around the world. In earth's last days, God is communicating with people and guiding them not only through the books of Daniel and Revelation, but also through contemporary individuals to whom He has given His Spirit.

SUMMARY AND CONCLUSION AND WHAT THIS TELLS US ABOUT JESUS

Revelation 12 gives us a glimpse of the great war between God and evil. It opens with a description of heaven's invasion of planet Earth through the birth of the Messiah, and then it transitions to the conflict the church has with the red dragon—a.k.a. Satan—who attacks God's people with a flood of deception. Again we see the 1,260-year period during which God's Word was suppressed and His people oppressed.

We also catch a glimpse of God's people, who remain faithful despite the attacks of the devil. They hold on to God's commandments and are blessed by the gift of prophecy that is operating among them in the person of Ellen White. From heaven's standpoint, Christmas is a celebration of Heaven's invasion of this sin-sick world in order to save it—to save the people who live here.

The great controversy is a fight not only to vindicate God's character, but also to capture the allegiance of humanity. In this setting the "red dragon" is not only the devil, but also our hearts. The Bible says that the human heart is full of sin, and consequently, is a source of deception (Jeremiah 17:9). Whenever Jesus enters our lives or convicts us of sin, we tend to resist. We tell ourselves that we are fine and don't need to change—and when we believe ourselves, we, in effect, devour the loving influence of our Savior, destroying it.

Jesus wants to be born into our worlds—not just into planet Earth, but into our hearts and minds. The next time you sense God leading you to make a change or a commitment to Him, remember the picture of the red dragon. When you feel the urge to reject what God is doing in your heart, become a dragon slayer. Pray to Jesus, asking Him to give you the strength to endure.

ENDNOTES

1. Philip Yancey, _The Jesus I Never Knew_ (Grand Rapids, Mich.: Zondervan, 2000), 43.
2. Ellen G. White, _Review and Herald,_ January 20 1903.

Chapter 23
The Making of 666
Revelation 13a

The dreaded number 666 spawns countless theories and speculations, and it strikes fear in the hearts of many who see it. When Ron and Nancy Reagan moved into their Bel Air home in California in 1979, the house had the number 666. They changed it to 668.[1]

Psychologists have noticed the panicky sensation that this number induces in some people. Just as we have names for fears of such things as water (*hydrophobia*), confined spaces (*claustrophobia*), and trees (*dendrophobia*), so we also have a term for the fear of the awful triple six: *hexakosioihexekontahexaphobia*.*

I'll wait a little longer in case you're still in the midst of pronouncing the word.

So, where does this number come from? Why is it associated with evil, and why are people so paranoid about it?

You'll find the answer in Revelation 13. The number is the product of two spiritual business partners who are working with the dragon, Satan, against the kingdom of God. These three "beast buddies" have been working as a team down through history, one after the other, seeking to undermine God's authority and to substitute a false system of worship in place of our worship of Him. This false worship is characterized by a mark—a symbol—that reveals fallen humanity's choice to side with the enemy of Jesus. The issue the next two chapters discuss is that of worship.

We begin with a sea monster.

The sea monster

"The dragon stood on the shore of the sea. And I saw a beast coming out of the sea. It had ten horns and seven heads, with ten crowns on its horns, and on each head a blasphemous name. The beast I saw resembled a leopard, but had feet like those of a bear and a mouth like that of a lion. The dragon gave the beast his power and his throne and great authority. One of the heads of the beast seemed to have

---

* Google it.

had a fatal wound, but the fatal wound had been healed. The whole world was filled with wonder and followed the beast" (Revelation 13:1–3, NIV).

This thing looks like something Napoleon Dynamite would draw. Remember the liger bred for skills and magic? If you don't know what I'm talking about, you're probably over fifty years old. But that's OK; I'm glad you're reading this anyway. Seriously. Don't feel bad. You really haven't missed anything—except the best dumb movie of all time. In any case, this chapter begins with a beast that's hanging out with the dragon (Satan) and that looks something like this:

Hastily Drawn Image 23.1

Sea Monster

Ten Horns

Bandages healing deadly wound

Yay! My evil friend!

When I was a seminary student, one of my professors asked if we thought the beasts were literal (real) or symbolic (representing something else). Surprisingly, a few people chose literal. That's the correct answer! In the last days, a great sea monster will emerge out of one of the oceans and like Godzilla wreak havoc upon the globe. If you don't know who Godzilla is, you're probably under fifty years old. That's OK—glad you're here too.

Of course, I'm lying. The creatures in Revelation 13 most definitely are symbolic. You know this if you've read *Prophecies of Daniel Made Simple*. The book of Daniel tells us that the beasts and horns pictured there stand for kingdoms and powers, and the beast we're discussing bears a striking resemblance to the creatures in Daniel 7.

As for the sea, Revelation doesn't hint around. It directly tells us that waters are symbolic of people (Revelation 17:15). So, the emergence of this beast from the sea means that it comes from a place where there's a multitude of people.

As for its strange appearance, a little dissecting reveals its relationship to Daniel's beasts.

Describing a vision he's had, Daniel says, "There before me were the four winds of heaven churning up the great sea. *Four great beasts,* each different from the others, came up out of the sea" (Daniel 7:2, 3; emphasis added).

Right away we see a couple parallels with Revelation 13: waters and beasts. We're on the right path—let's keep analyzing this monster.

Here are the four beasts Daniel saw in his vision, as recorded in Daniel 7 (you'd already be acquainted with these if you had that book I keep mentioning):

- An eagle-winged lion (verse 4)
- A bear with a back problem having a snack (verse 5)
- A four-winged and four-headed leopard (verse 6)
- An iron-toothed terror with ten horns (verse 7)

Daniel is told that this menagerie of monsters represents kings or kingdoms that follow one another (verses 17, 23), and the ten horns represent ten kings/kingdoms that arise out of the fourth beast/kingdom—all of them functioning at the same time.

What's the connection to Revelation's sea monster? John said it was like a leopard, but it had feet like a bear's and a mouth like a lion's and ten horns. Revelation's sea monster is built from parts of Daniel's four beasts, which also came out of the sea.

But Daniel's vision has more that helps us understand the vision recorded in Revelation 13. Daniel wrote, "I considered the horns, and behold, there came up among them another horn, a little one, before which three of the first horns were plucked up by the roots. And behold, in this horn were eyes like the eyes of a man, and a mouth speaking great things" (Daniel 7:8). The next few verses (20–25) point out ten characteristics of this little horn.

1. It's a geopolitical power that arises *after* the ten horns.
2. It uproots three of the ten horns.
3. It has eyes like a human being.
4. It speaks boastfully.
5. It carries on a war against the "saints" (God's people).
6. It's a different kind of power from the other horns (kings/kingdoms).
7. It speaks against the Most High.
8. It oppresses the saints (God's people).
9. It tries to change times and laws.

10. It rules for a time, times, and half a time.

Again we run into this 1,260-year period. Whatever power the little horn represents rules from 538 to 1798.

Take a good look at this list. Sear it into your brain.

Got it?

Great.

Now back to the sea monster.

Back to the sea monster

"And they worshiped the dragon, for he had given his authority to the beast, and *they worshiped the beast,* saying, 'Who is like the beast, and who can fight against it?' And the beast was given a mouth uttering haughty and *blasphemous words,* and it was allowed to *exercise authority for forty-two months.* It opened its mouth to *utter blasphemies against God, blaspheming his name and his dwelling, that is, those who dwell in heaven.* Also it was allowed to *make war on the saints* and to conquer them. And authority was given it over every tribe and people and language and nation" (Revelation 13:4–7; emphasis added).

We can see that the sea monster is a religious power as well as a political power, because it accepts worship. The text also says it utters blasphemies against God. One year when I worked at summer camp, my friend and I videoed ourselves baptizing a turtle, and then we showed that video to the campers. Our camp director was less than pleased. He said our video was "blasphemous."

Now, I'll admit that baptizing the turtle and showing our video of that service to the campers were mistakes. In fact, I'll even admit that what we did was definitely sacrilegious (in that we were mocking religion). But blasphemy is far more serious than sacrilege.

The Gospel of Mark gives us a definition of blasphemy: "When Jesus saw their faith, he said to the paralytic, 'Son, your sins are forgiven.' Now some of the scribes were sitting there, questioning in their hearts, 'Why does this man speak like that? *He is blaspheming! Who can forgive sins but God alone?*'" (Mark 2:5–7; emphasis added). Blasphemy is claiming to be God when you aren't.

This sea monster has some ego issues. Not only does it try to usurp Jesus' place in heaven, but it also attacks God's people—for forty-two months. A brief comparison reveals that this diabolical creature is one and the same as the little horn in Daniel 7. It is a composite—a mixture—of all the beast powers hostile to God's people and has many of the characteristics of the little horn.

1. It's a political power that also receives worship.
2. It claims to have the power to forgive sins.
3. It rules for 1,260 years (a time, times, and half a time).

4. It blasphemes God, attempting to take His place.
5. It makes war against the "saints."

Only one historical entity fits this description.

In the first few centuries after Christ's resurrection, Christianity's status was uncertain, and Christians endured persecutions from both the Jews and the Romans. The early church was governed by a college of bishops (not a school), who ruled from various places, such as: Antioch, Jerusalem, Alexandria, Carthage, and, of course, Rome.

After a few years, Stephen, the bishop (leader) of Christians in Rome got a little grabby about power. An argument broke out regarding baptism, and Stephen, the bishop of Rome, repudiated the position that had been set forth by some of the other leading bishops, including Cyprian, bishop of the church at Carthage.

Cyprian reminded Stephen that there is no "I" in team. He wrote, "Thence, through the changes of times and successions, the ordering of the bishops and the plan of the Church flow onwards; so that the Church is *founded upon the bishops,* and every act of the Church is controlled by these same rulers."[2]

Bishops plural was the point. No single church leader was to have authority over the others.

Firmillian, bishop of Caesarea, joined Cyprian in about A.D. 256, saying,

> *They who are at Rome do not observe those things in all cases which are handed down from the beginning, and vainly pretend the authority of the apos-tles.* . . . Do not deceive yourself, *since he is really the schismatic who has made himself an apostate* from the communion of ecclesiastical unity. For while you think that all may be excommunicated by you, *you have excommuni-cated yourself alone from all.* . . . I, therefore, the prisoner of the Lord, be-seech you that ye walk worthy of the vocation wherewith ye are called.[3]

In other words, the bishop of Rome was breaking away from all the others and splitting the church by claiming superior authority. His power trip even inspired him to change some things that were "from the beginning." Remember, Daniel said the little horn would "think to change times and laws."

From outlaw to official

While Christianity was an outlaw for the first few centuries of its existence, it became the official religion of the Roman Empire in the fourth century, when the emperor Constantine became a convert. The church at Rome felt superior and be-gan making moves to establish its supreme authority—especially as barbarian tribes began to invade and destabilize the capital of the empire.

Then, to escape the bearded barbarians, the emperor moved the capital from

Rome to Istanbul (a city in Turkey—the country, not the bird), and changed the name of the new capital to Constantinople (after the emperor). The emperor's move from Rome left a power vacuum, which the church was glad to fill. One historian says, "The center of the Empire was now at Constantinople, which claimed to be the new Rome not only politically but also ecclesiastically. As a reaction, the ecclesiastical authorities in Rome claimed that the ecclesiastical primacy of Rome—which had developed *de facto* out of the political primacy of that city—was based *de jure* on the Lord's words to Peter, whose vicar the pope was."[4]

Basically, when the government moved out, the church took its place—kind of like a squatter, which is kind of a gross-sounding name for someone who lives in an abandoned house. Only these squatters began claiming Rome as their own. They based their claim on a misunderstanding of a Bible verse.

The verse is Matthew 16:18. Jesus says to Peter, " 'And I tell you, you are Peter, and on this rock I will build my church, and the gates of hell shall not prevail against it.' " The Roman Church believes Peter was the rock on which Jesus built His church. They say Peter was the first pope and conclude that therefore the Roman Church has supreme authority.

However, in the verse we're examining, Jesus used two different words that mean "rock." Peter's name, *petros* in Greek, means "pebble," and the word translated "rock" in the phrase "on this rock" is *petra,* which means a large mass of rock. In other words, Jesus was actually contrasting Peter, the pebble, with the solid rock on which He would build His church.

If these words of Jesus gave Peter some superior status, none of the apostles recognized it. As a matter of fact, several years later, Paul gets in Peter's face and calls him out for being a racist (Galatians 2:11, 12). Oh snap! And Peter would soon try to dissociate himself from Jesus—three times, no less (John 18:25–27). Pretty shaky foundation on which to build a church! Yet Jesus worked through His disciples despite their weakness. The Roman bishop isn't the foundation of the church; Jesus is (Ephesians 2:20).

As the barbarian tribes were defeated, the Roman Church/medieval Christian church rose to power. The following story shows just how crazy powerful the church became.

In 1076, Pope Gregory excommunicated King Henry IV because of some of his relationship choices with the ladies.* He also told Henry's subjects that if Henry didn't repent of his sins, they didn't have to obey him.

Sassy.

Even though Henry was the most powerful monarch (not the butterfly) in Europe, the pope had the ace in the card deck of authority. The rebellious ruler found himself in a bit of a pickle, so, having no other option, he traveled to the pope's

---

* To excommunicate someone is to remove that person from the church—and from heaven, because the church taught that there was no salvation outside of it.

winter castle in Canossa, Italy. But the pope refused to see him. So, King Henry IV stood barefoot outside in the cold for three days in penitence. Then the pope spoke with him and allowed him back into the church. Who was the more powerful?

Power corrupts

The church became so powerful that it began to accept praise that belongs only to God. In 1512, Christopher Marcellus said of Pope Julius II, "Thou art the Shepherd, thou art the Physician, thou art the Governor, thou art the Husbandman, finally, *thou art another God on earth.*"[5] The pope must have liked the compliment; at least, he never corrected Marcellus. Compliments like this became the standard fare. One of the characteristics of the beast was its speaking blasphemies. These "compliments" certainly fill the bill.

The medieval church was also a bully. Its violent outreach programs included the Crusades (kill the Muslims!), the Inquisition (kill the heretics!), and the Thirty Years' War (kill the Protestants!). These evangelistic endeavors resulted in millions of deaths.

And finally, this church sought to change times and laws by replacing observance of the seventh-day Sabbath of the fourth commandment with Sunday keeping. Writers in the early centuries had pointed out the widespread keeping of the seventh-day Sabbath as a day of worship:

- **Josephus** (A.D. 100): "It will be found that throughout the whole of that period not merely have our laws stood the test of our own use, but they have to an ever-increasing extent excited the emulation of the world at large. . . . There is not one city, Greek or barbarian, nor a single nation, *to which our custom of abstaining from work on the seventh-day has not spread.*"[6]
- **Socrates Scholasticus** (A.D. 380–450): "Although *almost all churches throughout the world celebrate the sacred mysteries on Sabbath of every week,* yet *the Christians of Alexandria and at Rome, on account of some ancient tradition, have ceased to do this.*"[7]
- **Sozomen** (A.D. 400–450): "*The people of Constantinople and almost everywhere, assemble together on the Sabbath,* as well as on the first day of the week, *which custom is never observed at Rome or at Alexandria.*"[8]

While everyone else enjoyed worshiping on the seventh day, the jokers in Rome and Alexandria apparently threw their own party on Sundays. Justin Martyr (A.D. 100–ca. 165) writes that Christians kept Sunday from the early times. But guess where he lived? That's right—Rome.

We started this chapter with 666, and we haven't yet figured out where it came from or what it means. But we're going to take a break here—time for you to learn a little more about the change from Sabbath to Sunday, and time for me to rest. (In the process, you'll actually get to sample a bit from *Prophecies of Daniel Made Simple!*)

And we'll get back to 666. I promise.

ENDNOTES

1. "The Reagans: First Family Easing Into Private Life," *Los Angeles Times,* November 19, 1988.
2. Cyprian, Epistle XXVII.
3. Firmillian, bishop of Caesarea to Cyprian, 5, 6, 24 (emphasis added).
4. Justo Gonzalez, *History of Christian Thought,* vol. II, 139.
5. Fifth Lateran Council (emphasis added).
6. Josephus, *Against Apion,* vol. 2, 39, 40 (emphasis added).
7. Socrates Scholasticus, *Ecclesiastical History,* ch. XXII (emphasis added).
8. Sozomen, *Ecclesiastical History,* ch. XIX (emphasis added).

Intermission and Commercial
Sabbath Versus Sunday

All God's acts, everything He does, is important. So when He makes a set of laws for the people He created, those laws are bound to be important. Changing them, then, is no small matter.

Sometimes you have to go backward in order to go forward. Because God's law is a primary theme in the book of Daniel, and because Revelation is so strongly influenced by Daniel, we need to start there.

As has been mentioned a shameful number of times, I have already written a book on Daniel. Now, I'm offering you—the consumer and Bible student—a free preview of its contents. This allows me to be lazy and take a break. Enjoy the study below. I'll meet you back in Revelation 13 when you've read the following.[1]

On A.D. March 7, 321, Emperor Constantine passed a law that stated, "On the venerable day of the sun [Sunday, in other words] let magistrates and people residing in cities rest, and let all workshops be closed."

A mandatory day off? How can you argue with that? Because Christianity and paganism were learning to coexist in the now Holy Roman Empire (thanks to Constantine, who made Christianity legal instead of lethal), Sunday was chosen because it had meaning for both Christians (since Jesus rose on Sunday) and pagans (who worshiped the sun). It was a political law meant to unite the citizens of the empire. But as time went on, it took on religious overtones.

In the same year that the Ostrogoths got the boot, A.D. 538, the Catholic Church held the Third Council of Orleans (in France, not Louisiana). At this meeting, a statement known as the Twenty-eighth Canon found its way into church law. It says that on "Sunday[,] . . . agricultural labor ought to be laid aside, in order that people may not be prevented from attending church."

While that statement may seem pretty unthreatening, it carries the same tone as your mother does when she says, "I'd like you to clean your room." That statement isn't a wish—it's a subtle command. If you don't believe me, try responding with,

"Yeah, that would be nice. Well, I have some video games to get to, so I'll see you later."

Sunday or Sabbath—who cares?

A mandatory day of worship might seem like a minor matter (like not brushing your teeth), but a closer look reveals that its results are far more serious (halitosis, gingivitis, and a lifetime without kissing).

By the middle of the second century, the practice of observing Sunday as a day of worship in honor of the Resurrection was widespread. About A.D. 160, Justin Martyr said, "Sunday is the day on which we hold our common assembly"[2] (a.k.a. church). A number of arguments were made for worshiping on Sunday instead of Sabbath, one of the stronger ones being that by Jesus' day the Sabbath had become a tad crusty with all kinds of dos and don'ts—such as how far you could walk, how much you could carry, and even how often you could go the bathroom. Christians wanted to distance themselves from that kind of legalism. In fact, they wanted to get rid of everything that connected them with the Jews because Rome and the Jews were at odds with each other—and it was obvious Rome was going to come out on top; it had already decimated Jerusalem and the Jewish temple.

However, while people in places such as Rome (Justin Martyr's hometown) and Alexandria (a city with a really cool library) began keeping Sunday holy, everyone else continued holding services on Sabbath. Christians in Egypt (pyramids), Turkey (not the bird), Palestine (hometown of lots of fighting), France (croissants), Italy (the Mario brothers), and more got their church time on day number seven instead of day number one. Conflict about the day of worship increased as Roman Catholicism's political and religious power grew and it tried its best to phase out Sabbath worship wherever it could. Not only did it exercise its influence, but it was sassy about it.

During the Protestant Reformation (in which Martin Luther and his peeps challenged the pope and his authority), a Catholic scholar named Johann Eck taunted Luther by saying, "Scripture teaches: 'Remember to hallow the Sabbath day; six days shall you labor and do all your work, but the seventh day is the Sabbath day of the Lord your God,' etc. Yet the church has changed the Sabbath into Sunday on its own authority, on which you [Luther] have no Scripture." What made this an incredible burn on Luther was that he prided himself on getting all his theology from the Bible and not from the church.

It seems everybody has trouble with consistency!

However, Scripture is consistent on the topic of the Sabbath, the day of worship; it always points to the seventh day. The Sabbath is the first thing Scripture says God made holy (Genesis 2:3). It is number four among the Ten Commandments (Exodus 20:11). Jesus kept it (Luke 4:16). It's more than a day; it's sacred time that God Himself established—so all those who tamper with it and try to reschedule it are, by their actions, saying they think they have the same authority that God has—they're equal to God. But only God can change God's laws.

It's a shame that some people think otherwise—people such as Petrus de Ancharano, who in 1400 said, "The pope can modify divine law, since his power is not of man, but of God, and he acts in the place of God upon earth, with the fullest power of binding and loosing his sheep."[3] And then there's Gaspar de Fosso, archbishop of Reggio, who, at the Council of Trent in 1562, stated, "The Sabbath, the most glorious day in the law, has been changed into the Lord's Day [Sunday]. . . . These and other similar matters have not ceased by virtue of Christ's teaching, but they have been changed by the authority of the church."[4]

Daniel said the little horn would "think to change the times and the law." The Sabbath is a *law* about *time*. Unfortunately, while God's Sabbath is the seventh day of the week, people think that now, God's day is Sunday. This little switcheroo causes a major problem. It shows that something or someone wants to take God's place in your life and in the lives of everyone else on the planet. And it wants to do so in such a way as to make people think they are worshiping God when in reality they are following something else entirely.

Our salvation is dependent upon Jesus Christ; anything that replaces Him puts our salvation in jeopardy. We must not choose to put more stock in human-made rules and systems than in those that God has given us.

The truth of Sabbath is multifaceted, but in this prophecy the issue at stake is the question of whose authority we follow: God's, or that of the little horn? Do we look to Scripture or to man-made tradition? Do we accept God's system of truth or that of human beings? The choice is ours—along with the consequences.

Now back to your regularly scheduled book chapter.

ENDNOTES

1. The rest of this intermission is taken from Seth Pierce, *Prophecies of Daniel for Teens* (Nampa, Idaho: Pacific Press®, 2011), 75, 76.
2. Justin Martyr, "Weekly Worship of the Christians," chap. 67 in *The First Apology of Justin,* vol. 1 of *The Ante-Nicene Fathers,* 186.
3. Petrus de Ancharano, quoted in Lucius Ferraris, "Papa," article 2 in *Prompta Bibliotheca,* vol. 6 (Venice: Gaspar Storti, 1772), 29.
4. Gaspar de Fosso, quoted in Mansi, *Sacrorum Conciliorum,* 33:529, 530.

Chapter 24
Now Back to Your Regularly Scheduled Chapter
Revelation 13b

The era of the sea monster power lasted from 538 to 1798, when the French general Berthier took the pope captive. The pope died in captivity, which seems a fitting image of his church's loss of power and influence and is the "deadly" wound prophesied in Revelation 13:3.

In the middle of the reign of the medieval Christian church, great religious leaders such as Martin Luther and John Calvin and thousands of laypeople from all levels of society made the painful decision to leave the "mother church." This movement, known as the Protestant Reformation,* took place because thousands of people recognized that the church God had meant to be beautiful had been transformed into something beastly.

Martin Luther said that unless the leaders of the Roman Church changed their tune, "they are guilty of all the souls that perish under this miserable captivity, and the papacy is truly the kingdom of Babylon, yes, the kingdom of the real Antichrist."[1] John Calvin also saw the problem. He wrote, "Daniel and Paul foretold that Antichrist would sit in the temple of God (Dan. 9:27; 2 Thess. 2:4); we regard the Roman Pontiff as the leader and standard-bearer of that wicked and abominable kingdom."[2]

These are strong comments, but we must realize that leaving one's church is extremely painful—like going through a divorce. Painful as it is, though, followers of Jesus often have to choose between man-made traditions and God's Word.

At this point a lot of people like to put on a smug face and say something like

* "Protestant" because the people in the movement were protesting the evils of the corrupt church.

Notes

"See? Organized religion is bad." But however intelligent these people think themselves to be, they always squirm when asked if they prefer *disorganized* religion. Just because something is evil now doesn't mean that it was evil to begin with. Think of how wonderful love is—and then think of all the horrible things people do in the name of love.

Incidentally, *Babylon* represents *false* religion. The name has come to mean "confusion"—which is what results when people reject organization.

So we have identified the sea beast as representing the medieval Christian church. In 1798, the church was injured and its power was broken for a while. But that wasn't the time of trouble that Scripture says Christians will experience in the last days. We'll get to that eventually, but first there's another beast to identify—one that arises from the earth in the 1700s to take up where the sea monster left off.

Earth creature

"Then I saw another beast *rising out of the earth. It had two horns like a lamb and it spoke like a dragon.* It exercises *all the authority of the first beast* in its presence, and *makes the earth and its inhabitants worship the first beast,* whose mortal wound was healed" (Revelation 13:11, 12; emphasis added).

Hastily Drawn Image 24.1

Earth Beast

If the sea represents masses of people, a densely populated area, then dry land must represent a sparsely populated area—like Dawson, Nebraska, population 146.

This strange creature that arises out of the earth has horns like those of a lamb (which is a symbol of Jesus; see John 1:29). But though it looks cute and harmless, it has breath like that of a dragon (a symbol of Satan). It aims to get everyone to worship the sea monster, even if it must force them to do it. What we have is a religious power that appears to be Christian but practices something else: Falstianity.

Only one power arose during the 1700s that professed to offer religious liberty and has worldwide power and influence: the United States.

The Bible says, "By the signs that it is allowed to work in the presence of the beast it deceives those who dwell on earth, *telling them to make an image for the beast that was wounded by the sword and yet lived*" (Revelation 13:14; emphasis added).

What means does this image of the beast use? What is the hallmark of all false religions?

Force. Coercion.

I think being an American is an awesome privilege. But I must admit that there have been occasions when America hasn't extended freedom to everyone. That was true even when this country was in its infancy. Jamestown, one of the first settlements, had laws enforcing worship:

> Those who failed to come to services twice daily would first lose their food for the day. A second offense brought a whipping, and a third six months in the galleys. To break the Sabbath "by any gaming, public or private" or to miss church on Sunday was, on the third offense, a capital crime. . . . In short order the first English settlement had become not an outpost of freedom or an inspired missionary base but a New World stage on which the Old World imposed its most suffocating and absolutist tactics.[3]

A person could be executed for not worshiping correctly. Not quite the "land of the free," was it? Unfortunately, that wasn't the only instance. Ray Allen Billington tells us that in the middle of the seventeenth century,

> the Virginia House of Burgesses provided that thereafter no "popish recusants" were to hold office in the colony and that any priest entering its borders was to leave immediately on being warned by the governor. Catholics were likewise disenfranchised and threatened with other persecution. . . . So general was this anti-Catholic sentiment in America that by 1700 a Catholic could enjoy full civil and religious rights only in Rhode Island, and even [t]here it is doubtful what the interpretation of the liberal statutes might have been.[4]

Weird that Protestants were now behaving just like the leaders of the church they left. American Protestants were making an image—a likeness—of the beast they had rejected and emigrated to escape. Now, people who were Catholics faced persecution. Doesn't sound right, does it?

By the 1800s, America had a constitution that promised religious liberty. Despite that, however, various states and localities enacted "blue laws" that forbade work on Sunday (the human-made Sabbath) and classified people who broke them as criminals. In 1883, for example, a Sunday law enacted in Arkansas led to the arrest of twenty-one people.

People who claimed to be Christians derided their neighbors whose religious beliefs and practices differed from theirs. Want a sample? How's this, from a man named Josiah Strong: "If the opponents of the Bible do not like our Government and its Christian features, let them go to some wild, desolate land, and in the name of the Devil, and for the sake of the Devil, subdue it, and set up a government of their own on infidel and atheistic ideas; and then if they can stand it, stay there until they die."[5]

Nice. I would love to have sat by Josiah in church. I bet he was great with kids.

In 1888, H. W. Blair introduced a *loooooong*-titled mess of a piece of legislation into Congress: "A Bill to Secure to the People the Enjoyment of the First Day of the Week, Commonly Known as the Lord's Day, as a Day of Rest, and to Promote Its Observance as a Day of Religious Worship." Yikes. This windy law had the intention of forcing people to worship—the very thing Daniel tells us the Babylonians did to his three companions (Daniel 3).

Historians point out that even in the 1900s, those who chose to worship on the seventh-day Sabbath often had to struggle with their employers, who wanted them to work on their day of rest. "The Christian who is committed to voluntary seventh-day Sabbath observance acts without government compulsion. On the contrary, he often endures *direct economic hardship* because of his inner compulsion to 'keep holy' the seventh day."[6]

I show you this so you can see how false religion works—especially in the area of obscuring God's fourth commandment. This is the spirit of the beasts and the dragon.*

Now we move to their magic number.

The mark

"Also it causes all, both small and great, both rich and poor, both free and slave, to be marked on the right hand or the forehead, so that no one can buy or sell unless he has the mark, that is, the name of the beast or the number of its name. This calls for wisdom: let the one who has understanding calculate the number of the beast,

---

* Seventh-day Sabbath keepers in America can be thankful that organizations such as the North American Religious Liberty Association have fought against religious discrimination, and now many employers are willing to make accommodations for such things as Sabbath observance.

Going Deeper

The leaders of the Hittites carried seals that indicated their authority. The seals communicated the name, the title, and the domain of the persons carrying them. Read Exodus 20:8-11 and see if you can find these elements in the fourth commandment. How is this commandment a seal of God's authority?

for it is the number of a man, and his number is 666" (Revelation 13:16–18).

Many people speculate that this mark of the beast could be a computer chip, a bar code, or some unsightly symbol tattooed into the foreheads of the unsuspecting. But Scripture gives us a much more potent explanation. In Old Testament times, God told an angel to mark His faithful people so they wouldn't be destroyed when the unfaithful were punished (Ezekiel 9:3, 4). In Revelation, the mark is a symbol of affiliation with the one whom the marked person serves (Revelation 7:2, 3; 14:11; 22:4).

The location of the mark would have stimulated the memory circuits of John's Jewish homies. Way back in the book of Deuteronomy, God tells His people to keep His commandments (including the seventh-day Sabbath) tied as "symbols on your hands and bind them on your foreheads" (Deuteronomy 6:8, NIV; see also verses 4–9). Taking this literally, some Jews have written brief passages of Hebrew Scripture on pieces of papyrus (or paper) and placed these notes in little black boxes called *tefillin* that they then tied on their hands and/or their foreheads. Foreheads and hands represent belief and practice.

When Christ seals us with His Spirit (whose job it is to lead us into truth, see John 16:13), we conform our beliefs and actions to His will. Likewise, the marks in the forehead or hand indicate either acceptance or at least conformity to the will and claims of the beasts and dragon. The allusion to the Ten Commandments reveals what the conflict involves: recognition of the Creator's authority or that of created beings.

We see this conflict, the choice human beings must make, in the claim of the Roman Catholic Church, the modern version of the medieval Christian church, that it has the authority to change God's fourth commandment. An article in the *Catholic Record* states, "Sunday is founded, not on Scripture, but on tradition, and is distinctly a Catholic institution."[7] This admission was reiterated almost thirty years later: "Sunday is our mark of authority. . . . The Church is above the Bible, and this transference of Sabbath observance is proof of that fact."[8]

Catholics aren't the only ones to recognize who made the change. Hank Hanegraaf, the "Bible Answer Man," defends Sunday observance as biblical, but in the middle of his defense, he gives credit to early church tradition. He stated on his Web site, "The early Christian church changed the day of worship from Saturday to Sunday."[9] So much for Bible answers.

But God calls the Sabbath a sign between Himself and His people (Ezekiel 20:12). And in the fourth commandment, He tells His people to remember the Sabbath as a sign of His Creatorship (Exodus 20:8–11). Good intentions aren't enough. What we believe and what we do matter, because our beliefs and our actions reveal who actually has our allegiance. The Bible tells us that those who follow God will worship Him in "spirit and truth" (John 4:24). This means that our Christianity, our worship, our commitment, requires more than just energetic music and exciting preaching. There must be an inner core of truth.

And that brings us back to the mysterious number 666.

666

Some people suggest that *gematria,* an ancient Jewish system of assigning numbers to letters, gives us the key to understanding 666. This approach says that the numbers of the letters in the name of the antichrist will add up to 666. Many apply this to an inscription allegedly on the inside of a papal tiara.* (And yes, I realize princesses also wear tiaras.) The problem is that many other names also yield the number 666.

Babylonian mathematics was based on the numbers six and sixty. An amulet popular among the priests of Babylon bore the inscription below. Notice that it contains the numbers from one to six, that it has six rows and six columns, and that the total of each row and of each column is 111 (kind of like Sudoku). The six rows, then, total 666, and so do the six columns.

1	32	34	3	35	6
30	8	27	28	11	7
20	24	15	16	13	23
19	17	21	22	18	14
10	26	12	9	29	25
31	4	2	33	5	36

While this approach is warmer, it doesn't quite fit the bill. What help can we find in Scripture itself?

The number occurs in Ezra 2:13, which says the "sons" of Adonikam number 666. Don't get too excited—Nehemiah 7:18 says he had 667 sons. Adonikam could have had another son between Ezra's and Nehemiah's accounts. But it seems to be a random number in a whole list of different numbers, none of which have any special significance.

The number also occurs in 1 Kings 10:14 and 2 Chronicles 9:13. These passages state that King Solomon's yearly revenue included 666 talents of gold. The context indicates that about this time, Solomon married an Egyptian princess and bought military supplies from the nation that had enslaved the Israelites, and Israel began

---

* The alleged inscription reads *Vicarius Filii Dei,* which means vicar of the Son of God. If you're interested in this idea, you can see my recommended reading at the end of this book for a . . . uh . . . recommendation.

Going Deeper

A lot of people don't like prophecy because of all the beasts. But it was Jesus who chose to use beasts in the prophecies He gave to Daniel and John. What reason might He have had for using such monstrous creatures?

_____

_____

_____

_____

_____

_____

_____

_____

_____

_____

_____

_____

_____

_____

_____

_____

_____

Notes

drifting away from God. Perhaps the number symbolized God's people becoming self-important and self-sufficient. For crying out loud, they were buying military supplies from their former oppressors! That's like Superman buying kryptonite from Lex Luther, or the local police purchasing drugs for their personal use.[10]

We have already seen that in Scripture, the number seven represents completeness and perfection. The Sabbath, for instance, was created on the seventh day. So the number 666 is called a "man's number," something short of perfection, while the Sabbath appears to be a symbol of God's divine authority. Any religion that uses force to achieve its goals bears the mark of the beast—as do the people who, for whatever reason, join that religion. It's Falstianity, if you will.

As we move into Revelation 14, the worship war between the dragon and the Lamb escalates—and the Sabbath issue becomes more evident.

SUMMARY AND CONCLUSION AND WHAT THIS TELLS US ABOUT JESUS

This chapter describes the worship war between Satan and Jesus. The dragon in chapter 12 works through the sea monster, the medieval Christian church and, surprisingly, also through the earth creature, the United States, to cover up God's law, especially the Sabbath, and to institute a false worship that glorifies human beings. The medieval Christian church reached a low point around 1798, just as the United States was establishing itself. But that doesn't mean all persecution related to religion had ceased. Protestants did their share of it too. The mark of the beast is forced religion, and the number 666 represents that as well. The Sabbath/Sunday controversy is a concrete example of false religion's attempts to establish its authority above that of God. As we move into chapter 14, we'll see the warning that in earth's last days, the Sabbath issue—as well as God's role as Creator—will especially be the sites of conflict.

Passion is an essential ingredient in our faith—but so is truth. Passion doesn't always check the facts, and we're easily deceived when we don't spend time studying God's Word. Then we're susceptible to being swept away when we feel intense emotions. The Bible says God's Spirit leads us to worship not only with our emotions, but also with our minds. So ask God's Spirit to keep both your heart and your mind engaged at all times. When we lose either one, we're in danger of slipping into false religion.

We learn a lot about Jesus when we see Him in contrast to false religion. He is a God of love, and He gives people the freedom to choose—even if they choose to do something stupid. Jesus characterizes Falstianity as monstrous because He considers oppressive powers to be monstrous. In our conduct as Christians, no matter how much passion—or truth—we have, we still must ask Jesus to fill us with His love so we don't act like monsters.

ENDNOTES

1. Martin Luther, *A Prelude on the Babylonian Captivity of the Church,* p. 536.

2. John Calvin, *Institutes of the Christian Religion,* 4.2.12.

3. Jon Meacham, *American Gospel* (New York: Random House, 2007), 43, 44.

4. Ray Allen Billington, *The Protestant Crusade* (New York: Rinehart and Company, 1938), 7, 9.

5. Josiah Strong, *Our Country,* 1885.

6. Warren L. Johns, *Dateline Sunday* (Mountain View, Calif.: Pacific Press®, 1967).

7. *Catholic Record,* September 17, 1893.

8. *Catholic Record,* September 1, 1923.

9. http://www.equip.org/bible_answers/why-do-christians-worship-on-sunday-rather -than-on-the-sabbath/

10. Rob Bell and Don Golden, *Jesus Wants to Save Christians* (Grand Rapids, Mich.: Zondervan, 2008), 38–43.

Notes

Chapter 25
The Three Angels
Revelation 14

Before the Webbernet, the iPhone, or even the radio (that thing that makes sounds in your car), people had to rely on more primitive means of communication over long distances.

By primitive, I mean the carrier pigeon. These birds flew from mobile military forces to their headquarters with messages tied to their scrawny little legs. They were amazing. For me, that's saying a lot, since most birds annoy me—especially pet birds. Having experienced the difficulty of potty-training cats, dogs, and humans, I can't fathom trying to accomplish the same task with a creature capable of flight. I have endured several visits with bird-owning friends. They're always quick to towel me off apologetically when a little accident happens, but that doesn't change the fact that I think birds are awful pets.

They don't cuddle.

They won't be quiet.

I remember being annoyed by birds even in the wild. My friends and I would head out to play a game of baseball or football only to find the ball field littered with cylindrical leftovers from the geese that had thrown a party there the day before. We couldn't slide into second base or tackle without being mindful of where we landed—or what we landed in. Geese also act like they own the bike paths, hissing at you when you walk by—or charging at you if they're in a particularly foul mood.

Carrier pigeons, though, served useful purposes. During both world wars, these brave birds, which were equipped with natural homing devices (which is why they're also called "homing pigeons"), would carry messages from the front lines to their home base.

A pigeon named The Mocker flew fifty-two missions before being hurt. And another, Cher Ami, delivered the message it was carrying despite losing both an eye and a foot to bullets. The information it brought was what the officers needed to save a bunch of American infantrymen.

However, the prize for being the most epic pigeon warrior of all time goes to

Mercury. Launched with a hundred other pigeons, Mercury flew 480 miles nonstop (with no inflight meals or movies). Mercury was the only pigeon to make it home, and thus the only one to deliver the message that had been entrusted to it.

Revelation 14 is an important passage. It's especially important for Adventists. It pictures three angels flying through the air carrying special messages. The messages focus on the great war between God and the dragon (Satan), informing God's people what they are to pass along to the rest of humanity in response to the dragon's attacks.

Before John sees the messages about that super great war though, he sees the reward of those who belong to the Lamb. Here's assurance that despite the dangers of that war, those who give themselves to God will survive and stand on Mount Zion.

"Then I looked, and behold, on Mount Zion stood the Lamb, and with him 144,000 who had his name and his Father's name written on their foreheads" (Revelation 14:1).

In this chapter of Revelation, we see the contrast between those who have remained faithful to Jesus and experience redemption and the beast buddies who follow their evil overlords mindlessly. Mount Zion is symbolic of God's ultimate government (Psalms 2:6; 48:1, 2). Joel prophesied that it would be the place of deliverance for God's people (Joel 2:32). The passage goes on to portray them as singing songs of victory (Revelation 14:2, 3), and it says they have "not defiled themselves with women, for they are virgins" (verse 4).

We've already seen that the number 144,000 is symbolic rather than literal, so when John writes that those who comprise this group are virgins, he isn't saying that they've had no intimate relations with the opposite sex. The Bible calls God's people "virgins" when they've been faithful to Him rather than becoming involved with other religions, other gods. False religion is often likened to what I call a "shady lady." (We'll explore that more fully later on.) Just in case the symbols aren't clear enough, the next few verses illuminate the character of God's end-time resistance troops by telling us they follow Jesus in every way and are "blameless" (verse 5).

Much of the rest of Revelation describes the end-time conflict. Before Jesus gets into that, though, He wants to encourage John—to assure him that those who are committed to God will be victorious. So Revelation 14 opens with a preview that lets John know that no matter how bleak the battles become, Jesus and His followers win. As we return to what must happen before that happy ending, we see three angels, or messengers, electrify the skies above a war-torn world.

The first angel

"Then I saw another angel flying directly overhead, with an eternal gospel to proclaim to those who dwell on earth, to every nation and tribe and language and people. And he said with a loud voice, 'Fear God and give him glory, because the hour of his judgment has come, and worship him who made heaven and earth, the sea and the springs of water' " (verses 6, 7).

The first angel lights the earth with a worldwide proclamation of the gospel. The message goes to "those who dwell on the earth," meaning to those who haven't yet become followers of Jesus. This gospel is special because it comes at a time of judgment. The angel is warning that time is short—Jesus has begun His final work in the heavenly sanctuary.

This angel tells those who are listening to remember that God is the Creator. In 1844, Jesus began the second phase of His ministry as the Divine High Priest, ushering in the judgment and the time of the end. In that year, Robert Chambers published a book titled *Vestiges of the Natural History of Creation*. (Riveting title, isn't it!) This book called into question the biblical teaching that God created the world and all life on it—which inspired Charles Darwin to write *On the Origin of Species*. Darwin's book gave the theory of evolution the push it needed to be accepted—including the idea that people and apes are descended from the same ancestors—an idea many people still hold rather than believing that God created human beings.

Early Adventists studied this first angel's message intently and saw not only confirmation that they were living in the time of judgment, but also a reference to the neglected seventh-day Sabbath. Notice that the angel said, "Worship him who made heaven and earth, the sea and the springs of water." His words closely reflect the words God wrote on the stone tablet: "For in six days *the* LORD *made heaven and earth, the sea, and all that is in them,* and rested on the seventh day. Therefore the LORD blessed the Sabbath day and made it holy" (Exodus 20:11; emphasis added).

Notice the similarity?

So did the Adventists.

The fourth commandment is a memorial meant to remind us that God is our Creator. Those early Adventists realized that in addition to proclaiming the gospel in light of the judgment going on in heaven, they were also to proclaim the truth about the Sabbath. This would restore true worship of the God who gave us the Ten Commandments.

Another attack on God's Creatorship came from something called *spiritualism*. The root of this idea goes back to Greek paganism, which wormed its way into Jewish and Christian thought. The basic premise is that people are two-part creatures: they're made of physical bodies that house immaterial souls—and it's the soul that's the important part, and it's inherently immortal.

Hastily Drawn Image 25.1

What spiritualistic ideas do you see in movies, television, and video games that are popular today?

_____

_____

_____

_____

_____

_____

_____

Spiritualism

But the very first lie the devil told Eve was, " 'You will not surely die' " (Genesis 3:4). The Bible says that God alone is immortal (Romans 1:23; 1 Timothy 1:17; 6:16), and of course, if He is the only One who has immortality, He is the only One who can give it to anyone else. The Christian's hope for life beyond death is the second coming of Jesus, when He will give His followers immortality.

Consider how the Bible portrays God's creation of the first human being: "The Lord God formed man of the dust of the ground, and breathed into his nostrils the breath of life; and man became a living soul" (Genesis 2:7, KJV). Not an immortal soul, but a living soul.

Hastily Drawn Image 25.2

WRONG   **YES!**

The human soul, or person, is the combination of two essential parts: the physical

_____

_____

_____

_____

_____

_____

_____

_____

_____

_____

_____

_____

_____

_____

_____

body and the breath of life. The soul isn't the complete human person. It doesn't exist apart from the body.

Hastily Drawn Image 25.3

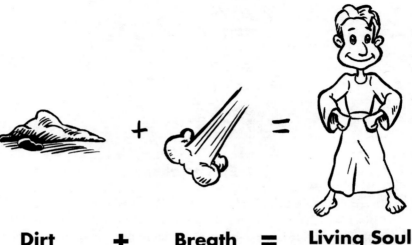

Dirt   +   Breath = Living Soul

Spiritualism became popular in the 1800s. The fundamental belief of this religion is that "the existence and personal identity of the individual continue after the change called death."[1] Through Ouija boards, spiritualist mediums, and other means, people contacted what they believed were their dead friends and relatives. But if, when humans die, they "sleep" until the resurrection (sleep is an important biblical metaphor for death; see, foe example, John 11:11–14; 1 Thessalonians 4:15), then who do you think is talking to people "from beyond the grave"? And suppose your dear ole saintly grandma died. If you thought you were actually contacting her through spiritualism, and she told you things that contradicted the Bible, would you believe the Bible, or would you believe your grandma?

Here's another interesting connection to 1844: The invention of the telegraph and the Morse code enabled people to communicate swiftly across great distances, something they hadn't been able to do before. It was cooler than a new iPhone. The first time Samuel Morse (inventor—well, actually co-inventor—of the Morse code, in case your mind is moving a little slow today) sent a message a significant distance, the message said, "What hath God wrought?" He sent that message in 1844.

While attending a séance not long after that, a Reverend Asahel Jervis received what he said was an accurate message from beyond the grave. When that happened, he exclaimed, "God's telegraph has outdone Morse's altogether."[2] In other words, he was claiming that spiritualism was an acceptable—even God-ordained—practice.

But God has consistently forbidden our consulting spiritualism in any of its forms (see, for example, Isaiah 8:19, 20). If the dead are asleep, and God isn't communicating through spiritualistic mediums, who do you suppose is?

That old serpent—the devil, Satan—was pulling out all the stops to distract people or mislead them so they would miss the message of Revelation's three angels.

The second angel

"Another angel, a second, followed, saying, 'Fallen, fallen is Babylon the great, she who made all nations drink the wine of the passion of her sexual immorality' " (Revelation 14:8).

Falling down and drinking go hand in hand—YouTube verifies this with countless hilarious videos. In this case, however, the picture on display isn't funny. The second angel says Babylon has biffed it. Babylon is a symbol of false or corrupt religion and the enemy of God's people (see Isaiah 21:9 and the book of Daniel).

The foul drink that the nations guzzle represents Babylon's falsehoods, which intoxicate people so that they abandon God (Jeremiah 25). These drunks end up chugging down another round—but this one comes from God's cup, which contains the wine of God's wrath (see the commentary on the third angel that follows). This wine sends the devotees of Babylon to eternal destruction. (Note to self: avoid anything that tastes like wrath.)

The Reformers had been motivated by the corruption of the majority church of their day, and the preachers of the Great Awakening had been motivated by the coldness and lifelessness of the churches of their day. Similarly, the early Advent believers noticed that the churches around them had stopped expecting Jesus' return. Instead, they aimed at perfecting life in this old world—believing that Jesus would come when they had cleaned everything up.

The second angel filled the early Advent believers with a sense of urgency. They preached that we can't create a perfect world. Usually, when we try, we end up killing our neighbors, going crazy, or going broke. This isn't to say we shouldn't do our part to make the world a better place—most Christians could stand to be a bit more helpful in this world. But we must realize that perfection won't come through human effort.

When the early Adventists began preaching the soon return of Jesus, many of the very churches that had once been passionate about His return became hostile. The world still denies the return of Jesus and mocks people who believe it and preach it. The war between good and evil continues—and the messages that the angels brought will be relevant till the end.

The third angel

"And another angel, a third, followed them, saying with a loud voice, 'If anyone worships the beast and its image and receives a mark on his forehead or on his hand, he also will drink the wine of God's wrath, poured full strength into the cup of his

Going Deeper

Christian historians point out that Christians adopted the Greek idea of an immortal soul because they were under persecution. Why would anyone be persecuted for not believing in an immortal soul? Or was that idea more attractive than the Bible doctrine to people who were facing death?

Notes

anger, and he will be tormented with fire and sulfur in the presence of the holy angels and in the presence of the Lamb. And the smoke of their torment goes up forever and ever, and they have no rest, day or night, these worshipers of the beast and its image, and whoever receives the mark of its name' " (Revelation 14:9–11).

The third angel reveals the consequences of not listening to the first two angels. Those who persist in following false religion are treated to a sip of wrath wine—a sip of unmixed, undiluted wine. In Bible times, people often mixed water into the wine they drank, diluting its potency. We do the same thing with juices that we give to little kids—diluting the juices with water so the kids aren't overwhelmed by the awesome power of a sugar rush. God's unmixed wrath means His justice without the addition of His grace and mercy. Undiluted, it is that justice that destroys the wicked.

Many people are uncomfortable with this picture of a "wrathful" God carrying out the judgment's sentence of capital punishment. It's true that some people picture God's wrath in a way that portrays God as no better than the devil. They picture Him as an enraged, all-powerful Deity who delights in torturing some of the poor, unfortunate beings He created.

Sometimes murderers apply much more force than needed to end their victim's life—shooting seventeen bullets into the victim, for instance, when the first bullet had obviously done the job. Often, overkill is evidence that the killer knew and may have even cared about the victim at one time. In these cases, the murderer may have felt so deeply hurt or angered by the victim that rage drives him or her to strike again and again until eventually the rage dissipates.

So, Revelation's portrayal of God as full of undiluted wrath toward the wicked—wrath that is only satisfied when "the smoke of their torment goes up forever and ever, and they have no rest, day or night" (verse 11) can make Him appear to be overwhelmed with rage. However, God's wrath isn't like human anger. It's the natural response God has toward sin and rebellion. And the perpetual torment represents the eternal *consequences* of the judgment. Jude wrote that Sodom and Gomorrah "serve as an example [of the fate of the wicked] by undergoing punishment of eternal fire" (Jude 7). Yet, obviously, those cities aren't burning today. Eternal fire doesn't burn forever. It burns until what it's burning is forever destroyed, is gone forever.

While we're talking about the wicked being destroyed, we should remember that God repeatedly warns people of the consequences of sin. Even when Jesus is about to return to earth, He still does all He can to convince the people of the world to turn away from their beastly buddies and turn to Him instead. The death of the wicked hurts God deeply (see Ezekiel 33:11).

Calling people from their service to the beasts and dragon is tough work. And it's unpopular, exposing those who do it to persecution. The third angel's message speaks to this—and ends with an assurance, a promise: "Here is a call for the endurance of the saints, those who keep the commandments of God and their faith in Jesus. And I heard a voice from heaven saying, 'Write this: Blessed are the dead who die in the Lord from now on.' 'Blessed indeed,' says the Spirit, 'that they may rest from their labors, for their deeds follow them!' " (Revelation 14:12, 13).

Anyone who has run a marathon or who has had a twenty-four-hour flu knows how agony can make time seem to drag slowly by. As the end approaches, God's people will have to endure the world's rejection because of their faithfulness to Jesus—faithfulness particularly expressed by their continuing to trust in Jesus and to keep His commandments, including the seventh-day Sabbath.

But heaven offers encouragement. Those who pass away while hoping in Jesus can be at peace. They have the hope—the promise, really—of a resurrection. This is in stark contrast to the end of those who become buddies with the beasts.

Revelation 14 ends by picturing the fate of the faithful and the rebellious as harvests. First, Jesus Himself comes on a cloud, wearing a crown, and reaps the fully ripe from the world: "Then I looked, and behold, a white cloud, and seated on the cloud one like a son of man, with a golden crown on his head, and a sharp sickle in his hand. And another angel came out of the temple, calling with a loud voice to him who sat on the cloud, 'Put in your sickle, and reap, for the hour to reap has come, for the harvest of the earth is fully ripe.' So he who sat on the cloud swung his sickle across the earth, and the earth was reaped" (verses 14–16).

Despite the menacing appearance of sickles, this first harvest is a positive one. It represents the gathering of God's people and their being taking to heaven at Jesus' second coming.

The second harvest, on the other hand, looks more like something a cloaked skeleton would appreciate. "Then another angel came out of the temple in heaven, and he too had a sharp sickle. And another angel came out from the altar, the angel who has authority over the fire, and he called with a loud voice to the one who had the sharp sickle, 'Put in your sickle and gather the clusters from the vine of the earth, for its grapes are ripe.' So the angel swung his sickle across the earth and gathered the grape harvest of the earth and threw it into the great winepress of the wrath of God. And the winepress was trodden outside the city, and blood flowed from the winepress, as high as a horse's bridle, for 1,600 stadia" (verses 17–20).

The meaning of this graphic, gory harvest is pretty straightforward. Those harvested are crushed in God's winepress, which no doubt squeezes more from the grapes than any other winepress can.

The blood flood represents the completeness of the destruction of evil (see Joel 3:13); it isn't meant to be taken literally. God uses intense word pictures to impress upon our hearts and minds the eventual end of those who embrace evil. The next two chapters, which cover the seven last plagues, expand upon this painful theme of punishment.

Going Deeper

The people God raises up in the last days are called a "remnant." They are the people who remain faithful after everyone else has abandoned truth. We Adventists consider ourselves to be the remnant because Adventists are the only people who have embraced the truths spoken of in Revelation 14. This doesn't mean we are better than other Christians or that we will be the only people who are saved. However, the time will come when everyone will be forced to choose between truth and error. How can we share with our brothers and sisters in Christ what we have discovered without making them think we consider them to be heathens, or at least less than fully Christian?

_____

_____

_____

_____

_____

_____

_____

SUMMARY AND CONCLUSION

Revelation 14 opens with a preview that pictures Jesus' followers rejoicing in victory. Here is assurance that they will be redeemed despite the terrors they will endure because they have been faithful witnesses for Jesus. Next we saw three angels, or messengers, and hear the divine messages they deliver. They represent God's end-time people who are to bring God's final messages to all of earth's inhabitants.

The first angel delivers the gospel with a sense of urgency as Jesus is finishing His work as the Divine High Priest before He returns to earth. This first angel calls the world to worship the Creator, which alludes also to the forgotten seventh-day Sabbath. Seventh-day Adventists have made it their mission to preach the love of Jesus as the end approaches, while at the same time directing worship to the Creator and drawing attention to God's forgotten truths such as the Sabbath.

The second angel warns that in the time just before Jesus' return, false religion will be widespread. The time is swiftly coming when these false religions will be totally corrupt, and those who remain within them at that time will become the objects of God's wrath.

The third angel adds to the warning of the second angel vivid images of the final and complete destruction of those who reject the gospel and true worship and who remain in the beastly system of the dragon.

When Jesus returns, there will be two harvests—one to gather in the righteous, and one that collects those who accept the ways of the beasts of Revelation 13. While the image of God's wrath can be disturbing, we must remember that it is not a petty human emotion but the natural reaction of a Holy Being to sin. Eventually, those who haven't accepted Jesus' gift of salvation will face the awful consequences of their decision.

The question, then, is how *you* will respond to the gospel while mercy and grace are still available. Will you accept the free gift of salvation? Will you choose to keep God's commandments and to trust Jesus no matter how hard life becomes? Which harvest will you experience—the first one, which gathers people to heaven, or the second one, which gathers people to the opposite place?

This chapter reveals that in the end time, people who are committed to Jesus will carry His message to the world. There's no limit as to how many can join Him—but Jesus values truth. Ever since sin came into existence, there have been forces that have tried to distort who Jesus is, and He will not let those lies go unanswered.

While no one likes persecution or the thought of having to "endure" anything, the Bible clearly says that if we place our trust and hope in Jesus, He will help us. Note, for instance, this promise in Jude's epistle: "Now to him who is able to keep you from stumbling and to present you blameless before the presence of his glory with great joy, to the only God, our Savior, through Jesus Christ our Lord, be glory, majesty, dominion, and authority, before all time and now and forever. Amen" (Jude 24, 25).

May you choose Jesus, and may He give you strength and courage to stand for the truth in the end times.

ENDNOTES

1. The Declaration of Principles of the National Spiritualist Association of Churches (NSAC) #4.
2. Barbara Weisberg, *Talking to the Dead: Kate and Maggie Fox and the Rise of Spiritualism* (New York: Harper One, 2005).

The Wrath of God
Revelation 15-18

Chapter 26
Game Over
Revelation 15

Going Deeper

What analogy can you imagine that explains God's wrath without portraying Him as a monster?

_____

_____

_____

_____

_____

_____

_____

_____

_____

_____

_____

_____

_____

_____

_____

_____

_____

_____

The famous story "The Three Little Pigs" treats us to a narrative in which anthropomorphized (people-ified) pigs experiment with various architectural designs. The first pig selects straw as the basic material he will use in his dwelling, and he creates a fluffy, yellow hut. The second porker picks sticks with which he builds himself a rickety domicile. The third—arguably the most intelligent of the three piggies—goes with the red brick option. All three build their dwellings in record time, completing them just before the arrival of a problem: a wolf with a taste for bacon.

Mr. Wolf (*Canis lupus* to his scientific friends; the Big Bad Wolf to children all over the world) approaches the house made of fluff and there begins what has become a famous dialogue. (Mr. Wolf can speak because he, too, has been anthropomorphized.)

The Big Bad Wolf says, "Little pig, little pig, let me come in."

Not to be outdone by Mr. Wolf, Piggy Number One fires back the witty retort: "Not by the hair on my chinny, chin chin."

This outrageous sass provokes Mr. Wolf to violence: "Then I'll huff, and I'll puff, and I'll blow your house down!"

Mr. Wolf carries out his threat post haste, and Piggy Number One finds himself exposed to the elements—and to the razor sharp teeth of the hungry wolf. So, he runs to the stick house that his brother built, crying, *"Wee-wee-wee!"* all the way.

There, Mr. Wolf and Piggy Number Two carry on the very same interaction as Mr. Wolf and Piggy Number One had, and it ends in the very same way—Mr. Wolf expels a forceful wind, it collapses the stick house, and the pigs run to the house of their intellectually superior brother.

Mr. Wolf, of course, follows them and makes the same request, and Piggy Number Three says No in the same way: "Not by the hair of my chinny, chin chin." But this house withstands the Big Bad Wolf's huffs and puffs, and his futile attempts to topple the brick estate nearly make him pass out.

So, pulling the old Santa Claus maneuver, the Big Bad Wolf scales the house and

Notes

tries to drop down the chimney. However, in a sick twist, the pigs crank up the fire, which roasts the miserable villain on his way down the chimney.

While I certainly don't want to compare God to a wolf, the analogy helps us understand the difficult subject of God's wrath. When Adam and Eve ate the forbidden fruit, they became sinful, bringing into the life of every human being after them what is to us a sinister element, but one that, in God's presence, collapses and combusts. So, to be able to enter God's glorious presence, humans must be covered by an act of grace (see Genesis 3:21).

The Old Testament sanctuary system and the sacrifice of Jesus were designed not only to obtain forgiveness for sins committed, but also to transform people's characters so they become more like God's. God has given us character-building materials with which to fortify ourselves. Those who choose to reject them will be destroyed—not because some crazed killer swinging a sickle will slice and dice the wicked, but because those people have rejected the perfect materials God wanted to give them and have chosen instead to build with materials that contain sin, which collapses and combusts in the presence of Jesus.

The sea of glass

"Then I saw another sign in heaven, great and amazing, seven angels with seven plagues, which are the last, for with them the wrath of God is finished. And I saw what appeared to be a sea of glass mingled with fire—and also those who had conquered the beast and its image and the number of its name, standing beside the sea of glass with harps of God in their hands" (Revelation 15:1, 2).

The curtain is closing on the evil of this world. The seven trumpets were partial judgments, falling on only one-third of the various elements affected. They're meant to warn people about the impending final judgment. With this chapter, we have arrived at the end time, and before John is shown the effects of the seven last plagues, he is given another vision (like that of Revelation 14) of the reward God's victorious people will enjoy. Before we look at the wrathful plagues, we're given a glimpse of the beautiful fiery sea.

A huge basin called the "laver" (not the "lever," which is used to trigger trapdoors—like the one I would love to install in my office) stood at the entrance to God's wilderness sanctuary, and later, in front of the temple in Jerusalem (Exodus 30:18; 1 Kings 7:23–26). It was filled with water so the priests could wash themselves before they entered the sanctuary/temple. The first laver was cast from copper mirrors the Egyptians gave the Israelites as they began their exodus (see . . . uh . . . the book of Exodus).

The laver was also called the "Great Sea" and the "Brazen Sea," and here in Revelation, the "sea of glass" (Revelation 4:6; 15:2). Symbolically, it alludes to the Exodus: Jesus has led His people through the turbulent seas of the end times just as Moses led the Israelites through the Red Sea as they escaped from Egypt (Exodus

14). Triumphant and safe, God's people sing the song of Moses and of the Lamb (Revelation 15:3, 4)—which adds to the Exodus allusion (see Exodus 15). As for God's enemies—it's game over.

Revelation 15:1–4 comes before another scary part of the book. Like Revelation 7 and Revelation 14:1–5, it shows the ultimate victory of God's people, assuring us that Jesus can and will enable us to make it through the tough times He's about to reveal.

The close of probation—a.k.a. game over

"After this I looked, and the sanctuary of the tent of witness in heaven was opened, and out of the sanctuary came the seven angels with the seven plagues, clothed in pure, bright linen, with golden sashes around their chests. And one of the four living creatures gave to the seven angels seven golden bowls full of the wrath of God who lives forever and ever, and the sanctuary was filled with smoke from the glory of God and from his power, and no one could enter the sanctuary until the seven plagues of the seven angels were finished" (Revelation 15:5–8).

When I was growing up, there was nothing my siblings and I enjoyed more than an outing to Chuck E. Cheese's. The combination of stale pizza and mind-numbing video games filled our hearts with joy.

Once inside, we begged and pleaded for tokens—precious, precious tokens—so we could play the arcade games. Then we stood in front of our favorite machines and plunked coin after coin into them as we tried to push our scores higher or maybe even to beat the machine.

Unfortunately, our financial resources—or rather, my mom's financial resources—weren't infinite. Our onscreen characters would perish, and then the one-word question, "Continue?" would blink off and on as the machine began a countdown. Panic and pleading ensued, but, alas, we couldn't afford any more tokens.

"Game Over."

Eventually, someone invented the gaming console—a machine that can dwell in one's home and that runs solely on sweet electricity and doesn't require those miserable tokens. But, alas, those who did this kind of gaming still experienced that dreadful end. Sometimes your game ended because you ran out of lives, and sometimes it ended because you forgot to save the game. Whatever the reason, the result was the same: "Game Over."

The last verses of Revelation 15, just before the angels pour out the plagues, picture the sanctuary being opened (Revelation 15:5–8). As we have already seen, when God's sanctuary is open, the Ten Commandments are visible (Revelation 11:19). That's appropriate since the "covenant"—the agreement between God and His people—is founded on the big Ten (Exodus 19; 20). While we can't earn eternal life by keeping God's law, when God gives us eternal life as a gift, we love Him for His mercy. And, as Jesus Himself said, those who love Him will keep His

Going Deeper

How can we understand God's love when just being in His presence destroys evil?

_____

_____

_____

_____

_____

_____

_____

_____

_____

_____

_____

_____

_____

_____

_____

_____

_____

_____

_____

_____

_____

_____

_____

commandments (John 14:15). In fact, keeping God's law is one of the evidences that we are truly following Jesus (James 2:12).

The devil wants to undermine God's law to steal worship away from the Creator and make people miserable. Unfortunately, many people strip off the garments of God's truth, clothe themselves with sin, and then enter God's presence. That's the equivalent of dowsing oneself in gasoline and then running into a burning building.

In Old Testament times, when God filled the sanctuary or temple with His awesome glory, no one—not even the priests on duty—could go inside (Exodus 40:34, 35; 1 Kings 8:10, 11; 2 Chronicles 5:13, 14). When at this point in Revelation, God's glory prevents people and priests from entering the temple, we know this means that Jesus has ceased His intercession for His people. Those who are wicked will remain so because they've reached the point where regardless of how much longer Jesus continues to woo them, they will refuse Him.

The choices have been made.

The lines are drawn—for eternity.

We say that the time of probation has ended. No one will ever again change sides.

Revelation 16 pictures the results of people's decision to build their characters with sin instead of with salvation. Like the first two pigs in the children's story, the wicked have chosen to build their lives with things that cannot stand in the presence of God. Now He shows how He will respond to the cries for justice from the victims of the wicked.

The end of evil is at hand.

Game over.

SUMMARY AND CONCLUSION
AND WHAT THIS TELLS US ABOUT JESUS

Revelation 15 gives us a glimpse of God's redeemed resistance fighters—the people who have placed their faith in Jesus and kept His commandments. They stand by a glassy sea and sing the song of victory that reminds us of the great deliverance of God's people recounted in the book of Exodus.

Then we see seven angels preparing to pour the plagues upon those who have made their final decision—which is to join the beast buddies instead of the people of God. The smoke that fills the sanctuary symbolizes Christ ending His ministry on behalf of sinners. God will now take the final steps toward ending sin. All His wrath will be poured out.

As we have seen, God's wrath is not some petty human emotion. Rather, it is the natural consequence of choosing to build one's life with sin instead of with salvation. Having to destroy anything He created breaks God's heart, but He cannot allow evil to continue to ruin the world.

Jesus isn't a monster, though the devil would like to make Him look like one. While God's wrath is an awesome force, it doesn't contain any evil or vindictiveness. Jesus is love, and love means freedom. It means letting people go if they choose to go.

While it's easy to become discouraged when we see all the garbage people do to each other, we can find hope in the promise that someday soon God will make things right. Our cries for justice are being heard.

Are we living like Jesus while we wait? What materials are we using as we build our characters? Have we chosen God's law of love or Satan's law of selfishness?

Be sure you choose materials that can stand in the presence of God's glory.

Going Deeper

In what ways can we build our characters without becoming legalistic?

Chapter 27
Wrath Soup
Revelation 16

In Mexico, a traditional soup called *menudo* is lovingly crafted for special occasions. Among its special ingredients are onions, cilantro—and cow stomach!

Not a fan of cow stomach? A vegetarian, you say? Then you might enjoy a treat prepared by the Chagga tribe, who live at the base of Mount Kilimanjaro. The Chaggas are known for a soup called *kiburu,* which is made from sweet bananas, beans, dirt, and the occasional twig.

For those not partial to dirt and twigs, there are many more kinds of soup. In Tanzania, you can be invigorated by a steaming hot bowl of *supu,* a tasty blend of goat lungs, heart, liver, head, cow stomach, intestines, and tongue. On a good day, you may even find a bonus hoof or tail swirling around in the steamy mix.

If you have more exotic tastes, pop over to China for a serving of bird's nest soup. This delicacy costs between thirty and one hundred bucks a bowl. The recipe calls for the nest of the Swiftlet, the main ingredient of which is the bird's saliva. When placed in water, it takes on a gelatinous consistency that jiggles all the way down to a person's stomach.

Revelation 15 introduces us to seven bowls full of what I'll call "wrath soup." Each has a different flavor—none of them pleasant. John tells us what the angels' mission is: "I heard a loud voice from the temple telling the seven angels, 'Go and pour out on the earth the seven bowls of the wrath of God' " (Revelation 16:1). These soups haven't been served yet; they'll be dished out just before Jesus returns.

As unpleasant as the plagues caused by the contents of bowls will be, they're all designed to cure the world from its sin-sickness and to comfort those who have been beaten and abused unjustly. The number seven represents completeness—in this case, the complete evisceration of evil.

There is some disagreement as to whether the plagues are literal or symbolic. Some Bible students who look for a literal fulfillment cite scriptural examples of literal plagues: those that fell on Egypt, on unfaithful Israel in Old Testament times, on Jerusalem in A.D. 70, and on apostate Christianity (specifically, the invasion of the Roman Empire by the barbarian tribes). God certainly can bring about super-natural punishment of those who persecute His people.

However, other Bible students see the plagues as alluding to spiritual events that occur before God literally destroys the wicked. I'll show both as we move through this seven-course wrath soup extravaganza.

Bowl one: Sore soup

"The first angel . . . poured out his bowl on the earth, and harmful and painful sores came upon the people who bore the mark of the beast and worshiped its image" (Revelation 16:2).

The word translated "sore" here is the word used in the Greek Old Testament to describe the sixth plague that fell on Egypt (Exodus 9:10, 11). This word is also used to describe the sores that tortured poor Job when God tested him (Job 2:7). Like leprosy, this malady could serve as either a divine test or a divine punishment, or it could simply be the consequence of living in a sinful world (Leviticus 13; Deuteronomy 28:27).

If literal, all those who have endorsed or used coercion in spiritual matters will suffer a supernatural rash that no ointment or lotion can cure—a literal mark of the beast!

Interpreted symbolically, this plague means that now, those who have been op-pressing God's people will themselves be oppressed. And while the first trumpet affected only one-third of the earth, Sore Soup is universal.

Bowls two and three: Bloody water soup

"The second angel poured out his bowl into the sea, and it became like the blood of a corpse, and every living thing died that was in the sea. The third angel poured out his bowl into the rivers and the springs of water, and they became blood. And I heard the angel in charge of the waters say, 'Just are you, O Holy One, who is and who was, for you brought these judgments. For they have shed the blood of saints and prophets, and you have given them blood to drink. It is what they deserve!' And I heard the altar saying, 'Yes, Lord God the Almighty, true and just are your judgments!' " (Revelation 16:3–7).

The second trumpet pictured a mountain being thrown into the sea and bloody-ing everything, and the third trumpet spoke of water being made bitter. Both look back to the plague of blood that messed up Egypt's great Nile River (Exodus 7:17–21). This plague was particularly embarrassing for the pharaoh because he was considered to be the god responsible for the preservation of Egypt's main water source. Having the Nile turn red and rot like a corpse under his rule didn't exactly help him earn deity-points in Egypt.

The literal interpretation of these plagues suggests a total eco-meltdown that particularly involves the loss of earth's water supply. Those who have polluted

Going Deeper

The name *Hadad-rimmon* is mentioned in Zechariah 12:10, 11. He was an ancient pagan god whose firstborn son, according Canaanite legend, was killed by another god. Some people see this as an allusion to God sacrificing His only Son. Read all of Zechariah 12. Do these verses refer to Jesus? Why would John reference both a story about mourning the loss of Israel's last good king and the loss of a pagan god when he was writing about Armageddon?

nature with their greed and carelessness now experience famine and thirst beyond everything ever seen before. The good news is that Scripture has God on record as promising to feed and care for His people in times like these (Isaiah 41:17, 18; 33:16).

The symbolic interpretation suggests that since those who prefer Falstianity have fouled the streams of truth, now blood is all they will have to quench their spiritual thirst.

The mention of the altar speaking could be a follow-up on the "souls" who cried out for justice (Revelation 6:9). They now declare that justice is being done and that God is fair in His dealings with humankind. The long wait for vindication and justice is over.

Bowl four: Scorched soup

"The fourth angel poured out his bowl on the sun, and it was allowed to scorch people with fire. They were scorched by the fierce heat, and they cursed the name of God who had power over these plagues. They did not repent and give him glory" (Revelation 16:8, 9).

No one likes sunburns. Recently, on a trip to Southern California, I chose to lounge by the luxurious hotel pool for a few hours. I found a lovely spot with a chair, a table, and an umbrella. The shade didn't cover my legs below the knees, but I had already embraced the spirit of laziness and decided against going back to the hotel room for some sun block.

It's amazing how many shades of red a pair of sun-deprived Seattle legs can turn in three hours' exposure to the elements. When it was time for me to go, I believe the official color of my legs was "lobster"—which turns out to be a rather uncomfortable color to wear. Sunburns can make you seethe with pain, swelling, and blistering.

Those partaking of the scorched—the burnt, the nasty—soup are in agony. But instead of apologizing or pleading for mercy, they curse God. Even when they experience the consequence of sin, they persist in their attacks on God! Again, we aren't seeing here people who made a few mistakes. These are folks who have willfully embraced evil and deception despite being fully aware of the results.

Taken literally, this plague pictures the worst sunburn in history. It parallels the sixth seal, in which people plead for the relief a landslide that covered them would provide (Revelation 6:15, 16). The Bible promises that those who follow God will have His protection from the sun (Isaiah 49:10). But the wicked have abandoned their only hope of a covering—Jesus—and now face exposure to complete and utter holiness. The pain is extreme, but it doesn't wipe out humanity, because three more flavors of wrath soup are yet to be served.

The symbolic interpretation says that this plague parallels the spiritual darkness that accompanied the fourth trumpet. The wicked filled the earth with darkness, so now it's appropriate that they face exposure to the full brightness of the Son (Malachi 4:2; Revelation 1:16). In the presence of God, they now are seen for what they really are—wicked and pitiful. Yet they don't repent. They're just like the stubborn pharaoh of old who, despite being in the midst of the plagues, refused to acknowledge God (Exodus 5:2).

Bowl five: Darkness soup

"The fifth angel poured out his bowl on the throne of the beast, and its kingdom was plunged into darkness. People gnawed their tongues in anguish and cursed the God of heaven for their pain and sores. They did not repent of their deeds" (Revelation 16:10, 11).

This serving is directed at the heart of the beast's rule. Revelation 13 pictured the dragon (Satan) working through the sea beast (the medieval Christian church) and the earth beast (the United States) to set up a false system of worship. We saw samples from history, but they were small scale compared to what will happen when the plagues are poured out. At that time, these "beasts" will have produced a worldwide system of false religion combined with political power. Many believe the "throne" spoken of here to be the papal throne, where someone impersonating Christ will sit.

The darkness in this plague is an allusion to the darkness that fell upon Egypt before the pharaoh allowed Israel to leave (Exodus 10:21–23). The darkness was another direct attack on the pharaoh's claims of divinity. He was considered to be the incarnation of the sun god Ra—the giver of light. Like that pharaoh, the wicked will persist in cursing God despite the plague.

The literal interpretation suggests that the darkness is terror that falls on the beast powers that have been terrorizing God's people.

The symbolic interpretation sees this darkness as paralleling the fifth trumpet, which describes a bottomless pit of persecutions. Now God's plagues darken the world of the persecuting beast power. This darkness also suggests isolation.

Several years ago I toured Alcatraz—San Francisco's island prison. The tour guide showed us a cell where unruly prisoners were punished by solitary confinement in total darkness. This cell, called "the hole," was so small that its occupant had barely enough room to move. To keep their sanity, prisoners confined there would invent activities. For example, a prisoner might pry the buttons off his clothes, flick them away, and then search the dark cell for them.

The darkness of the fifth plague—whether literal or symbolic—drives its victims mad.

Bowl six: Demon frog soup—a.k.a. Armageddon

"The sixth angel poured out his bowl on the great river Euphrates, and its water was dried up, to prepare the way for the kings from the east. And I saw, coming out of the mouth of the dragon and out of the mouth of the beast and out of the mouth

Going Deeper

If John is referring to Zechariah 12, how does the story of a pagan god losing his son relate to the last plague that fell on Egypt (see Exodus 11:6)? Since a pharaoh's first-born was considered divine, his death was the death of the family religion. How does this relate to Exodus 12:12?

of the false prophet, three unclean spirits like frogs. For they are demonic spirits, performing signs, who go abroad to the kings of the whole world, to assemble them for battle on the great day of God the Almighty" (Revelation 16:12–14).

The sixth bowl of wrath soup contains a plethora of alarming ingredients that are even worse than bird spit. Like Egypt, Babylon had held God's people captive. The Euphrates River ran through Babylon, providing the city with water when it was besieged. But the forces of the Medes and the Persians, under the command of the Persian King Cyrus, who came from the east, dammed the river, creating a weak spot in Babylon's defenses that allowed them to conquer the city and its empire (Isaiah 44:27, 28; Jeremiah 50:38). Eventually, then, Cyrus and those who followed him upon the throne released God's people, allowing them to return to Jerusalem and eventually to rebuild the city and the temple.

The meaning is clear: end-time Babylon will lose its power and be overthrown by a new King—Jesus.

The next three ingredients are supplied when the evil trinity—the dragon, the beast (the sea beast), and the false prophet (the land beast)—burp up three unclean spirits, which look like nasty frogs.

The Egyptians worshiped a fertility goddess named Heket that had a head like a frog. When the plague of frogs came (Exodus 8), the frogs were everywhere—including in people's beds. So the fertility of the Egyptians was shut down by a plague that mocked their goddess of fertility.

First-century Jews associated frogs with tricksters and demonic water spirits. Frogs also hibernate. In other words, they disappear for a time and then reappear, a seemingly supernatural event. As we noted earlier in this book, the devil has used seemingly supernatural events such as spiritualism to lead people to call into question God's Creatorship. In the end times, deception will flourish like never before and lead many people astray. Signs, wonders, and miracles will bamboozle the senses and cause the careless to lose their solid footing in God's truth.

This doesn't mean God won't do miracles; He does and they are great. We just need to be aware that false religion seeks to trick people by inserting errors amid what otherwise are great spiritual experiences. These deceptions are meant to build their forces for an assault on God's coming kingdom, just as the inhabitants of ancient Babel attempted to build a tower so they could protect themselves and wouldn't have to pay attention to God.

The plague of frogs was the last one that the pharaoh's magicians were able to imitate. From that time on, they couldn't deceive people as to the limits of their powers.

The final ingredient in Demon Frog Soup is rather spicy. "And they assembled them at the place that in Hebrew is called Armageddon" (Revelation 16:16).

"Armageddon" is a great name for a Transformer (a Decepticon, to be specific). It's a combination of two Hebrew words: *har* ("mountain") and *Meggido* (which is a geographical location and not to be confused with Megatron, who is a Decepticon).

So where and/or what is this mysterious place?

Some interpretations suggest it's a literal place in the Middle East, like Palestine or Israel. Others say it refers to the place where God flung fire upon the altar Elijah built (1 Kings 18). They see similarities in that showdown between false and true religion atop a mountain close to the plain of Megiddo and the end-time showdown. However, we find some specific items within the Old Testament that help us pinpoint Armageddon and what it means for those sipping out of this sixth bowl of wrath soup.

Second Chronicles records one of the saddest moments in Israel's history. Tragically, King Josiah, a good man who enacted great reforms to keep God's people on track, was killed by Pharaoh Neco on the "plain of Megiddo" (2 Chronicles 35:20–27). Josiah was the last great king of Israel. When he died, a deep sadness blanketed his subjects. The prophet Zechariah alluded to this event when he wrote of the death of Hadad-rimmon—an entity thought to be either a pagan god or a location on the plain of Megiddo (Zechariah 12:10, 11). The plain, then, is a place of severe sadness and loss.

Daniel 11:45, which speaks of earth's final conflict, connects Armageddon with a "glorious holy mountain," which almost certainly refers to Jerusalem, God's city (see Psalm 48:1, 2; Galatians 4:26). This imagery makes sense since the prophecy of Daniel 2 pictures a mountain, representing the kingdom of God, that smashes all the earthly kingdoms to pieces.

What we have in Armageddon, then, is nothing short of the wicked powers of the world preparing to attack God's kingdom at the very time it is to descend from heaven (Revelation 3:12; 21:2). The assault isn't limited to some place in the Middle East: the text says this call to arms goes to the kings of the *whole* world. Ultimately, then, this sixth bowl of wrath soup represents the end-time forces of the trinity of beasts preparing to assault the kingdom of God.

So how is this a plague?

It's a set-up. The battle they're preparing to initiate will result in deep mourning and loss—the very emotions God's people felt when the forces of evil killed their beloved leaders. The battle of Armageddon is an end-time conflict between God and the kingdom of darkness. There will be a literal conflict between God and those who have chosen the way of the dragon, and the conflict is also symbolic of the spiritual choices we need to make to be on the winning side. Armageddon will be devastating for the forces of darkness, and it will liberate the people of God.

Squished into Revelation's description of this sixth soup is a little reference to Laodicea, the slacker church that thought it was rich but that had no relationship with Jesus (Revelation 16:15). It is placed here to warn God's people that if they aren't careful, they will be as susceptible to deception as all the others. All of us need

Going Deeper

The Greek word translated "war" is *pol mos,* which is the root of the English word *polemic.* The word refers to an aggressive argument meant to refute an opposing opinion or idea. In what way is Armageddon a war of ideas?

_____

_____

_____

_____

_____

_____

_____

_____

_____

_____

_____

_____

_____

_____

_____

_____

_____

_____

_____

_____

_____

to keep our focus on a relationship with Jesus so we can survive the battles still to come.

As the forces of darkness mourn their inevitable defeat, God serves the final bowl of wrath, which removes evil forever.

Bowl seven: Chaos soup

"The seventh angel poured out his bowl into the air, and a loud voice came out of the temple, from the throne, saying, 'It is done' " (Revelation 16:17).

The smell of soup cooking on a hot stove can permeate an entire house, making everyone in it feel warm and inducing in the hungry a waterfall of saliva. So, the last bowl of wrath soup affects the whole world—but it doesn't make everyone feel warm and cozy. It pushes the whole world into chaos. The Bible says, "There were flashes of lightning, rumblings, peals of thunder, and a great earthquake such as there had never been since man was on the earth, so great was that earthquake. The great city was split into three parts, and the cities of the nations fell, and God remembered Babylon the great, to make her drain the cup of the wine of the fury of his wrath" (verses 18, 19).

Welcome to God's full and complete judgment.

As the world becomes chaotic, we must remember that God is still in control. The chaos isn't the product of confusion; people have known about the end for a long time. God has warned them. Now the world is being "de-created," or "unmade"— something that we'll look at later. The point here is that the wicked world is being broken apart so God can remove sin and suffering from the universe. The imagery, again, comes from the Hebrew Scriptures (see Job 38:22, 23; Isaiah 28:15, 18).

The union of the dragon, beast, and false prophet—Babylon's all-star team of evil—is finally broken up. At the command of the Creator—the One who has always been in control—the world they've sought to control turns on them. Babylon is broken, crushed, as "every island fled away, and no mountains were to be found. And great hailstones, about one hundred pounds each, fell from heaven on people; and they cursed God for the plague of the hail, because the plague was so severe" (Revelation 16:20, 21).

That is some epic hail! People who are struck by marble-size hailstones say, "Ouch!" People who are struck by hundred-pound hailstones don't say anything at all.

Just as the Egyptians responded to the plague of hail by hardening their hearts and refusing to obey God (Exodus 9:34, 35), so the people who experience the final plague of hail curse God—because their hearts are harder than the hail that's falling on them. Like a loving parent, God has told His children what will happen if they reject His grace. The undesirable consequences that follow aren't a matter of God taking revenge upon people who have dared to disagree with Him. They're just the natural consequences that result when people break the laws upon which this universe is founded. Yet the wicked blame God for the miserable consequences they suffer. Their selfishness is so overwhelming that they consider their own willful mistakes to be His fault.

The final bowl of wrath soup fulfills the prophecy in Daniel 12:1 that when Jesus takes a stand, the earth is plunged into a "time of trouble" worse than anything it has ever before seen. Yet that prophecy also says that God's people "shall be delivered" from that trouble.

SUMMARY AND CONCLUSION
AND WHAT THIS TELLS US ABOUT JESUS

Revelation 16 portrays the final judgments poured out upon this sin-sick world. Those who have been persecuted by Babylon's unholy trinity—the dragon (Satan), the sea beast (the apostate Catholic Church), and the earth beast (the United States)—are comforted as justice is served. The removal of evil in all its forms—including politically minded religion, New Age/spiritualism, and secularism—is complete.

Students of the Bible may differ as to whether the plagues are meant to be understood primarily as literal or symbolic events. However, many of those who regard the earlier plagues as symbolic think the sixth and seventh are meant to be taken as literal. The battle of Armageddon, which isn't restricted to a specific geographical area, is the final showdown between God and Satan before Jesus returns. Satan does his best to build an army as God establishes His kingdom, but the effort is futile in light of the Creator's awesome power. The world will be destroyed along with the evil in it when Jesus returns.

The wrath of God isn't a petty emotional reaction; it's the natural consequence of sin. We may find it hard to picture our loving Savior destroying anything. Many times people read passages like the ones in this chapter and conclude that God the Father must be the One who destroys—which leads to the (unintended) conclusion that Jesus is the loving God who saves us from the angry, hardhearted Father. That view is one of the worst lies the dragon has tried to foist upon people.

John 3:16 portrays the Father as full of love for the world. It says that it was because of the Father's love for us that Jesus was sent to save humanity. Jesus' heart breaks at the thought, the reality, that He has to wipe out the world He made with such care and create it again.

Unfortunately, even when the wicked are experiencing the consequences of the choices they've made, they blame Jesus and curse Him. This should be a wake-up call to us. As we wait for Jesus' final judgments to fall on the world, we need to look at the choices we're making. If we are lost, it won't be because God doesn't love us or because He hasn't made any effort to reach us. Jesus is reaching out to everyone right now, asking all of us to accept His free gift of salvation, which will protect us from the plagues.

If you've given yourself to Jesus, begin thinking about how you can be a healing force in the world. While God is the Master Chef in charge of serving the wrath soup that will ultimately heal the world, you can serve literal soup to the homeless. You can bring the warmth of your friendship to the lonely, and the comfort of your words to those who are hurting. Serve the love of Jesus to everyone around you, so as many as possible will attend the grand wedding feast in heaven instead of dining on God's wrath when Jesus comes (Matthew 22).

Chapter 28
Beauty and the Beast
Revelation 17

I'm the father of two girls, so I'm well acquainted with Disney Princess movies, such as *Beauty and the Beast*. No doubt you've heard of that one, so I'll just summarize it—taking special care to ruin the ending for those who haven't seen it yet.

Belle (a French word that means "beauty," not the English word that means "ding-dong") lives in a quaint village in the French countryside with her eccentric inventor father, Maurice. He goes on a trip with his latest invention, takes a wrong turn into the dark, scary woods, and winds up stranded in an ancient castle. This castle is the site of an exchange that got a little hairy—a prissy prince refused to let an elderly woman come in out of the harsh weather.

Rude.

Naturally, the old woman morphed into a powerful enchantress and turned the bratty prince into a beast. His only hope was a wilted rose under a glass. If he could convince someone to love him before the last petal on the rose fell, he would return to normality. If he couldn't, he was doomed to live in his beastly form for the rest of his life.

Rude.

Maurice encounters Beast (or Prince, because he apparently never had any sort of real first name, like George) and Beast throws him into the dungeon, some other stuff happens, and eventually Belle takes her father's place in the dungeon. This is followed by several whimsical songs and the defeating of a villain, which nearly costs Beast his life. That makes everyone sad, until Belle either cries on his shoulder or kisses him—I really don't know which because I'd fallen asleep by this part of the movie.

When I woke up, Belle and whatever-his-name-is were living happily ever after in a home video library near you—or, at least they will be near you when Disney releases the movie again and charges you a beastly price.

Revelation 17 is a story about a beauty and a beast. Unfortunately, it lacks the whimsy of Disney's version: While the beauty is alluring, she's downright nasty and seduces many people by her wiles.

Most princesses ride pretty ponies. This shady lady rides a snarling scarlet beast. She is the personification of all that is devilish, and she dooms people to an eternity separated from God. And neither the beauty nor the beast has a happy ending. For obvious reasons, Disney has passed on the script.

The shady lady

"Then one of the seven angels who had the seven bowls came and said to me, 'Come, I will show you the judgment of the great prostitute who is seated on many waters, with whom the kings of the earth have committed sexual immorality, and with the wine of whose sexual immorality the dwellers on earth have become drunk' " (Revelation 17:1, 2).

Gross.

John says the shady lady was seated on "many waters" (verse 1). That means people all over the world support her (verse 15). This woman is in league with false religion, which is what a prostitute represents in the prophecies of the Old Testament (Isaiah 1:21; 23:17; Jeremiah 3:1; Ezekiel 16:26–29; Hosea 3; 4; Nahum 3:4). This beauty of Revelation 17 tempts the leaders of the world to turn away from God and enjoy what seems to be an attractive alternative.

The Bible describes the beauty's scandalous ensemble: "And he carried me away in the Spirit into a wilderness, and I saw a woman sitting on a scarlet beast that was full of blasphemous names, and it had seven heads and ten horns. The woman was arrayed in purple and scarlet, and adorned with gold and jewels and pearls, holding in her hand a golden cup full of abominations and the impurities of her sexual immorality. And on her forehead was written a name of mystery: 'Babylon the great, mother of prostitutes and of earth's abominations.' And I saw the woman, drunk with the blood of the saints, the blood of the martyrs of Jesus. When I saw her, I marveled greatly" (Revelation 17:3–6).

Hastily Drawn Image 28.1

Blasphemy

Blasphemy

Blasphemy

Seven Hills

Blasphemy

Beauty and the Beast

Going Deeper

Do you see faith and politics combining today? Where?

The gnarly red dragon had chased the church into the wilderness, so it's fitting that this system of false religion is itself in the wilderness when it receives its punishment. Some commentators see the wilderness as representing the United States, a relatively unpopulated area when it first comes on the scene.

The shady lady (a.k.a. false religion) is decked out in expensive garments and flashy accessories, and she's holding a golden cup filled to the brim with abominations —a drink with the bold flavor of lies (1 Kings 11:7; Isaiah 44:15, 19, 20). And no shady lady would be complete without a gaudy tattoo on her forehead. This one has the word *mystery* scrawled above her eyebrows. This word can refer to the gospel (Revelation 10:7), but in this case it refers to iniquity (which means lawlessness; see 2 Thessalonians 2:7). The religion this woman represents disregards God's law and leads people into breaking it.

All this is bad enough, but there's worse to come. First, a question: What do all mothers have in common besides the advantageous genetic mutation known as "eyes in the back of her head"?

That's right, they all have children.

Believe it or not, this shady lady is a mother too. Toward the end of time, false Christianity will have spawned many distinct distortions, all of which have in common the forsaking of God's commandments and a focus on saints and priests and prelates rather than on Jesus. The contrast between this dark figure and the sunny woman who represents God's church in Revelation 12 really makes the differences apparent.

Notes

_____

_____

_____

_____

_____

_____

_____

_____

_____

_____

_____

_____

_____

_____

_____

_____

_____

_____

_____

_____

_____

_____

_____

_____

_____

_____

_____

_____

_____

_____

_____

Revelation 12   Revelation 17

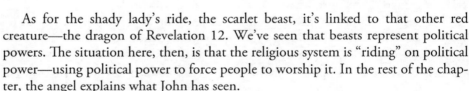

Star crown

No guile in mouth

Clothed with sun

Stands on the moon

VS.

Blasphemy

Mouth full of blasphemy

Offensive tattoo

Wears gaudy jewelry

Red and purple dress

Stands on an ugly red beast too big to fit into this picture

As for the shady lady's ride, the scarlet beast, it's linked to that other red creature—the dragon of Revelation 12. We've seen that beasts represent political powers. The situation here, then, is that the religious system is "riding" on political power—using political power to force people to worship it. In the rest of the chapter, the angel explains what John has seen.

The scarlet beast

"The beast that you saw was, and is not, and is about to rise from the bottomless pit and go to destruction. And the dwellers on earth whose names have not been written in the book of life from the foundation of the world will marvel to see the beast, because it was and is not and is to come" (Revelation 17:8).

In Revelation 4:8, God was described as the One who "was and is and is to come." Twice in in this verse the beast is described in almost the same words, and its apparent likeness to God makes the people who have rejected Him "marvel" at the beast (see Revelation 13:3). The abyss indicates the demonic origin of the beast (see Revelation 11:7).

The next verse says, "This calls for a mind with wisdom: the seven heads are seven mountains on which the woman is seated" (Revelation 17:9). Many people argue about whether this means Rome or Jerusalem or Constantinople, all of which were supposedly built on seven hills. But this information is about as helpful as Apple's attempt to replace Google Maps on the iPhone.*

They aren't hills; they're symbols. The text clearly says, "This calls for a mind with wisdom: *the seven heads are seven mountains* on which the woman is seated; *they are also seven kings,* five of whom have fallen, one is, the other has not yet come, and when he does come he must remain only a little while" (verses 9, 10; emphasis added). The chapter gives us one more clue to the beast's identity: "As for the beast that was and is not, it is an eighth but it belongs to the seven, and it goes to destruction" (verse 11).

OK, now let's break this down. Seven kings—seven rulers or governments—are associated with the beast power. Five are dead, one was operating in John's day, and another was yet to come. This power "was" and "is not," meaning that at one time it had power, but then it lost that power (see the parallel in Revelation 13:3). Then we have an "eighth" that seems to be an extension of whoever the future "seventh" king is. So,

- Five kings related to the beast are dead.
- Number six is ruling when John writes.
- Number seven will rule in the future, will fall for a time, and then will return to life.
- There will be an eighth, but it will really be an extension of number seven.

Who are these seven kings—these seven powers? Bible scholars differ a bit regarding whom they represent. I'll give what I think is the interpretation with the most support.

Most Bible scholars agree that the five fallen powers are Egypt, Assyria, Babylon, Media-Persia, and Greece. Each of these powers had oppressed God's people, and by John's time all of them had become history.

Of course, Rome was the power "that is"—the power that was ruling when John received the Revelation—and Rome didn't appreciate those who were faithful to the Lord Jesus Christ (see Revelation 1:9). The Roman Empire had already been colliding with Christianity for years, and it would continue to collide with it until a pack of wild bearded barbarians began to break up the empire—which opened the way for the next oppressor of God's people.

By A.D. 538, Falstianity (the medieval Christian church) was able to assume political power, and it ran with that power until 1798. Revelation 13:3 says this power (the sea beast) was to receive a "mortal wound" that in time would be healed.

---

* Oh snap—I went there. For the technologically challenged, Apple abandoned the reliable GPS program it had gotten from Google and created one itself. But that one stank, misleading people (literally!) so that they got lost. Fortunately (for us), the man who made the app for Apple was fired, and Google was welcomed back with open arms . . . at least by Apple's customers.

Going Deeper

Many Catholics have planted their faith firmly in Jesus and devote themselves to service throughout the world. How should we relate to Catholic people who love Jesus but practice rituals that distort His character?

_____

_____

_____

_____

_____

_____

_____

_____

_____

_____

_____

_____

_____

_____

_____

_____

_____

_____

_____

And eventually, the emerging United States—the land beast, which had the horns of a lamb but spoke like a dragon (also in Revelation 13)—would help the sea beast regain power through forcing people to worship it.

According to this prophecy, before Jesus returns, the United States, influenced by spiritualism and by Protestants who value tradition more than they do God's commandments, will help the medieval Christian church, now known as the Roman Catholic Church, to regain the power and the position it held in the past (see Revelation 17:8).* That church will then attempt to make all human beings accept its traditions in place of biblical doctrines and practices. In this sense, the medieval Christian church—with all its political oppressive power—will have returned to life. So, the end times will see a return of a distorted Christianity that was founded on man-made traditions and that has worldwide control.

"And the ten horns that you saw are ten kings who have not yet received royal power, but they are to receive authority as kings for one hour, together with the beast. These are of one mind, and they hand over their power and authority to the beast. They will make war on the Lamb, and the Lamb will conquer them, for he is Lord of lords and King of kings, and those with him are called and chosen and faithful" (Revelation 17:12–14).

The iron-toothed terror of Daniel 7 provides an interesting parallel to these ten horns. That beastly mess also had ten horns. They represented the ten barbarian tribes that tore the Roman Empire apart. This suggests that the ten kings are powers—possibly European powers (the troublesome "toes" came from northern Europe)—that lend their power to the beast.

The basic picture is that the secular powers of the world have aligned with false religion. The shady lady is distorted Christianity supported by the political powers that Satan controls.

But the ride is over.

The end of an ugly relationship

"And the ten horns that you saw, they and the beast will hate the prostitute. They will make her desolate and naked, and devour her flesh and burn her up with fire, for God has put it into their hearts to carry out his purpose by being of one mind and handing over their royal power to the beast, until the words of God are fulfilled" (verses 16, 17).

What's worse than being bucked off of a wild bull? Being attacked by a beast that strips off your clothes, eats your flesh, and then torches your remains. The beast and the ten horns abandon the shady lady when the earthly rulers realize what a mistake

---

* Many people feel very strongly that Catholicism has been the foremost evil power since John's day. The headquarters of the medieval Christian church was located in Rome; however, until the time of the Reformation, it really was the only Christian church, which is why I have referred to it using the more generic term "the medieval Christian church."

they made when they chose to follow her. Those who reject Jesus and assault His beloved people never live happily ever after.

SUMMARY AND CONCLUSION
AND WHAT THIS TELLS US ABOUT JESUS

Revelation 17 begins the section of Revelation that records the fall of all the evil powers that have plagued God's people. One of the angels who served the wrath soup takes John where he can see the fall of false religion. The prostitute represents the reemergence of the oppressive medieval Christian church. Forceful, false, and fighting to replace Jesus, it sits atop the political powers of the world (such as the United States)—using them to seduce men and women away from God's love and His commandments.

The seven hills represent seven powers that have oppressed God's people down through human history—the first five being Egypt, Assyria, Babylon, Media-Persia, and Greece; the sixth power, which was ruling in John's day, being Rome; and seventh, which was still to come, being the medieval Christian church, which would fall, but then return to power as the eighth that belongs to the seventh. The ten kings represent earthly powers, possibly within Europe, all of which have lent their support to the false system of worship.

So, Revelation 17 pictures Babylon and its attempts to lead people astray. While many people look for an antichrist that is dark, bleak, and scary, the devil works silently within Christianity to hide error in truth and in this way lead people away from God. Even though we love our churches, pastors, and teachers, we must constantly verify all we see and hear by the words of Scripture.

Revelation 17 tells us that Jesus won't let evil last forever. No matter how strong it becomes, it will crumble in His presence.

Going Deeper

How would you sum up the main point of Revelation 17?

_____

_____

_____

_____

_____

_____

_____

_____

_____

_____

_____

_____

_____

_____

_____

_____

_____

_____

_____

_____

_____

_____

_____

Chapter 29
We Better Get Outta Here!
Revelation 18

Like many desperate parents, my father and stepmom gave my siblings and me notebooks so we could draw during the church service. They hoped this would not only keep us occupied so they could listen to the sermon, but that it would also increase our creativity. Maybe we would even draw a picture that was related to the sermon or to a Bible story or to the memory verse. Instead, however, they were blessed with a random assortment of glorious nonsense.

My brother Ben created what was by far the greatest piece of art to come out of those Sabbath morning sessions. He drew a cartoon good enough to have been in that off-the-wall comic strip *The Far Side*. The thought bubble stated the obvious, but that is exactly what made it hysterical. While I don't have a scan of the original, it's my privilege to reproduce its essence for you.

Hastily Drawn Reproduction 29.1

Gorgeous, isn't it?

And quite true to life.

We often find ourselves in places and situations that have us crying, "I better get outta here!" Whether it is an unhealthy relationship or a dead-end job, our success in life often depends on recognizing when it's time to make our exit.

Revelation 17 portrays the fall of Babylon the prostitute as the kings/powers of the world withdraw their support. Revelation 18 views Babylon as a city, and sees its fall from the perspective of those who have supported it: the kings, wealthy business people, and successful sailors.

Babylon has fallen. It is now dead. A literal interpretation sees the wealth of the world crumbling—to the horror of all the people whose wealth depends on her. A symbolic interpretation suggests that those who profited from selling people a spiritual bill of goods are now forever out of business. Their power is gone. False Christianity—the worldwide deception that has led people away from Jesus—has finally been judged and declared guilty, and now the sentence is being executed. As this is happening, another angel—not one of those serving wrath soup—appears and illuminates the world with the last warning: You better get outta there!

The fourth angel

"After this I saw another angel coming down from heaven, having great authority, and the earth was made bright with his glory. And he called out with a mighty voice, 'Fallen, fallen is Babylon the great! She has become a dwelling place for demons, a haunt for every unclean spirit, a haunt for every unclean bird, a haunt for every unclean and detestable beast. For all nations have drunk the wine of the passion of her sexual immorality, and the kings of the earth have committed immorality with her, and the merchants of the earth have grown rich from the power of her luxurious living' " (Revelation 18:1–3).

This angel, known as the fourth angel (because four comes after three; wow—a free math lesson!), builds on the messages of the three angels of Revelation 14 (especially verse 8). The announcement is given because what was going on in Babylon has now been intensified. When the three angels spoke, Babylon was making people drink the wine of fornication. Now Babylon is the home of devils. Paul warned that in the last days people will prefer what demons teach over God's truth (1 Timothy 4:1). But just as ancient Babylon tumbled (Isaiah 21:9; Jeremiah 51:45), so will end-time Babylon. Though this fourth angel's message still hasn't been fulfilled and may not be for a while yet, we shouldn't ignore the warning.

In fact, at this point John hears "another voice," this one from heaven, "saying, 'Come out of her, *my people,* lest you take part in her sins, lest you share in her plagues; for her sins are heaped high as heaven, and God has remembered her iniquities' " (Revelation 18:4, 5; emphasis added.)

Winston, a ninety-pound malamute, lives in my house. He's a sweet and obedient

Which analogy—a prostitute or a city—tells the most regarding Babylon/ Falstianity?

_____

_____

_____

_____

_____

_____

_____

_____

_____

_____

_____

_____

_____

_____

_____

_____

_____

_____

_____

_____

_____

_____

dog—except when there's food around. Then he's a thief, and a bold one. Whenever someone leaves food on the table or the counter, Winston helps himself to it. So far he has consumed hot dog buns, Cadbury chocolate eggs, pasta, cookies, entire loaves of bread, and an assortment of other items I had planned on enjoying.

His raids on counter tops and the table threaten his health, and they always make a mess. When he got into a bag of chocolate-covered peanuts, he sucked the chocolate right off and left slimy nuts strewn across the living-room floor. The only hope we have of stopping him from consuming the goods is if I see him moving in for the kill and cry out to him in a loud, sharp voice: *"Winston, NO!"*

Winston's response is immediate—he flinches, turns, and heads away.

The voice from heaven calls out to "my people"—letting us know that it's our Master who is shouting (Exodus 3:7; 5:1). He's telling us, "Get out!" "No!" "Leave it!" in the hope of keeping people from consuming Falstianity, which—far from being a nutritious snack, is a health-threatening morsel.

The text says that Falstianity's sin is a great steaming pile that reaches up to heaven—reminding us of the Tower of Babel (Genesis 11:4), of Sodom and Gomorrah (Genesis 18:20, 21), and of Nineveh (Jonah 1:2). It's time to leave this spiritual counterfeit as Martin Luther, Philip Melanchthon, John Calvin, and so many other faithful followers of Jesus left their churches when those churches became corrupt.

Early as well as modern Adventists who are working to restore the Ten Commandments, the full recognition of Jesus' role as Creator, and the reality of the soon coming of Jesus sometimes find other Christians intensely hostile to their message. When supposedly Christian groups willfully reject God's end-time truth or when individuals convicted by that truth find no spiritual support in the church they've been attending, they must choose between Jesus and Falstianity.

Next, the voice from heaven said, "Pay her back as she herself has paid back others, and repay her double for her deeds; mix a double portion for her in the cup she mixed" (Revelation 18:6).

There's a legal philosophy named *lex talionis*. Essentially, this philosophy says that the amount of and kind of punishment the guilty receive should roughly coincide with the crime they have committed (see, for example, Jeremiah 50:29). In other words, steal someone else's food, and yours is taken. Burn his house down, and yours is burnt down. Whatever the case, the results are not happy. The powers that have invested in Falstianity's success now weep for their loss.

The crying kings, mourning merchants, and sad sailors

"And the kings of the earth, who committed sexual immorality and lived in luxury with her, will weep and wail over her when they see the smoke of her burning. . . . And the merchants of the earth weep and mourn for her, since no one buys their cargo anymore. . . . The merchants of these wares, who gained wealth from her, will stand far off, in fear of her torment, weeping and mourning aloud. . . . 'In a single hour all this wealth has been laid waste.' And all shipmasters and seafaring men, sailors and all whose trade is on the sea, stood far off and cried out as they saw the smoke of her burning, 'What city was like the great city?' " (Revelation 18:9–18).

Literal interpretations suggest that the power afforded the political leaders that allied with Falstianity, as well as the luxury it brought, all burns at Jesus' coming. Symbolically, it's simply a loss of power: as Falstianity is now discredited and abandoned, its ambitions go up in smoke.

As for the merchants . . . Frequently the game show *Wheel of Fortune* features an unfortunate soul who, after making big bucks, spins the wheel and lands on the section labeled Bankruptcy. That contestant's money is zeroed out instantly. The audience groans, but the other players secretly grin with glee. The bankrupt contestant tries to smile bravely, as though it's all part of the fun. But you know he or she wants to climb atop the wheel like a rabid monkey and rip it to shreds.

Interpreters who take the literal view of Revelation's prophecies suggest that the fall of Falstianity initiates an economic collapse greater than any that's happened previously. At that point—and especially in light of Jesus' coming—money matters very little. Nature is in chaos, and the world is ending, so who cares what's in anyone else's bank account?

Those who see the visions John is reporting as symbolic believe this part could be picturing the fate of those who supported Falstianity by selling its falsehoods, and that their problem is that no one believes them now. They've been exposed as the ultimate Snake oil salesmen.*

Some commentators suggest that the list of now worthless goods (verses 9–20) covers all the items necessary to maintain a temple's services. This would be an interesting contrast, since the world was led astray by focusing on an earthly temple/religion while the true followers of Jesus maintained their focus on His ministry in the heavenly temple.

The text mentions that the "fruit" that the merchants long for is gone. We feel bad when fruit rots, because fruit is delicious and we hate to see it wasted. In this case the fruit represents what the merchants who profited from Falstianity desired. They should instead have aimed for the "fruit of the Spirit," which is love that leads to a solid character (Galatians 5:22).

The *Titanic* of worldly wealth has struck the iceberg of solid Truth. The wealthy sailors who made money either in literal goods or symbolically, in deceptions, cry out at the sight that made the kings cry. As they watch Falstianity sink, they mourn her loss. Their cry is similar to that of those who wept for the city of Tyre in Old Testament times (Isaiah 23:8: Ezekiel 27:32).

---

* "Snake oil salesmen" sell products that don't do what the salesmen claim they do. I capitalized Snake as a reference to Satan, whom Scripture likens to a snake. I know—clever, isn't it?

Going Deeper

What are some common ways we can make our faith mirror ourselves instead of Jesus?

Watch out for falling rocks!

"Then a mighty angel took up a stone like a great millstone and threw it into the sea, saying, 'So will Babylon the great city be thrown down with violence, and will be found no more' " (Revelation 18:21).

Think of it as the most epic cannonball ever performed.* Revelation 8:8, 9 pictures an angel tossing a mountain into the sea, at which a third of the life therein goes belly up. Now we have an angel tossing a millstone—a really big rock used for grinding grain—into the sea. Thousands of years of scientific study have revealed that heavy rocks sink in water. I know it sounds like crazy talk, but they do—they sink right to the bottom.

Pool toy manufacturers use this principle to make big money. They create colorful dive sticks that sink to the pool floor for people to fetch. Money also works—coins that is. You can try throwing dollar bills into the water, but it would be a better use of your time to just mail them to me.

In any case, the idea in Revelation is that Babylon will sink just like the stone—and it will sink so deep that no one will be able to retrieve it.

Revelation 18 ends with the imagery of Falstianity's music ending and its light going out because its people have shed the blood of so many of God's people (Revelation 18:22–24).

SUMMARY AND CONCLUSION
AND WHAT THIS TELLS US ABOUT JESUS

We have seen Babylon portrayed as a prostitute and now as a city—a "death room" that leads people to their destruction. These two metaphors picture the same fall from different perspectives. This chapter shows us the finality of Falstianity's demise, and the reactions of all those who had been supporters. Strange that even though the kings, merchants, and sailors were the cause of her fall (as led by God), they still are full of regret as she sinks into the depths. From the literal perspective, this chapter of Revelation shows us the economic collapse of the world, and from the symbolic perspective, this chapter indicates that the time is coming when all those who have profited through promoting spiritual deceptions will see their profits end.

Self-seeking religion always ends in disappointment.

Sin is a disease no human being can cure. It runs into our very core, causing us to weep at losing the things that are destroying us. We need Jesus as our Savior; no human effort can match what He has done for us.

Religions that elevate humans above God are headed for a fall—hence the urgent call to "Come out!" of Falstianity, wherever they may be. We are to

---

* A cannonball is a jump (rather than a dive) into water—a jump that's done so as to splash as much water as possible as high and wide as possible.

constantly reflect Jesus and lead people to focus on Him rather than on ourselves. There comes a moment when we have to choose what is right in Jesus despite our emotional connections to what has been crafted in human institutions and traditions. This is when the model of the remnant makes a change and looks like this:

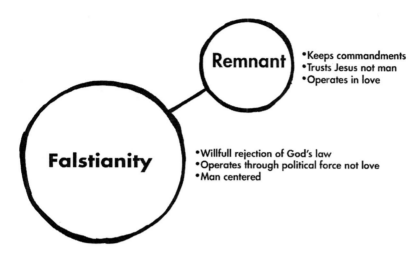

Remnant
- Keeps commandments
- Trusts Jesus not man
- Operates in love

Falstianity
- Willfull rejection of God's law
- Operates through political force not love
- Man centered

This chapter tells us a lot about Jesus. Again, we see that God continues to warn people right up to Falstianity's fall. And He doesn't make just one or two mild suggestions—He reaches out as strongly as He can to save all of us.

Is the church you attend built around Jesus or around the members?

Time is short.

Choose Jesus.

The Final Exit of Evil
Revelation 19 and 20

Chapter 30
Enter the Hero and Exit the Villains
Revelation 19

In high school I participated in a drama ministry called Streetlight. We performed at a variety of venues, including a large youth church attached to a huge megachurch. I played a variety of characters, none of which were as intimidating or curious as Bible Man—a big-talking, Scripture-quoting superhero who helped young people thwart the devil's temptations. Playing this character required the wearing of a spandex unitard—perfect for a 120-pound guy who was subject to the tough social system of high school.

On one occasion, hundreds of youth watched as two other actors set the scene. One of them was playing the role of a teenager, and the other played a malicious demon who was tempting the teen to cheat on a test. The dialogue was building toward a crisis point as the tempted teen teetered on the edge of giving in. At that point I was supposed to dash on stage in a ratty cape and the gray spandex with a giant *B* (for Bible Man) emblazoned on my chest.

This could be the moment when my social life and any coolness points that I had managed to get vanished as hundreds of kids gazed upon my scrawny frame displayed in a ridiculous outfit. What made it potentially even more humiliating was that until shortly before this performance, I had been dyeing my hair red. To get my hair back to its natural blond color, I bleached it. But that hadn't removed all the red, so under some stage lights, my hair was an effervescent blond that glowed pink.

When my cue came, I said a quick prayer, swallowed hard, and then dashed toward center stage to stop the demonic assault on the teenager.

The crowd reacted immediately—screaming, cheering, and applauding. They absolutely lost their minds over the hero of the drama.

Strengthened by their support, I rebuked the demon with a myriad of Bible passages, saving the day.

Everybody loves a hero.

Revelation 19 pictures the epic moment when Jesus finally shows up on earth again to end evil and take His people to heaven. What He wears is far cooler than anything made out of spandex—even with a cape. Raw glory, holiness, power, and justice flow from the Source of love and pulse throughout the world, shattering the hold of wickedness once and for all. As soon as people realize He's coming, songs and prayers of praise erupt from all directions.

The Hero has arrived.

Cue the music

"After this I heard what seemed to be the loud voice of a great multitude in heaven, crying out, 'Hallelujah! Salvation and glory and power belong to our God' " (Revelation 19:1).

John is given a picture of what is called the "already but not yet." In other words, before picturing the demise of Falstianity, Revelation 19 jumps ahead with a vision of the total victory of the redeemed and their trip to heaven. Victory is so certain that we can rejoice now, before it actually is ours.

Revelation 19 is the only place in Scripture where the word *hallelujah* appears. This word of praise is reserved for, and in anticipation of, Christ's coming.

The second verse rejoices in God's fairness in that He has "avenged" His faithful followers. The word *avenge* is a legal term that points to God's covenant (His agreement) with His people. It may also call attention to God's answer to the souls pictured in Revelation 6:9–11 as crying out for justice.

Verse 3 of chapter 19 speaks of the "smoke" of Falstianity's destruction going up "forever." We're to understand that as being figurative.

How do we know that?

When Hannah brought her sweet son Samuel to the temple, she said he would "dwell there forever" (1 Samuel 1:22). If we take her words literally, we can all hang out with Sam the prophet tonight, because he must still be alive and living in a temple somewhere, right?

No, Hannah meant she was giving Samuel to serve the Lord *permanently*—for the rest of his life. That's the point of the passage. It refers to the *permanence* of Falstianity's punishment. That system will never again live, so those whom it has tormented won't ever have to fear it again.

More beings join in the rejoicing over the fall of the wicked (Revelation 19:4)—which raises an important question: Are God's people gloating over the death of their enemies? Are they actually praising God for destroying people? It's one thing to scramble out of your house to proclaim to all who might be cheering for some other team that *your* team is better and *their* team is headed for a loss. Who hasn't done that? And who hasn't laughed right in a sibling's face when they've beaten that sibling at a video game?

Perfectly appropriate.

However, when people are imploding in God's presence, saying "Hallelujah!" seems weird.

But the saved aren't gloating over the death of the lost. God has clearly said that He takes no delight in the death of the wicked (Ezekiel 33:11). The hallelujahs have everything to do with God's justice and the end of evil itself. They're not expressing joy at the death of the people who committed the evil.

The wedding

"Then I heard what seemed to be the voice of a great multitude, like the roar of many waters and like the sound of mighty peals of thunder, crying out, 'Hallelujah! For the Lord our God the Almighty reigns. Let us rejoice and exult and give him the glory, for the marriage of the Lamb has come, and his Bride has made herself ready; it was granted her to clothe herself with fine linen, bright and pure'—for the fine linen is the righteous deeds of the saints. And the angel said to me, 'Write this: Blessed are those who are invited to the marriage supper of the Lamb.' And he said to me, 'These are the true words of God' " (Revelation 19:6–9).

It's wedding time—almost.

I say almost because the Greek word translated "reign" really means "began to reign." At the point pictured here, Jesus has come to reclaim His people, but that won't actually take place until the events described in Revelation 20 happen and the world is completely restored, made new.

In Bible times, weddings differed from weddings today. The process began when the couple was betrothed at the house of the bride's father. Becoming betrothed was like becoming engaged, except that people practically considered the couple already married. Following the betrothal, the groom paid the father of the bride some money, the "dowry," to make their betrothal all nice and official. Then the groom returned to his father's house to prepare a place where he and his wife would live. That was back when living with your parents was cool. When the groom had a place ready, he would go to the bride's home and bring her to his father's house for the wedding ceremony.

When marriage is used as a metaphor of our relationship to Jesus, He is the Groom. He paid the dowry for us with His blood, His life. Then He left to prepare a place for us in His Father's "house" in heaven, and now it's time for Him to claim His bride, His people. The "wedding" will take place in heaven.

In Bible times, while the bride was waiting for the groom, she was to prepare herself for the wedding and her new life. Still operating from the perspective of the end, Revelation 19:7 says God's people have done that.

The reference in verse 8 to "fine linen" alludes to Daniel 12:10, where God's people are said to "purify themselves and make themselves white." Revelation 19:8 says the "fine linen" is "the righteous deeds of the saints." The Bible warns about a

Revelation 19 features four "hallelujahs" (verses 1, 3, 4, 6) and one "praise" (verse 5). What does each of these worship expressions praise God for?

_____

_____

_____

_____

_____

_____

_____

_____

_____

_____

_____

_____

_____

_____

_____

_____

_____

_____

_____

_____

_____

_____

_____

faith that has no works (James 2:17–20), but that doesn't mean that we can work our way to heaven. Revelation 19:8 says it was "*granted her* [the bride] to clothe herself with fine linen bright and pure" (emphasis added). The idea is that good deeds come as a response to God's grace toward us and as the result of the spiritual power God's grace gives us.

Next, the passage says the people who are "invited" will be happy. This parallels the "Come out of her!" call in the previous chapter. Only those people who leave Falstianity can attend the wedding. Interestingly enough, the Greek word translated "church" in the New Testament means the "called out ones."

Wedding invitations are expensive. This one was bought with blood. Accept it. The wedding will be worth it.

The testimony of Jesus

"Then I fell down at his feet to worship him, but he said to me, 'You must not do that! I am a fellow servant with you and your brothers who hold to the testimony of Jesus. Worship God.' For the testimony of Jesus is the spirit of prophecy" (verse 10).

John mistakes the angel for God and is swiftly corrected. Before moving on, the angel tells the prophet that the "testimony of Jesus"—something that chapter 12 says God's end-time people will "hold to"—is the "spirit of prophecy."* This important phrase points to the Spirit who has spoken through all the prophets throughout history about Jesus. We are not only to recognize the gift of prophecy in the church, but we are also to follow it.

In most weddings today, it's the entrance of the bride in her beautiful white dress with the long train that impresses people. When she comes down the aisle, they stand and snap pictures. But in this next scene, it's the entrance of the Groom that's spectacular. Of course, He isn't wearing a white dress. Instead, He's riding a white horse, and He's at the head of a large army.

He doesn't fail to impress.

"Then I saw heaven opened, and behold, a white horse! The one sitting on it is called Faithful and True, and in righteousness he judges and makes war. His eyes are like a flame of fire, and on his head are many diadems, and he has a name written that no one knows but himself. He is clothed in a robe dipped in blood, and the name by which he is called is The Word of God. And the armies of heaven, arrayed in fine linen, white and pure, were following him on white horses" (verses 11–14).

The white horse hearkens back to Revelation 6:2, in which the first rider of the apocalypse goes forth on a white horse with the pure gospel to proclaim. The white horse is a symbol of victory.

Throughout Revelation, evil powers have attempted to crown themselves rulers over the universe—the dragon wearing seven crowns (Revelation 12:3), and the sea

---

* We discussed this concept in chapter 22 of this book.

beast wearing ten (Revelation 13:1). However, Jesus wears an unnumbered "many," signifying His absolute rule.

Four names

Most of us are blessed to have three names—a first, middle, and last, and some of us are lucky enough to have a fourth or even a fifth. Often these extra names are "pet names"—cutesy little things that our loved ones give us to show how they feel about us. These are names like Honey (normal), Cuddles (sort of normal), and Snuggle Poops (I don't want to know).

Revelation 19 contains four names of Jesus—each revealing something about His character. He's called

1. *Faithful and True* (Revelation 19:11; compare with Revelation 3:14). Jesus and His Word make a solid foundation on which we can build our lives. He is more trustworthy than anything else on which we could place our hope.
2. The name "that no one knows but himself" (Revelation 19:12). While Jesus is our Friend, He is also God, and there will always be more for us to learn about Him.
3. *The Word of God* (Revelation 19:13; cf. John 1). Jesus is the logic and reason behind all of creation. In Him, everything makes sense.
4. *King of kings and Lord of lords* (Revelation 19:16). Jesus is sovereign (in control) over the universe. Nothing happens without His permission. He is the ultimate Ruler.

Next, we have to discuss Jesus' choice of clothing—some sort of bloody, tie-dye number (verse 13). Scholars debate whether this refers to the blood of the martyrs or the blood of those whom Jesus slays as He avenges the martyrs. The words mirror Isaiah 63:1–6, which portrays a dialogue: "Why is your apparel red, and your garments like his who treads in the winepress? 'I have trodden the winepress alone, and from the peoples no one was with me; I trod them in my anger and trampled them in my wrath; their lifeblood spattered on my garments, and stained all my apparel. For the day of vengeance was in my heart, and my year of redemption had come' " (Isaiah 63:2–4).

Well, that's certainly graphic. We'll discuss God's wrath more in the next chapter. For now, just remember that the winepress is merely a symbol, not a literal gigantic winepress that turns human beings into a warm juice.

Too far? Sorry.

I think the image of Jesus' bloody garment refers to both His love for those slain on His behalf and His concern that justice be done. Jesus' justice and His love exist together in harmony. In fact, His justice is an aspect of His love. Jesus loves sinners, but He hates sin. His justice moves Him to bring an end to evil, and His love means He won't be torturing people forever in some hidden part of the galaxy.

The passage says that when Jesus comes, the "armies of heaven" come with Him (Revelation 19:14; cf. Jude 14, 15). When Jesus and His crew arrive on the scene, He unsheathes His weapon: "From his mouth comes a sharp sword with which to strike down the nations, and he will rule them with a rod of iron. He will tread the winepress of the fury of the wrath of God the Almighty. On his robe and on his thigh he has a name written, King of kings and Lord of lords" (Revelation 19:15, 16).

I love swords as much as anyone—because they *are* awesome. Just don't tell people you own any unless you want to commit social suicide.

The mouth sword isn't a literal device that extends a blade when one is about to fight—how dangerous would that be? It is the Word of God, which is said to be "sharper than any two-edged sword" (Hebrews 4:12). This passage also says Jesus is the Word of God. The point is that the Jesus who has the power to speak worlds into existence can also speak judgment upon those who have rejected His love and mercy.

Eat or be eaten?

"Then I saw an angel standing in the sun, and with a loud voice he called to all the birds that fly directly overhead, 'Come, gather for the great supper of God, to eat the flesh of kings, the flesh of captains, the flesh of mighty men, the flesh of horses and their riders, and the flesh of all men, both free and slave, both small and great' " (Revelation 19:17, 18).

While Jesus' people gather to feast on the food of heaven, those who have ignored the invitation to His wedding become a feast for the birds. Jesus warned this would happen (see Luke 17:37). The Bible says that the wicked who survive the tumultuous events of the end time will be slain by the brightness of Jesus' coming, and then the birds will tuck into the meal of flesh.

Ever have someone flip the lights on in your bedroom after you've been dozing a while and your eyes have adjusted to the sweet darkness of the night? How do you react when the glory of the light bulbs blazes through your dreams and sears your skull? Most likely, you grope for a pillow or a blanket to cover your head.

Kind of resembles Revelation 6:15, 16, which pictures the wicked pleading for the rocks to fall on them, doesn't it? No amount of cover can protect anyone from the burning, blinding light of the raw presence of God—except the cover of Jesus' blood and His grace.

"And I saw the beast and the kings of the earth with their armies gathered to make war against him who was sitting on the horse and against his army" (Revelation 19:19).

This sad gathering is the final attempt of the earthly religious-political powers to overthrow Jesus and His kingdom (see Revelation 16:16).

Epic failure.

"And the beast was captured, and with it the false prophet who in its presence had done the signs by which he deceived those who had received the mark of the beast and those who worshiped its image. These two were thrown alive into the lake of fire that burns with sulfur. And the rest were slain by the sword that came from the mouth of him who was sitting on the horse, and all the birds were gorged with their flesh" (Revelation 19:20, 21).

The sea beast (the devil-driven, religio-political power, a.k.a. Falstianity) and the false prophet (a.k.a. the earth beast, the United States, which gave authority to Falstianity) are tossed into an uncomfortably warm lake. The fire is symbolic—like the winepress. We'll look more carefully at the lake of fire in the next chapter. Here, the point is that the coalition of evil organizations and religions is eliminated, along with the wicked, who cannot stand before God.

No longer can the wicked hide behind their warped institutional machines: *corrupt* church organizations, *corrupt* government, and *corrupt* family structures. They are exposed, and they crumble and combust until they're gone forever. Never again will these institutions be able to hurt people. Nor can the wicked individuals. They perish at Christ's coming.

So, the villains make their exit when the Hero makes His entrance. Our anticipation of that glorious day should make us say Hallelujah.

SUMMARY AND CONCLUSION AND WHAT THIS TELLS US ABOUT JESUS

We have seen that it is during the persecutions and plagues of the end times that Jesus comes to save His people. Revelation 19 opens with a vision of the rejoicing that will fill heaven when the lengthy conflict is finally settled. It is so certain that God will fulfill the prophecies that are the hope of His people that the vision portrays it as already happening. The certainty that God will destroy evil and save His people should move us to sing praises to Him.

A wedding theme follows the praises with which this chapter begins. Those who have heeded the warnings in Revelation 14 and 18 and have accepted the invitation to follow Jesus rather than man-made gods are gathered to enjoy a feast in heaven.

The wedding metaphor is followed by a vivid description of Jesus as a military Hero arriving on the scene to save His people and destroy evil. The four names this chapter says He has reveal His character and the power of His Word.

At this point, the wicked who are still alive can't hide from His glory, and they perish at His appearing. The wicked powers represented by the beasts are

Going Deeper

What reasons might God have for using so many images to picture the destruction of the wicked (winepress, swords, fire, etc.)?

reduced to nothing—giving people nothing to hide behind. Revelation 20 details their final fiery fate.

Sometimes it can be hard to see Jesus amid all the gory imagery of these final chapters of Revelation. We need to remember that it was Jesus who gave the visions of Revelation to the prophet John, and everything in this book points to Jesus. Revelation 20 tells us that Jesus faithfully honors His promises—including His grand promise to take all who believe in Him to be with Him forever.

Jesus is our Hero. He has graciously invited us to His wedding, and He will give us strength to become more like Him even as we await His arrival and evil's exit. In the meantime, we should accept His invitation to the wedding feast. So, sing a little louder at church this week, and praise Him for the assurance that He will do what He has promised.

Chapter 31
The Memorable Moment
Revelation 20

Downing a cold drink after a hard workout.
Seeing your newborn child.
Scoring the game-winning point when people are watching.
Finding out you got the job.
Watching your team kick the last-second field goal that wins the Super Bowl.
Feasting until you fall into a food coma.
Descending into a sweet sleep after thinking you will die of illness in front of a toilet bowl.

These are beautiful moments—but they don't last. In fact, they pass so quickly that budding photographers risk destroying them as they try to capture them. And pain or boredom turns our thoughts away until we run across our sad little pictures. How many times have you looked at a photo and wished you could go back in time and enjoy the moment a bit longer? Revelation 20 is special because it presents a beautiful moment that lasts for a thousand years.

The pit
"Then I saw an angel coming down from heaven, holding in his hand the key to the bottomless pit and a great chain. And he seized the dragon, that ancient serpent, who is the devil and Satan, and bound him for a thousand years, and threw him into the pit, and shut it and sealed it over him, so that he might not deceive the nations any longer, until the thousand years were ended. After that he must be released for a little while" (Revelation 20:1–3).

We've seen the destruction of the wicked at Christ's coming (see 2 Thessalonians 2:8). Now there's a time of deliberation before the sentences determined in the final judgment are executed. During this time, the evil one who has masterminded all the pain throughout history will be imprisoned in what's called "the pit" (Revelation 20:1), or "the bottomless pit" (Revelation 9:1, 2; 17:8). The Greek word behind "pit" is

The millennium is a hot topic among some Christians. *Postmillennialists* believe that when humanity learns to work together, the world will achieve peace and then Jesus can come. They say the Second Advent comes after the millennium.

Dispensational premillennialists believe that Christ will come secretly, snatch His people off the earth, and take them to heaven before the end-time troubles start. The official Second Coming will take place seven years later, before the millennium begins, and at the Second Coming, people have another opportunity to accept Jesus.

Historical premillennialists (the view presented in this book) say Jesus comes to this world and takes His people to heaven after the end-time troubles but before the millennium. He returns to earth with His people after the millennium to create a new heaven and a new earth.

Amillennialists believe the millennium is purely symbolic and that the church is God's kingdom.

abussos, from which we've gotten the word *abyss.* In the LXX version* of Genesis 1:2, *abussos* is the Greek word translated by the English "deep," which describes the state of the earth before Creation week.

The demonic locorpions that were loosed upon the earth when the fifth trumpet was blown came from this bottomless pit (Revelation 9:1–3). So did the beast (Revelation 17:8). Now Satan is chained there—not with a high-grade metal chain bought at Home Depot, but by his circumstances: he can't leave the earth, and there's no one there that he can tempt. For the next thousand years he has nothing to do but contemplate his failure while staring into the heavens and realizing that somewhere the saints and their Savior are rejoicing.

So, the wicked are dead, and the devil is bound. Where are the good guys?

Millennial moment

"Then I saw thrones, and seated on them were those to whom the authority to judge was committed. Also I saw the souls of those who had been beheaded for the testimony of Jesus and for the word of God, and those who had not worshiped the beast or its image and had not received its mark on their foreheads or their hands. They came to life and reigned with Christ for a thousand years. The rest of the dead did not come to life until the thousand years were ended. This is the first resurrection. Blessed and holy is the one who shares in the first resurrection! Over such the second death has no power, but they will be priests of God and of Christ, and they will reign with him for a thousand years" (Revelation 20:4–6).

God's people spend this millennium with Jesus in heaven. Scholars debate whether this millennium is a literal one thousand years or simply symbolic of a long time. In any case, Jesus has taken His people off the earth while Satan "enjoys" his bleak time out.

The order of events can be confusing—especially the passage that gives us a glimpse of the saints reigning before it speaks of the resurrection. Fortunately, the Bible clarifies things for us. The apostle Paul told the Thessalonians that "we who are alive, who are left until the coming of the Lord, will not precede those who have fallen asleep. For the Lord himself will descend from heaven . . . And the dead in Christ will rise first. Then we who are alive, who are left, will be caught up together with them in the clouds to meet the Lord in the air, and so we will always be with the Lord" (1 Thessalonians 4:15–17).

So, those who died "in Christ" (Paul's words), including those who were martyred, "beheaded" (John's words), rise from their graves. They go first. But the believers who are alive when Jesus comes are "caught up together with them," and they all meet the Lord in the air. The wicked who are dead and buried when Jesus returns stay where they are, and Jesus' glory incinerates the wicked who are living.

We've just noted when Jesus resurrects the dead. Now let's consider just what

---

* A Greek translation of the Old Testament. Jesus and the disciples quoted from the LXX.

Continued...

the resurrected are like. Our scripture passages didn't picture ethereal souls coming down out of heaven and grabbing their old bodies. Paul clearly says that at the resurrection/Second Coming, "this perishable body will put on the imperishable, and this mortal body must put on immortality" (1 Corinthians 15:53). Those who are resurrected retain their physical bodies, but now they've been made immortal. The idea that we consist of mortal bodies and immortal souls isn't biblical. In fact, that's the foundational belief of spiritualism.

After all of life's considerable pain and its fleeting moments of joy, those of us who have trusted Jesus now get to bask in God's love in glorified new bodies—no sickness, no weight problems, no deformities. We are finally together with Jesus, and we don't need to take pictures to preserve that joy. This isn't some passing moment of joy, like those of our former life. This moment will last for a long time, and when it ends, life will only get better—forever.

But after the tears, hugs, kisses, and songs of joy, what do we do?

The passage says that those with Jesus were given "authority to judge." This judgment theme appears again in Revelation 20:12, when the "books are open" and people are judged based on what is written in them. This image draws upon Daniel 7:10, which says that "the court sat in judgment, and the books were opened." So, Scripture indicates that there is some sort of record of the choices people made.

The apostle Paul clarifies this matter too. He writes, "Do you not know that the saints will judge the world? . . . Do you not know that we are to judge angels?" (1 Corinthians 6:2, 3). Paul says God considers His people competent to judge both humans and angels.

But hold on—the saints are saved; the sinners are dead; and Satan is bound. So, who's left to judge?

No doubt we'll have hundreds of questions about who was saved and who wasn't. We'll be allowed to take our questions to God's records and see for ourselves whether He's been fair. Even before Satan planted doubts in Adam's and Eve's minds (see Genesis 3), he had deceived some of his fellow angels (Revelation 12:4, 7). God uses the millennium to vindicate His character. His allowing us to judge—giving us access to heaven's records—is an incredible act of openness and transparency.

Many people suggest that Christianity's God condemns people who question what He's said and done. But He allows and even encourages the honest asking of questions. It's the religion of the beast that demands unquestioning allegiance.

Final fight

"And when the thousand years are ended, Satan will be released from his prison and will come out to deceive the nations that are at the four corners of the earth, Gog and Magog, to gather them for battle; their number is like the sand of the sea. And they marched up over the broad plain of the earth and surrounded the camp of

Critique these views. Are they biblical?

the saints and the beloved city" (Revelation 20:7–9).

This part of the chapter portrays the resurrection of the wicked and the loosing of Satan from the pit. Like a mad dog breaking out of his fenced yard, he immediately launches himself out among the restored wicked to infect them with deceptions. As he has done so many times, he uses lies to get them to join with him, and then he makes them into an army with which he'll launch an assault on God's beautiful holy city. The time he's had to reflect on his actions has done nothing to reduce his hatred for Jesus. And his wicked homies are right there with him. None of them has changed.

So why has God resurrected them?

Simple—to prove His judgment has been correct. Those who died before Jesus' second coming died in their sin, disbelief, and rebellion against God. And those obliterated by Jesus' presence never had time to reflect on the fairness of His judgment. As they stand before God's great white throne, they realize just whom they have been rebelling against (verse 11).

The Bible says that those who have "done evil" will be resurrected to "judgment" (John 5:28, 29). The Bible also says (twice) that there will come a time when *every* knee will bow, and *every* tongue will confess that Jesus is Lord (Romans 14:11; Philippians 2:10, 11). The picture is of a memorable moment—memorable in a sad way—when those who have chosen to reject Jesus see their decisions for what they are and acknowledge that God's judgment is fair.

This great evil group is said to have been gathered from Gog and Magog.

Um . . . where?

These places figure in chapters 38 and 39 of Ezekiel's prophecy. They speak of God's enemies invading from the north, but they are symbols of all the enemies of God that have ever existed, and they head out to deceive everyone in all different directions. The numeric values assigned to the words *Gog* and *Magog* total seventy—the number that in Jewish tradition represented all the nations outside of Israel. This group's attack on God's New Jerusalem isn't Armageddon; that has already happened. At Armageddon, the wicked died "the first death." The time has come for the "second" death—the eternal death (see Daniel 12:2).

If this seems confusing, check out the following diagram.

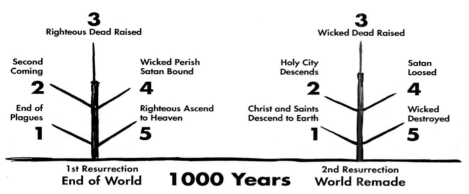

Hastily Drawn Diagram 31.1[1]

Between the Resurrection Trees

3
Righteous Dead Raised

Second Coming
2

Wicked Perish Satan Bound
4

End of Plagues
1

Righteous Ascend to Heaven
5

3
Wicked Dead Raised

Holy City Descends
2

Satan Loosed
4

Christ and Saints Descend to Earth
1

Wicked Destroyed
5

1st Resurrection
End of World   **1000 Years**   2nd Resurrection
World Remade

On earth: Satan left to think on what he's done
In heaven: Redeemed verify God's judgment

Ultimately, God's character is proven good, and the wicked—in acceptance of reality; not in worship—bend the knee and confess Jesus as Lord. What follows is one of the most difficult and uncomfortable teachings of Scripture: the death of evil in the flames of hell.

Into the fire

"Fire came down from heaven and consumed them, and the devil who had deceived them was thrown into the lake of fire and sulfur where the beast and the false prophet [a.k.a. the earth beast] were, and they will be tormented day and night forever and ever. . . . Death and Hades were thrown into the lake of fire. This is the second death, the lake of fire. And if anyone's name was not found written in the book of life, he was thrown into the lake of fire" (Revelation 20:9–14).

Some Christians love this passage. One man even told me that he took great comfort in the fact that his sister would burn in hell.

Yikes.

Other Christians hate this passage. They can't believe God would kill anyone. They think He'll save everyone.

That's not what this passage—or any other—says.

The Old Testament does picture God as destroying the incorrigibly wicked (for example, Genesis 6–8; 19:23–28; 2 Kings 1:9–12). Consequently, many people have grown up with an image of Him as some angry, wildly violent deity who enjoys sinner flambé. People have sometimes even portrayed the Father as the Old Testament God who has the hobby of punishing people. They see Jesus, in contrast, as being the New Testament God who came to save us from the cruel Divine Father.

Going Deeper

Millerite Christians struggled against postmillennialism, which most Christians at that time believed. The denominations that held the majority view became hostile to the Millerites and their conviction that Jesus' coming was soon. How much should Adventists engage with other people, with other Christians, to make the world a better place? What would you say to people who don't believe they should try to improve their community because, they say, "Jesus is coming soon"?

_____

_____

_____

_____

_____

_____

_____

_____

_____

_____

_____

But this picture isn't correct. Isaiah calls God's execution of sinners a "strange act" (Isaiah 28:21)—strange because He doesn't want to execute anyone (Ezekiel 33:11). Jesus said the Father loves sinners so much that He sent His Son to save them (John 3:16), and Peter said that God doesn't want anyone to die (2 Peter 3:9). And, on the other hand, Jesus spoke approvingly of people being cast into hell (see, for example, Matthew 23).

In fact, numerous metaphors in the Bible say in many ways that malicious sinners and their master will eventually be eliminated. If God were to excuse open rebellion, He would have to force salvation on people, and love isn't compatible with coercion. A God who truly loves people gives them the freedom to choose—but that doesn't mean He'll never hold them accountable for what they've done. We couldn't worship a "savior" who, when little children are gunned down while Satan laughs, just shrugs and says, "Oh well; they can always make more kids." That kind of indifference is horrifying.

Just what is this hell? *Gehenna*, one of the words translated "hell" in the New Testament, pictures it for us. Gehenna is the name of the place where Israelites sacrificed infants to the pagan god Molech ("the valley of the son of Hinnom"; 2 Chronicles 28:3; 33:6; Jeremiah 7:31; 19:2–6). In New Testament times, this valley was used as a garbage dump. The fire there burned continually—not because God had placed a bit of His eternal fire there, but because people kept feeding the fire with their trash. As we've seen earlier in this book, the phrases *eternal fire* and *forever,* as used of the punishment of the wicked, mean a fire that keeps burning until it has completely consumed whatever was put in it. Whatever was burned in it is gone forever.

While better than an eternally burning Hellscape, the image of bodies being consumed in a flaming garbage dump still isn't going to make it into children's stories or Bible picture books.*

Fire from God appears several times in John's vision (for example, Revelation 17:16; 18:8; 19:20), but essentially, there are just two of these fires. Just before the Second Coming, fire destroys the evil institutions represented by the sea beast and the land beast/false prophet, and at the end of the millennium, demons and unrepentant humans are destroyed by fire, clearing the way for God to cleanse this planet and create a new heaven and a new earth.

People who want us to remember that justice is a basic characteristic of God argue that the fire is literal, while those who don't want God to look like a monster contend that it is symbolic and point out that death is a natural consequence of sin. The people on each side have experiences (and baggage) that incline them to the positions they hold. Both are concerned that God's character—as seen in Revelation's portrayal of what He does in the judgment—be vindicated. Both point to Bible texts that apparently support their position.

---

* Can you imagine a felt set of this flaming garbage-dump hell?

The issues raised by hell are legion, requiring a book rather than just a portion of one chapter—so I'll leave you with what I hope is a helpful thought. The next time you want to pester a guitar-strumming friend, give some of the pegs a twist when he or she isn't looking. Don't be shy. Then go back to whatever it was you were doing and wait for your friend the rock star to play the instrument. Watch as he or she strums that first chord. Did you see that pained expression? The look of horror? Hilarious, isn't it? Now start running, because it won't take your friend long to figure out who meddled with that finely tuned instrument.

A guitar's strings will snap if you stretch them too tight, and they won't make any sound if you make them too loose. In order to sound the way they should, the strings must have the right amount of tension.

For us to understand God's wrath correctly, we must see it in perfect balance with His love, His mercy, His holiness, His grace, and all His other attributes. Scripture pictures the death of the wicked in many ways, and that may confuse us. But it makes what He is and what He does so clear that we can agree on them and rejoice in them.

1. God is love.
2. God is just.
3. God ends evil.

Come, Lord Jesus!

SUMMARY AND CONCLUSION
AND WHAT THIS TELLS US ABOUT JESUS

Revelation 20—with the help of 1 Thessalonians 4:13–18—gives us a glimpse of the order of end-time events, including the first and second resurrections and the first and second deaths. When Jesus comes, the living wicked perish, the dead in Christ are raised, and, together with the living followers of Jesus, they ascend to heaven. Then the devil is bound and cast into the abyss. During the next thousand years (the millennium), God allows the righteous to examine His records and judge whether or not He's been fair.

At the end of the thousand years, the wicked dead from all the ages are awakened and Satan is released. Still rebellious, the demons and the wicked prepare to assault the New Jerusalem, which God has brought to earth with the righteous inside. Standing before God's throne, the wicked soon realize that their attack is futile. They acknowledge their sins and confess that Jesus is Lord—not, however, out of repentance and a desire to serve Him, but merely as an admission that He is stronger than they. Then, to the sorrow of the saved, all those people—who had every opportunity to accept Jesus but

Going Deeper

Some people suggest that seventh-seal silence (Revelation 8:1) follows the destruction of the wicked. If this is true what would the silence mean or what purpose would it serve?

_____

_____

_____

_____

_____

_____

_____

_____

_____

_____

_____

_____

_____

_____

_____

_____

_____

_____

_____

didn't—perish, and the world is free from sin. The thousand-year-long memorable moment now becomes an eternal moment without evil.

In addition to the love and justice of Jesus, the idea that He would allow us to check His records amazes me. As God, He has no reason to care about what I think; after all, His rule is absolute. Yet He lets me ask questions. He lets me explore His reasons and His decisions. Jesus cares about what you think and how you feel. You can trust Him with your problems and your questions. Jesus invites us to have a faith that develops our minds as well as our hearts.

Revelation 20 is all about the end of evil and the saving of God's people. The chapter opens with Satan chained to a barren earth for a thousand years while God's people go to heaven to be with Him. It closes with the "second death" of the wicked, in preparation for the creation of a new heaven and a new earth.

ENDNOTE

1. This diagram is based on one in Kenneth Mathews, *Revelation Reveals Jesus* (Greeneville, Tenn.: Second Coming Publishing, 2012), 1043. Available at www.secondcomingpublishing .com.

The Reward of the Righteous
Revelation 21 and 22

Chapter 32
Extreme World Makeover
Revelation 21

"Driver—*move that bus*!"

At those words, the members of an unfortunate family who have been living in a deathtrap hold their breath. They're about to see their new world.

It all starts when someone sends a video of the family and their current living conditions to *Extreme Makeover: Home Edition,* a show on ABC that specializes in radically altering people's living space. Their video and the others that come in tell heart-rending stories—stories of lost jobs, illness, poverty, and/or natural disasters. They picture a house in such bad shape that you break out in a rash just thinking about going into it. Network executives select one that's a particularly effective tearjerker and pass it along to a team of designers and builders. Then, via our TVs, we join them on a grand tour of the house. The experts highlight problems like leaky roofs, moldy bathrooms, broken furnaces, exploding ovens, rat infestations, and/or anything else short of a toxic waste dump.

The crew interview the family, getting a sense of what would turn their life into a dream come true, and then the family is sent on a weeklong vacation—usually to a magical place like Disney World.

While the family is off enjoying the Magic Kingdom, the team takes sledgehammers, saws, flamethrowers, and bulldozers and rip the house to shreds—sweeping it away until no trace is left of the hellhole that has caused the family so much suffering.

And then the real work begins. Knowing the tastes, personalities, and stories of the family, the team begins to fashion a place that has everything that is meaningful and wonderful to them. For the child with respiratory problems, they install air purifiers. For the mother who had precious little space in which to cook meals for her children, they build a spacious kitchen filled with brand-new commercial appliances that gleam and shimmer. For the kid who longs to play a guitar but could never hope to buy one, they present a wall on which hang several autographed guitars from his favorite musicians.

When the family comes back from their magical vacation stay, they and their neighbors are positioned behind a big tour bus, which screens the new home from their view. When the bus pulls away and the dad, mom, and kids see their new home, they all cry out with joy. In fact, frequently they nearly pass out with joy. The sight overwhelms them. Their new house has been built to meet all their needs. It has everything they need to thrive. Surprises lurk behind every door, in every room. The new house represents a completely new reality—a new world.

The bulk of Revelation features Jesus and His servants working diligently in this old world. Chapters 19 and 20 take God's people on a thousand-year-long vacation in heaven and then back again to see the end of evil and the cleansing of the entire world with fire (see 2 Peter 3:10). Now John, having witnessed so much struggle and pain, finally breathes in the purified air of the world that has been demolished and remade—an extreme makeover.

Revelation 21 introduces us to what our future holds.

Our new world.

Our new home.

New world; no tears

"Then I saw a new heaven and a new earth, for the first heaven and the first earth had passed away, and the sea was no more" (Revelation 21:1).

Some elderly people have to go to a retirement home when they can no longer care for themselves and need help with their day-to-day functions. It's also a place where they can interact with others instead of wasting away in an empty house—one of the greatest challenges of growing old is becoming lonely.

When John saw the vision that we call Revelation, he was an old man stuck on an island. All of his oldest friends—the ones with whom he had walked with Jesus—were dead. Those friends who were still alive were far away across the sea. John was alone, maybe even wondering if he'd been forgotten.

Then Jesus came and gave him a vision that showed his place in the grand flow of history and that ends with a spectacular view of what God plans after the Second Coming. The text speaks of a new heaven and a new earth (Revelation 21:1). This won't be just a redo; the world in which John has suffered will be demolished and replaced, and the sea that now separates him from his loved ones will be no more.

The vision includes the New Jerusalem—God's capital of the universe. John says it will be like a bride who is adorned for her husband (verse 2). Again, we're talking about a makeover—a reconstruction of the world that has made it beautiful again. In fact, "all things" will be redone (verse 5). These words echo Isaiah 65:17, which says the makeover will be so complete that we won't even remember the old, broken world.

Next, the text tells us that God will live with us on this new earth. One of Jesus' names means "God with us" (Matthew 1:23)—only then, He'll be with us as the inaugurated King of the new earth. Many Christians seem to think that heaven is the ultimate destination for God's people, but this passage reminds us that God's plan is for us to live on the new earth with Jesus—not in some distant place furnished with clouds and harps.

And we're told the best part about this new home in one of the most beautiful texts in all of Scripture. This is a verse that you should tape to your mirror, put in your pocket, memorize, tell to your friends, Facebook, tweet, and text (not while driving) until it is settled permanently in your heart. The verse says, "He will wipe away every tear from their eyes, and death shall be no more, neither shall there be mourning, nor crying, nor pain anymore, for the former things have passed away" (Revelation 21:4).

That new home will have no cancer, no trips to the ER, no divorce, no cheating, no name calling, no violent parents, no drug abuse, no drunken driving, no war, no bug bites, no theater shootings, no school shootings, no hate, no crazies, no indifference, no Satan, and no sin.

In the New Jerusalem, everything negative is replaced by a positive. The root word of *Jerusalem* is *salem,* which is a form of *shalom,* which means "complete, whole, at peace." In the New Jerusalem, the world is at *shalom.*

"And he said to me, 'It is done! I am the Alpha and the Omega, the beginning and the end. To the thirsty I will give from the spring of the water of life without payment. The one who conquers will have this heritage, and I will be his God and he will be my son. But as for the cowardly, the faithless, the detestable, as for murderers, the sexually immoral, sorcerers, idolaters, and all liars, their portion will be in the lake that burns with fire and sulfur, which is the second death'" (Revelation 21:6–8).

Jesus restates what was said of Him in Revelation 1:8—He is the beginning and the end and everything in between. Nothing but life flows from the New Jerusalem, and none of the forces that would seek to ruin it can gain entrance. I've been in lots of cities: L.A., New York, Seattle, Dallas, Toronto, Vancouver, and even Lima, Peru. All of them have hospitals, police forces, firefighters, gas stations, cemeteries, and ghettos. These amenities practically identify a place as a city. But the New Jerusalem has none of them, yet it shines above and beyond anything ever imagined by earth's most brilliant city planners, architects, and *Extreme Makeover* crews.

New city

"Then came one of the seven angels who had the seven bowls full of the seven last plagues and spoke to me, saying, 'Come, I will show you the Bride, the wife of the Lamb.' And he carried me away in the Spirit to a great, high mountain, and showed me the holy city Jerusalem coming down out of heaven from God, having the glory of God, its radiance like a most rare jewel, like a jasper, clear as crystal" (Revelation 21:9–11).

Interesting that one of the angels who dumped wrath on the world acts as a tour

Going Deeper

Revelation 21 tells us that there won't be a temple in the New Jerusalem (see verse 22). What makes the temple superfluous there?

guide for the world made new. But God's servants are not angry, vengeful creatures. They operate with perfect love. Even when they pour out God's wrath, it isn't because they're itching to hurt people—they have to let people reap what they have sown. Fortunately, now the angel has more pleasant things to show the prophet.

The city is built in twelves—twelve gates, twelve angels, the twelve names of the twelve tribes of Israel, and twelve foundations bearing the names of the twelve apostles (verses 12–14). Now, I like the number twelve as much as anybody, but what's the deal? Perhaps twelve is the number of God's people: the twelve tribes being the number of His people in Old Testament times and the twelve apostles representing the number of His people in New Testament times.

The New Jerusalem is also said to have perpetually open gates on every side of the city—meaning that everyone from anywhere is welcome to live there. We never have to fear that Jesus didn't die for *us*. Neither our ethnicity, nor our grades in school, nor our money, nor our poverty, nor our gender disqualifies us from receiving God's love and salvation.

Next we see the shape of the city: it's a cube. Not a heart nor a cross. Just a three-dimensional square (verses 15–17).

The Bible tells us that the most sacred place of the sanctuary—where God's presence on earth was tangible—was a holy cube (1 Kings 6:20). The cube glitters with a host of different colored gems, representing the beautiful diversity of all those who have accepted God's invitation (Revelation 21:18–21; see also Exodus 28:17–20; 39:10–19).

And the city gates are said to be "single pearls." Besides being beautiful and valuable, pearls represent suffering. They're created when a grain of sand slips into the shell of an unfortunate oyster. The miserable oyster covers the grain of sand in layers of a milky white substance, that, when hardened, is a pearl. The irritation prods the oyster to produce something of value.

All those who enter the New Jerusalem have endured trials. They've been called names, mocked, and even killed because of their commitment to Christ. But life in the new world is more than adequate compensation for the suffering. As one author wrote of what we'll feel when we're there: "We tried to call up our greatest trials, but they looked so small compared with the far more exceeding and eternal weight of glory that surrounded us, that we could not speak them out, and we all cried out, Alleluia! heaven is cheap enough."[1]

Whatever you're going through, hang on to your faith. What God has planned for us is worth it.

The ultimate nightlight

"And I saw no temple in the city, for its temple is the Lord God the Almighty and the Lamb. And the city has no need of sun or moon to shine on it, for the glory of God gives it light, and its lamp is the Lamb" (Revelation 21:22).

Most nightlights are modeled on cute animals, action heroes, or scary-faced clowns. They all give off an eerie glow to comfort those who are afraid of the dark and show those of us desiring a midnight snack—or getting a midnight sick—where to find relief. But we won't need nightlights in the New Jerusalem. The light that shines from God is so bright that night ceases to exist. In fact, nothing spiritually or psychologically dark can exist anywhere near the New Jerusalem. And who needs nighttime anyway, when you don't need to sleep? Our new bodies won't run down, so they can stay awake to see our Lord and His marvelous creation. Our minds will never become exhausted, so we can learn and grow for eternity. Our voices will never fade or go off tune, so we can sing joyful songs of praise whenever we want and as loudly as we want.

The promise Jesus made so long ago has come true—He has prepared a place for us so we can be with Him forever (John 14:3).

Come, Lord Jesus!

SUMMARY AND CONCLUSION
AND WHAT THIS TELLS US ABOUT JESUS

This penultimate chapter reveals the long-awaited extreme makeover of planet Earth. At the end of the millennium, the New Jerusalem descends with God's people, and the wicked prepare their final assault, which doesn't have a chance of succeeding (Revelation 21:8, 27). Then the world is free from pain and free from sin's pollution, and the New Jerusalem is a city of peace.

Revelation 21 shows us that Jesus wants to be with His people. He designed a new place where He can dwell in the midst of us. The frequent mention of the city being continually open in all four directions and the beautiful diversity of gemstones both symbolize that Jesus loves us no matter who we are. He doesn't care what ethnicity you are, whether you're rich or poor, smart or simple or whatever. He came to save everyone—including you and me.

The care with which Jesus designed the city also reveals how much He loves us. While earthly contractors can design some cool features for the homes they build, none of them can remove pain, tears, or loneliness. Jesus takes note of every tear we cry (Psalm 56:8) so He can wipe them all away.

John's body bore witness to his age and to what he suffered as he had faithfully served Jesus. The Lord gave His disciple a glimpse of the new earth in order to fill him with hope so that he would persevere. He wants us to persevere too.

ENDNOTE

1. Ellen G. White, *Spiritual Gifts* (Washington, D.C.: Review and Herald®, 1944), 2:35.

Going Deeper

God reveals that everyone from every nation is welcome in His kingdom. What implications does this have for our relationships with other people—particularly with people we don't like? What does this suggest about who should be included in our churches?

Chapter 33
The Garden
Revelation 22

One of my first jobs was to be a superhero. Seriously. A woman handcrafted various costumes in her home—mostly of spandex*—and asked high school students to put them on—not for her own personal fashion show, but to wear to Perkins Family Restaurant. The superhero was to sit in the entry and paint various symbols on the faces of the little kids who came in.

The job was easy enough, but the shame was difficult to endure. In the first place, the spandex suit I wore wasn't shiny; it was fuzzy from use. Second, Christian Bale consumed six thousand calories a day to bulk up to the proper size to play Batman. I didn't have that kind of time or appetite, so I was a much leaner superhero—about 135 pounds compared to his 225. On top of that, whoever had worn that costume before had been a much larger Batman than I was, so the spandex was stretched out and the costume hung from my limbs like loose skin (though it held its own in all the wrong places).

That meant I had to wear shorts. In fact, the only piece of the costume that worked—and this was true for the Spiderman costume as well—was the mask.

The precious mask.

On the way to whichever Perkins would be hosting my festival of shame, I had to pause at the stoplights. The looks I received from other drivers were amazing. No one expects Spiderman to be driving a 1994 Taurus station wagon. But thanks to that mask, they never saw who I was.

When I got to my destination, I would set up my little art show. Much to my chagrin, it never failed that a cute girl from my high school or youth group would show up with her friends. Thinking it would be fun, and because they were pretty and nothing they did would ever be considered stupid, they inevitably decided to get their faces painted. The preservation of my fragile social status at school depended on that worn-out spandex.

This job, one of my first jobs, paid well: seventy-five bucks an hour. But the job

---

* I know, this stuff keeps cropping up in my life, doesn't it?

was a problem because it was too stressful.

Most first jobs are epic disasters, but Adam and Eve's was pretty sweet.

God creates a perfect garden world. Then He creates humans in His image. Next He puts them in the Garden "to work it"—not in the sassy, supermodel-runway-walk kind of way, but in the easiest, most-enjoyable-job-on-earth kind of way.

Think about it. Death hadn't entered the world yet, so how hard would it have been to "work" a garden? It's not like you could have killed anything, right? Basically, the job God gave the first humans was to eat fruit, name animals, and hang out with each other and with God. Not a bad set-up.

But then the devil took the war that began in heaven (Revelation 12:7) to humanity's workplace. Adam and Eve did the one thing God told them not to do—they ate fruit from the tree of the knowledge of good and evil.

So they lost the Garden.

They lost perfection.

And they gained pain, sickness, and death.

The "very good" world God created (Genesis 1:31) now had a very bad problem.

This is how the Bible begins, but it isn't how it ends—because "the free gift is not like the trespass. For if many died through one man's trespass, much more have the grace of God and the free gift by the grace of that one man Jesus Christ abounded for many" (Romans 5:15). The last chapter of the Bible says that Jesus will remove the curse and make the world good again, as He had created it to be so long ago (John 1:1–4).

Matter of fact, the first person to see Jesus after the resurrection confused Him with the "gardener" (John 20:15). The new Adam had returned from death to usher in new life.

Eden 2.0

"Then the angel showed me the river of the water of life, bright as crystal, flowing from the throne of God and of the Lamb through the middle of the street of the city; also, on either side of the river, the tree of life with its twelve kinds of fruit, yielding its fruit each month. The leaves of the tree were for the healing of the nations" (Revelation 22:1, 2).

Every time Apple releases upgraded software, people foam at the mouth and camp out to get it even if their old version still works. Beyond the realm of software, people rejoice over new cars. They strut in new clothes. And they bask in the glow of their new big-screen TVs. (And when you witness these things—especially the big-screen TV when all you own is a thirteen-inch laptop screen—you want an upgrade too.)

Revelation 22 tells about the greatest upgrade this world will ever witness.

Jesus prophesied, "Truly, I say to you, in the new world, when the Son of Man will sit on his glorious throne, you who have followed me will also sit on twelve

Going Deeper

Some say that humanity will be dependent on the fruit from the tree of life for eternal life. What makes sense about this idea? What doesn't?

_____

_____

_____

_____

_____

_____

_____

_____

_____

_____

_____

_____

_____

_____

_____

_____

_____

_____

_____

_____

_____

Notes

thrones, judging the twelve tribes of Israel" (Matthew 19:28). Underneath the English translation lies an interesting word that points to the nature of the upgrade of the world. The Greek word for *new* that Jesus chose was *palingenesia*. Do you see the name of a biblical book embedded in that word? That word means rebirth or regeneration. "Re-genesis."

At the end, the world will be restored to what it was in the beginning. The new earth is a new genesis—a fresh story to replace the old one that froze, glitched, and crashed.

A long-lost tree captures John's attention—the tree of life (Revelation 22:2). The last time the tree of life was on this world, it was in Eden—in Genesis (see Genesis 2:9; 3:22). The Greek word translated "tree" here is *xulon*. Most of the time the writers of the New Testament used a different word for tree: *dendron*. But Peter used the word *xulon* when he accused the religious leaders of hanging Jesus on a "tree" (Acts 5:30). *Xulon* can also mean "cross." Symbolically, Revelation's tree of life is the cross of Christ.

Literally, the tree of life was meant to be the source of eternal life for Adam and Eve—which is why God ended their access to it after they sinned (Genesis 3:22–24). On the new earth, that tree will overarch the great river of life that flows from God's throne, offering fruit freely to God's people as it did in the beginning. The healing leaves allude to the separation humanity has experienced, and their lame attempt to cover up their shame (Genesis 3:7).

After Adam and Eve sinned, the serpent was cursed (verse 15), the ground was cursed (verse 17), and one of their sons was cursed (for killing his brother; Genesis 4:11, 12). Revelation 22 says that nothing accursed will dwell in the new world. Now the curse is gone.

Shame is gone too. Adam and Eve tried to hide themselves from God when sin made them feel exposed. But the text says, "They will see His face" (Revelation 22:4). Our separation from God is over. We will live in a never-ending Eden. It will be good. Very good. Just the way Jesus always intended it to be.

Worship, sealing, and a warning

"I, John, am the one who heard and saw these things. And when I heard and saw them, I fell down to worship at the feet of the angel who showed them to me, but he said to me, 'You must not do that! I am a fellow servant with you and your brothers the prophets, and with those who keep the words of this book. Worship God' " (Revelation 22:8, 9).

After telling us what John saw of the new genesis, chapter 22 ends with several appeals to the readers in the hopes that they will join those who will get to see the new Eden.

Worship has been a major theme throughout Revelation. People have fought and died over the matter of who deserves their allegiance. John, overcome by what he's seen of the new earth, falls down in worship of his tour guide. He is immediately corrected. Later, the angel contrasts the true worshipers, who are allowed into the re-created world, with those who aren't permitted to be there (verses 14, 15). Whom you worship determines your destiny.

The Greek manuscripts of Revelation differ as to what John wrote in verse 14. Some—the older versions, which were written closer in time to John's day—say that in order to have access to the tree of life, God's faithful people "wash their robes" (see, for example, the ESV, NIV, and ASV). Other Greek manuscripts—more recent and generally considered to be further from what John wrote—say, "Do his commandments" (see, for example, the KJV and NKJV). We may not know which phrase was the original one, but we do know that we are saved only by Jesus' sacrifice (Romans 5:8, 9), and that in response to His love and grace, we keep His commandments (John 14:15). God's grace declares us righteous and also works in us to make us more like Him.*

"And he said to me, 'Do not seal up the words of the prophecy of this book, for the time is near. Let the evildoer still do evil, and the filthy still be filthy, and the righteous still do right, and the holy still be holy'" (Revelation 22:10, 11).

Revelation is not a book of secrets meant to hide truth from God's people. It is a revealing of Jesus. In Daniel's time, the prophecies contained in his book were sealed (Daniel 12:4). Now they are unsealed—which suggests that God wants us to study them so we are prepared to be sealed by His Spirit and led into the truths that will secure our salvation.

"I warn everyone who hears the words of the prophecy of this book: if anyone adds to them, God will add to him the plagues described in this book, and if anyone takes away from the words of the book of this prophecy, God will take away his share in the tree of life and in the holy city, which are described in this book" (Revelation 22:18, 19).

Sorry, math nerds. Put the calculators, protractors, and pocket protectors away. You can't add anything to nor subtract anything from this book (cf. Deuteronomy 4:1, 2; 12:32). While we are to expect the gift of prophecy to operate in the last days, the words here clearly state that whatever is prophesied should never supersede the truths in God's Word—only support them. Jesus warned that in the last days, false prophets would lead people astray (Mark 13:22). Pay attention to everything you see and hear, and always test it through the lens of Scripture no matter how good it seems to be or how much you trust the source from which it comes.

Soon

"And he said to me, 'These words are trustworthy and true. And the Lord, the God of the spirits of the prophets, has sent his angel to show his servants what must

---

* Revelation doesn't favor either interpretation; John recorded both ideas in other places in the book—see Revelation 7:13, 14; 12:17; 14:12.

Going Deeper

Take some time to imagine how we will feel to be a part of the new Genesis story. What will you do first? What will you ask Jesus? What will you say to Him?

229

soon take place. And behold, I am coming soon. Blessed is the one who keeps the words of the prophecy of this book' " (Revelation 22:6, 7).

Christ hasn't been back to earth in physical form for two thousand years. Yet in this chapter alone, the word *soon* is used three times in connection with His coming (verses 7, 12, 20). The longer time goes on, the harder it is to say that Jesus is coming soon. If we are honest with ourselves and Scripture, we must admit that nobody knows when Jesus will come (Matthew 25:13). Even after His resurrection, when His anxious apostles asked if He was going to set up His earthly kingdom at that time, He told them, " 'It is not for you to know times or seasons that the Father has fixed by his own authority' " (Acts 1:7). Instead of telling them when He would return, He reminded them of the work they were to do: spreading the gospel (verse 8).

Yet Scripture not only says *soon,* but does so multiple times. Think of "soon" as being relative. I can wait five minutes for almost anything, but my two-year-old daughter goes crazy when she has to wait five minutes for something she wants. God has been alive forever, so a measly two thousand years doesn't mean much to Him. The apostle Peter wrote, "Do not overlook this one fact, beloved, that with the Lord one day is as a thousand years, and a thousand years as one day. The Lord is not slow to fulfill his promise as some count slowness, but is patient toward you, not wishing that any should perish, but that all should reach repentance" (2 Peter 3:8, 9). This text is especially meaningful because Peter was writing to Christians about people who were mocking them because Jesus hadn't returned though He promised He would. Peter says Jesus hadn't returned because He wants to give as many people as possible the opportunity to accept Him.

The Bible also says that there will be a "falling away" (KJV) or "rebellion" before Jesus returns (2 Thessalonians 2:3). Perhaps the thought of prophecies still to be fulfilled has discouraged some people. But when Jesus arrived the first time, He fulfilled many prophecies in just three and a half years of ministry.

Four hundred years passed between Malachi's final words and Jesus' first advent, and Jesus arrived right on schedule, even if it wasn't on anyone else's schedule.

Perhaps a more down-to-earth thought will help too. When people die, it is as if Jesus has come for them, because the next thing they know is either the resurrection to eternal life or the resurrection to eternal death. We have no guarantee of a long life. We may have only a few years in which to make the choice that will result in eternal life or eternal death. And the last chapter of Revelation tells us that our decision regarding Christ won't change once He comes (Revelation 22:11). So, whatever the scenario—prophetic or personal—Jesus is coming soon.

The angel tells John that what he's seen and heard is trustworthy and true (verse 6). All the promises for which we hope will come to pass. Jesus is real, and He wants a relationship with us forever. He's preparing a perfect place for you and me while we trust His Word in a cursed world.

Those of us who have made our choice, who study prophecy, and who want to tell the world about Jesus join our hearts and voices with John's as he ends his book: "He who testifies to these things says, 'Surely I am coming soon.' Amen. Come, Lord Jesus! The grace of the Lord Jesus be with all. Amen" (Revelation 22:20, 21).

SUMMARY AND CONCLUSION
AND WHAT THIS TELLS US ABOUT JESUS

The final chapter of Revelation shows us the restoration of the world to be what Jesus created in the beginning. The story of the Bible begins and ends in a garden. The river of life flows from God's loving rule, and we see the literal lost tree of life arching over the river—the tree that also symbolizes the cross of Christ that saved humanity from destruction. Now, the curse is removed, and humanity experiences a new Genesis—a fresh story to be written into the countless ages of the future.

Revelation 22 emphasizes the "soon-ness" of Jesus' return. It is near in the sense that the prophecies about what will precede His coming are nearly all fulfilled, and it is near also in the sense that we may die at any time, and will then experience His coming as if it immediately followed our death. The prophecies in Scripture about other events have proven to be accurate, and those pertaining to the new earth and humanity's future are just as trustworthy. We must decide whom we will worship now, before it is too late.

The final chapter of Revelation tells us that Jesus finishes what He starts. He created the world, and He will restore it to His original plan. No matter what the world goes through or how difficult it is to resist the attacks of the enemies of God, Jesus is present and leading in our world and in our lives. As a matter of fact, at the end of Matthew's Gospel, Jesus makes a promise to His servants that can give us comfort as we await His return: "I am with you always, to the end of the age" (Matthew 28:20).

Notes

Chapter 34
X
Final Thought

You've seen many things in Revelation. Sometimes it's easy to forget that the whole book is about Jesus—not about horns, bowls of wrath soup, angels, or beasts. Jesus selected all these images to tell us something about Him. The beast reveals to us what God thinks about the oppressive powers of this world—and what will happen to them in the end. But we can find ourselves sidetracked into trying to match dates and current events to every little detail of Revelation and miss the big picture: Jesus Christ. So I want to leave you with a picture of Jesus.

We've discussed what a chiasm is. It's a particular kind of outline. The sections of the last half of a speech or paper organized as a chiasm parallel in reverse order the sections of the first half, and the main point of the presentation is at the center of the outline. It's called a chiasm because the outline looks like the left half of the Greek letter *chi:* X. (That *chi*—pronounced "ky"—looks like an X, doesn't it?)

The book of Revelation has a chiastic literary structure. It points to Jesus at the beginning, at the end, and especially at the center. Watch.

> **A** Revelation 1:8—" 'I am the Alpha and the Omega,' says the Lord God, 'who is and who was and who is to come, the Almighty.' "
> **A'** Revelation 22:13—" 'I am the Alpha and the Omega, the first and the last, the beginning and the end.' "

Jesus is the beginning and the end of Revelation.

Keeping in mind that when the Bible was written it wasn't divided into verses and chapters (can you imagine how fun it would be to try to look something up?), we can pinpoint the middle of the book as being around the middle of what we know as Revelation 14.[1] This is where we find the three angels, the first of whom preaches a very important message—an "everlasting gospel"—to everyone in every nation in every language about Jesus.

Jesus is quite literally the beginning, the middle, and the end of Revelation—and of world history.

Incidentally, in the first centuries of our era, the *chi* (not the Chinese *chi,* pronounced "chee" and used by ninjas) was a symbol for Christianity. Some even say that the original crosses used in crucifixion were shaped like an X instead of a T. X marks the spot where we find the greatest treasure in the world.

Wherever your studies take you from here, my prayer is that you will always find an ever brighter picture of Jesus and how much He loves you.

> The great controversy is ended. Sin and sinners are no more. The entire universe is clean. One pulse of harmony and gladness beats through the vast creation. From Him who created all, flow life and light and gladness, throughout the realms of illimitable space. From the minutest atom to the greatest world, all things, animate and inanimate, in their unshadowed beauty and perfect joy, declare that God is love.[2]

ENDNOTES

1. Jacques Doukhan, *Secrets of Revelation* (Hagerstown, Md.: Review and Herald®, 2002), 15.

2. Ellen G. White, *The Great Controversy* (Mountain View, Calif.: Pacific Press®, 1950), 678.

Recommended Reading

Prophecy: *Yes, these are written by Adventists, but I believe they are biblical and worth your time.*

Anderson, Roy Allan. *Unfolding the Revelation.* Mountain View, Calif.: Pacific Press®, 1974.

Case, Steve, and Daniel Wysong. *Jesus: 7 Keys for Finding Jesus in the Book of Revelation.* Carmichael, Calif.: Involve Youth, 2012.

Doukhan, Jacques. *Secrets of Revelation.* Hagerstown, Md.: Review and Herald®, 2002.

Knight, George. *The Apocalyptic Vision and the Neutering of Adventism.* Hagerstown, Md.: Review and Herald®, 2008.

Mathews, Kenneth. *Revelation Reveals Jesus.* Greeneville, Tenn.: Second Coming Publishing, 2012.

Maxwell, C. Mervyn. *God Cares,* Vol. 2. Nampa, Idaho: Pacific Press®, 1985.

Naden, Roy C. *The Lamb Among the Beasts.* Hagerstown, Md.: Review and Herald®, 1996.

Paulien, Jon. *Revelation: The Deep Things of God.* Hagerstown, Md.: Review and Herald®, 2004.

———. *Seven Keys: Unlocking the Secrets of Revelation.* Nampa, Idaho: Pacific Press®, 2009.

Pierce, Seth. *Prophecies of Daniel for Teens.* Nampa, Idaho: Pacific Press®, 2012.

Smith, Uriah. *The Prophecies of Daniel and the Revelation.* Hagerstown, Md.: Review and Herald®, 2006.

Stefanovic, Ranko. *The Revelation of Jesus Christ,* 2nd ed. Berrien Springs, Mich.: Andrews University Press, 2009.

The Immortality of the Soul and Hell: *These are important topics that many Christians are studying. The traditional view of eternal torment is giving way to God's truth. Some of these books are heavy, but they are worth reading.*

Bell, Rob. *Love Wins.* New York: Harper One, 2011.

Fudge, Edward. *The Fire That Consumes: A Biblical and Historical Study of the Doctrine of Final Punishment.* Eugene, Ore.: Cascade Books, 2011.

Gonzalez, Justo L. *A History of Christian Thought. Vol. 1: From the Beginnings to the Council of Chalcedon.* Nashville: Abingdon Press, 1987.

Ellen White: *A lot has been written about her life—both good and bad. These books provide an introduction to her life and to the issues connected with her ministry.*
Fagal, William. *101 Questions About Ellen White.* Nampa, Idaho: Pacific Press®, 2010.
Knight, George. *Meeting Ellen White: A Fresh Look at Her Life, Writings, and Major Themes.* Hagerstown, Md.: Review and Herald®, 2001.
Lake, Jud. *Ellen White Under Fire.* Nampa, Idaho: Pacific Press®, 2010.

Sabbath: *This is another concept Christians are gravitating to more and more. Here are a few suggestions if you want to go deeper. Some of these are pretty heavy reading—just in case you like that sort of thing.*
Du Preez, Ron. *Judging the Sabbath: Discovering What Can't Be Found in Colossians 2:16.* Berrien Springs, Mich.: Andrews University Press, 2008.
Heschel, Abraham Joshua. *The Sabbath.* New York, NY: Farrar Straus Giroux, 2005.
Tonstad, Sigve K. *The Lost Meaning of the Seventh Day.* Berrien Springs, Mich.: Andrews University Press, 2009.

Other Good Stuff: *You might enjoy these if you've read all of the books I've mentioned so far and have time to read more.*
Bell, Rob. *Jesus Wants to Save Christians.* Grand Rapids, Mich.: Zondervan, 2008.
Billington, Ray Allan. *The Protestant Crusade 1800–1860.* New York: Quadrangle Books, 1964.
Bockmann, Melanie Scherencel. *Convicted.* Hagerstown, Md.: Review and Herald®, 2012.
Howell, Greg and Melissa, with Seth Pierce. *Fusion.* Hagerstown, Md.: Review and Herald®, 2010.
Kinnamon, Dave, and Gabe Lyons. *unChristian: What a New Generation Really Thinks About Christianity.* Grand Rapids, Mich.: Baker Books, 2007.
Pierce, Seth. *What We Believe for Teens.* Nampa, Idaho: Pacific Press®, 2007.